RACING'S RETURN
from the
BRINK

RACING'S RETURN
from the
BRINK

The Incredible Comeback of
OLD ROSEBUD
and American Horse Racing

JAMES C. NICHOLSON

Copyright © 2025 by The University Press of Kentucky

Scholarly publisher for the Commonwealth,
serving Bellarmine University, Berea College,
Centre College of Kentucky, Eastern Kentucky University,
The Filson Historical Society, Georgetown College,
Kentucky Historical Society, Kentucky State University,
Morehead State University, Murray State University,
Northern Kentucky University, Spalding University,
Transylvania University, University of Kentucky,
University of Louisville, University of Pikeville,
and Western Kentucky University.
All rights reserved.

Editorial and Sales Offices: The University Press of Kentucky
663 South Limestone Street, Lexington, Kentucky 40508-4008
www.kentuckypress.com

Cataloging-in-Publication data is available from the Library of Congress.

ISBN 978-1-9859-0250-3 (hardcover : alk. paper)
ISBN 978-1-9859-0254-1 (epub)
ISBN 978-1-9859-0255-8 (pdf)

Member of the Association
of University Presses

To Boone and Lyle

Contents

Introduction 1
1. Origins 5
2. Freak 25
3. Roses 47
4. Miracle Horse 70
5. King of the Turf 94
6. Last Campaigns 122
Epilogue 144

Acknowledgments 147
Notes 149
Bibliography 170
Index 175

Introduction

Amid racetrack closures, spates of equine fatalities, criminal convictions of high-profile trainers, and a drug-related disqualification in America's most famous horse race, it can seem as if Thoroughbred racing in the United States has faced more bad news in the past several years than it did in the previous hundred. But if the sport's prospects for long-term viability appear uncertain now, they were far grimmer at the dawn of the twentieth century.

By one count, there had been more than three hundred American racetracks in the 1890s, but after a wave of antigambling legislation swept across the country at the turn of the century, scarcely two dozen remained by 1908. Following the shuttering of New York tracks in 1910, the only US states with top-level racing and legal gambling were Kentucky and Maryland, and activists were ready to snuff out the sport in those places as well. Antigambling crusades were part of a broader, multifaceted American reform movement that blossomed at the end of the nineteenth century. One historian described the underlying philosophy that fueled Progressive Era agitation as "the conviction that government should actively pursue the public interest in a society whose private sector seemed increasingly indifferent or hostile to that interest."[1]

Progressive crusaders seeking to end racetrack gambling, the financial lifeblood of horse racing, didn't necessarily have a problem with the sport itself. They certainly were not advocating on behalf of the racehorses that enjoyed lives of relative luxury, particularly as compared to the millions of beasts of burden that still pulled wagons and carriages through the streets of American cities, plowed fields, and carried soldiers into battle. Antigambling zealots who took aim at horse racing were primarily concerned with the kinds of people who were profiting from the sport and those they saw as victims of a rigged game. From the reformers' perspective, horse racing was part of an unsavory underworld existing adjacent to, but largely separate from, polite American society and its conventional mores and structures. It was a realm where newly minted millionaires could flaunt their affluence and where professional gamblers could reap fortunes of their own, seemingly out of thin air. The whole scene encapsulated, and even seemed to be accelerating, much of what made portions of the old guard uncomfortable about a quickly evolving American society and economy.

There had been intermittent American opposition to betting on horse racing since colonial times. Puritan Massachusetts banned all gambling for its propensity to promote idleness. Prerevolutionary Virginia barred regular folk from betting with elite planters so as not to upset the social order. The Continental Congress encouraged all American colonies to outlaw horse racing, the theater, and other amusements that would tend to produce "dissipation" during the Revolutionary War. In the early 1800s, horse racing had been frowned on by American patriots who thought it carried vestiges of the English aristocracy and hindered economic development and by various Protestant groups who warned that gambling was inconsistent with biblical principles. Still, it remained the most popular sport in the United States for most of the nineteenth century.[2]

Much of the hostility toward racing and gambling that emerged at the end of the 1800s was part of a broader reaction to changes wrought by industrialization, urbanization, and immigration. The levels of wealth and power amassed by the new robber baron class through the organization of corporate trusts, railroad conglomerates, and industrial monopolies amid pockets of desperate urban poverty in Gilded Age America would have been unfathomable just a few decades earlier. Progressive reformers resolved to tame the rougher edges of free-market industrial capitalism while preserving traditional American tenets of hard work and self-discipline as the path to prosperity, in an era when the difference between professional gamblers and Wall Street speculators was difficult to articulate. Some of the localized opposition to racing often boiled down to little more than political squabbling, but the more principled objections to the sport tended to pertain to the potential for chicanery and fraud when the distinction between the entities that operated the racetracks and those that controlled the gambling was sometimes hazy.[3]

National appetite for Progressive causes would crest by 1917 as the United States joined the allied war effort in Europe and President Woodrow Wilson established the Committee on Public Information to stoke support for military mobilization, but wartime exigencies facilitated a late flurry of social reform measures in the waning years of the Progressive movement. John Dos Passos, a prominent member of the Lost Generation of American writers, colorfully noted the growing centrality of branding, marketing, and hype in American business and politics of that era through a character in his cynical *U.S.A.* trilogy:

> Whether you like it or not, the molding of the public mind is one of the most important things that goes on in this country. If it wasn't for that, American business would be in a pretty pickle. . . . Now we may like the way American business does things or we may not like it, but it's a historical fact like the Himalaya Mountains, and no amount of kidding is going to change it. It's only through publicrelations [*sic*] work that business is protected from wildeyed cranks and demagogues who are always ready to throw a monkeywrench into the industrial machine.[4]

Opportune promotion from pillars of the Thoroughbred racing community, including Jockey Club chair August Belmont II and Churchill Downs general manager Matt Winn, helped to sell policymakers and the American public on the notion that horse racing was vital to national security, at a time when Pancho Villa's deadly raid on a New Mexico border town—and the US military's failure to apprehend the revolutionary bandit—was fresh in Americans' minds. Dexterous advocacy by some of horse racing's most influential figures played on broader American fears regarding military impotence, helping the sport to avoid the fate of vice industries like prostitution and alcohol production that were effectively outlawed during World War I in the name of protecting American troops and devoting all available resources to winning in the European trenches.

Luminary Thoroughbreds are, to some degree, a product of the sportswriters who mythologize them, and most enduring racehorse biographies follow familiar formats. Some depict an underdog that overcomes adversity to earn a lasting place in the hearts of its backers, while others portray a superhorse that seems to possess otherworldly abilities. Old Rosebud exemplified aspects of both but fits neatly into neither category. Had he raced in a different era, Old Rosebud's status as a gelding (castrated horse) would scarcely have been noteworthy, beyond its elimination of any residual monetary value for the horse as a breeding animal. But as concerns over waning American virility seeped into public discourse, and some of horse racing's most powerful voices pushed to ban geldings as part of their effort to frame the Thoroughbred industry as critical to national defense, Old Rosebud's lack of testicles made him a somewhat improbable candidate for equine celebrity.

With American horse racing clinging to a precarious existence in the 1910s, Old Rosebud would reach a level of fame rarely achieved by four-legged animals. But without some deft and determined promotion of Thoroughbred racing—in the face of widespread efforts to destroy it—he might have been the last great American racehorse.

1

Origins

Frank Weir had high hopes for his undersized, dirt-colored gelding stabled at Terrazas Park in Ciudad Juárez, just across the river from El Paso, but he kept them to himself. During the Mexican Revolution of the 1910s, Juárez and the rest of the state of Chihuahua were often contested territory. The American-owned racetrack could operate only with the tacit permission of whatever faction was in control of the region at the time, and racing officials had to check the shifting political winds before tendering the requisite concession payments. Horse racing had thus far been undisturbed by the revolutionary violence that had spread across Mexico, but Weir did not want to draw unneeded attention to his unraced two-year-old. As the trainer later observed, "If the Mexicans had fancied that we considered him a good horse, we might have found him missing some morning."[1]

Old Rosebud's legs were a bit stubby. He was slightly swaybacked and lop-eared. His longish neck seemed mismatched to his largish head. But he had a broad chest, a good shoulder, an intelligent eye, powerful hindquarters, and a quick turn of foot. Lightning-fast breezes as a yearling had flabbergasted his trainer and riders back in Kentucky before he was shipped to Mexico for the start of the racing season. By early February 1913, the young horse was ready to race.

Terrazas had served as a wintertime destination for American racing enthusiasts since its inaugural meeting in 1909. After a flurry of state-level antigambling crusades had nearly ended the sport in the first decade of the twentieth century, there were few warm-weather options for racing. California and Florida would soon join Arkansas, Tennessee, and Louisiana on the list of states where gambling on horses was proscribed. A consortium of American businessmen and racing executives teamed with Alberto Terrazas, son of the largest land and cattle baron in North America, to form the Juárez Jockey Club. Terrazas would serve as president of the association. A bon vivant nephew of Wall Street giant James R. Keene named Jack Follansbee, who was also a Harvard friend of media mogul William Randolph Hearst and oversaw a portion of the Hearst family's million-acre Mexican properties, would be vice president. The group constructed a stately concrete grandstand, stables, and a nine-furlong oval. Matt Winn, general manager of Churchill Downs, home of the Kentucky Derby, assumed the same title at Terrazas Park and assembled a team that included first-rate starter Mars Cassidy and other top racing officials.

El Paso hotels catered to a growing American tourist trade in the busy transcontinental railroad hub. Socialites, stars of stage and screen, conventioneers, outlaws, businessmen, prospectors, and prostitutes could walk or take the streetcar across the Rio Grande to the races. "They had few rules and regulations," Winn recalled of an El Paso that retained more than a trace of the old West. "If you wanted fun, of any kind whatsoever, you needed only to walk a block or two, and there it was."[2]

Mexico had experienced more than three decades of political stability and economic growth under Porfirio Díaz's "constitutional dictatorship," which was supported by a large police force and the Catholic Church. During Díaz's reign, which began in 1876, the Mexican railroad system was modernized, thousands of new factories were built, and exports increased fivefold. By 1910, there were more than three thousand mines operating in Mexico, producing tons of silver, zinc, lead, copper, and iron. Most were owned by American interests. A nascent oil industry was dominated by American and British companies, and foreign investors enjoyed tax exemptions and protections in the courts. Not everyone in Mexico was sharing in the prosperity, however. By 1910, eight hundred landowners controlled 90 percent of Mexican land. Most Mexicans lived in a state of peonage, and 80 percent were illiterate. Americans owned one hundred million acres in Mexico and had more capital invested there than Mexicans did. Concerns about the political, social, and economic ramifications of rapid industrial growth produced a push for change. In the United States, similar apprehensions prompted a wave of Progressive reform, while in Mexico, they led to revolution.[3]

When the seventy-nine-year-old Díaz reneged on a promise not to seek another presidential term in 1910, wealthy cotton planter Francisco Madero announced his intent to challenge Díaz for the Mexican presidency. The vegetarian spiritualist Madero was not initially seen as a serious threat to the long-time dictator. But when it was apparent that Madero was receiving significant support, Díaz accused the challenger of fomenting rebellion and sent him to prison. Released from confinement following Díaz's claim of a landslide election win, Madero fled to Texas, declared the election a fraud, and called for revolution. Various guerrillas, including an outlaw with obscure origins calling himself Francisco "Pancho" Villa, recruited thousands of drifters, vaqueros, malcontents, and adventurers to the revolutionary cause. In May 1911, militants aligned with Madero (including those led by Villa) defeated federal forces at Ciudad Juárez and captured the city. In a decade of violence during the Mexican Revolution, as many as a million Mexicans would lose their lives.[4]

That American horsemen (they were nearly all men at that time) would choose to race in a literal war zone illustrates the condition of the sport in the United States—somewhere between precarious and dismal—in the early twentieth century. The Juárez course quickly became an important part of the diminishing American horse-racing landscape. In 1913, the *Daily Racing Form* called Terrazas Park "one of the great tracks of America." At a time when Kentucky and Maryland were the only states with high-level racing and legal on-track gambling, there were not many facilities in serious contention for such a designation.[5]

Old Rosebud made his racing debut on February 9, 1913, in the Yucatan Stakes, a 3.5-furlong dash for two-year-olds. Carrying a purse of $940, it was the featured event on a Sunday afternoon of racing at Terrazas.

After two scratches, blamed on the muddy conditions, a solid field of six remained, at least half of which would be stakes winners by year's end. Jockey Charley Peak had the mount on Old Rosebud. The talented but hot-headed rider from Arkansas had been suspended indefinitely for rough riding in Kentucky the previous summer and had just arrived in Mexico. Depending on the weather, the racing surface at Juárez could be as hard as brick or as sticky as glue. When Rosebud made his way to the starting line for the first time, it was a sea of gummy sludge. The little gelding found it much to his liking. He darted to the lead in the opening yards of the short race and pranced on to an easy six-length win.

Three weeks later, with Peak serving a suspension for an on-track infraction, young lightweight jockey Johnny McCabe would ride Rosebud in the gelding's second afternoon appearance on the Juárez oval, a three-hundred-dollar half-mile allowance, the opening race on a Wednesday card.[6] Though he had been riding for Weir for a couple of years, the teenaged McCabe was still relatively inexperienced and among the smallest riders in America. He had talent but was developing a reputation for questionable judgment on the racetrack, including an inclination to ignore officials' instructions behind the webbed, spring-loaded barriers resembling a badminton net that demarcated the starting line at early twentieth-century American tracks. McCabe was primed for a breakout year, having recovered from a dislocated wrist and a fractured leg suffered in racetrack spills months earlier. Old Rosebud's stellar unveiling pushed the precocious gelding to favored status among the bettors, at 2–5. After some fractiousness at the barrier, which would earn McCabe a reprimand from starter Mars Cassidy, Rosebud settled a couple of lengths off a quick pace. When McCabe relaxed his hold, his horse shot past

Old Rosebud, ridden by Johnny McCabe, was not considered to be the prettiest of horses, but he was precocious and very fast as a two-year-old in 1913. (Keeneland Library Cook Collection)

the front-runners. Within a few jumps, he was three lengths clear of the field. Already decelerating as the finish line approached, he was five lengths ahead of his nearest foe at the wire. There would be tougher races ahead, but those who had seen him run in Mexico wondered if there were any faster two-year-olds in North America.

Glowing descriptions in the American sporting press of Old Rosebud's eye-catching wins marked a return to national limelight for Frank Weir as the trainer neared his fiftieth birthday. Born in 1863 near Aurora, Illinois, forty miles west of Chicago, Weir had been a drugstore clerk as a teenager. Drawn to the outdoors, he traded his apothecary apron for a chance to work in the midwestern racing circuit, where smaller racetracks dotted the region and horse racing enjoyed broad popularity. By the time he turned twenty-one, he was training on his own.

Weir would win more than 1,700 races and purses totaling almost $1 million in his four decades as a trainer, but he took a meandering path to the top of the sport. Within a few years, he had assembled a competitive string that he raced at rough-and-tumble, notoriously corrupt tracks in New Jersey. Weir earned a reputation as a top-rate conditioner who could find the right races for his horses, though critics noted that he seemed to win with long shots at an anomalous rate.[7]

In 1893, Weir saddled the winners of 150 races at Gloucester—a short-lived, semilegal track unaffiliated with any national or regional racing association, where offseason racing was held at a facility constructed atop a landfill near the Delaware River. The track was adjacent to a low-grade resort that contained an amusement park, hotel, and casino, all accessible by ferryboat from Philadelphia. The *New York Tribune* described Gloucester's clientele as "murderers, highwaymen, burglars, pickpockets . . . and petty swindlers of all sorts" who gambled "with the proceeds of their crimes," while the track's defenders emphasized the hundreds of jobs it supported and the thousands of patrons who enjoyed wholesome diversion far removed from urban bustle. Weir's success there afforded him the chance to build a large home in Gloucester City, where he lived with his wife and two young children. But a slate of antigambling officials would be voted into positions of power that fall, amid the start of an economic depression that would galvanize an assortment of reformist causes later categorized as Progressive. A leading Republican voice in the push to end horse racing in the Garden State vowed to "protect

Frank Weir was among the top trainers on the East Coast before the shutdown of New York racing in 1910. (Keeneland Library Cook Collection)

New Jersey from the horde of gamblers and thieves who thrived during the recent Democratic regime."[8]

Some of the most influential advocates of Progressive causes at the end of the nineteenth century included a new generation of journalists and publishers disdainfully labeled *muckrakers* by their opponents. No media figure was more powerful than William Randolph Hearst, son of a stupendously wealthy forty-niner miner and founder of the first American corporate media conglomerate. In 1887, at age twenty-three, Hearst began publishing the *San Francisco Examiner*, which his dad had acquired as payment on a gambling debt and maintained as a means to enhance his political power. The young Hearst dramatically increased circulation through a combination of flamboyant promotion and colorful reporting that focused on sports, crime, and what would come to be derisively called *yellow journalism*. Soon, Hearst's media empire, producing a blurry combination of news, propaganda, and entertainment, would include several major newspapers, muckraking magazines, a wire service, newsreels, and syndicated cartoons. A reliably prolabor, antimonopoly, and anticorruption editorial bent would earn him plenty of powerful enemies.

Hearst would join other publishers in supporting the cause of Cuban independence from Spain. He sent artist Frederic Remington to illustrate his newspapers' coverage of the revolutionary upheaval. When a disappointed Remington wired Hearst to report that all was quiet and there was no war on the horizon, Hearst famously is supposed to have replied, "Please remain. You furnish the pictures, and I'll furnish the war." That this line would later be attached in popular memory to the subsequent conflict between the United States and Spain only underscored a growing public faith in the power of the press and public-relations machines to influence American policy. Hearst's claims that he had been primarily responsible for causing the American military intervention in Cuba through his constant barrage of incendiary anti-Spanish articles were dubious. But the Spanish-American War would earn the United States a place among Western imperial powers and accelerate the rise toward national political prominence of Theodore Roosevelt, who would bring the first tinge of Progressivism to the White House on his ascension to the presidency.[9]

By 1894, New Jersey had enacted antigambling legislation, bolstered three years later by a constitutional amendment, that would halt horse racing there for half a century. To prevent New York racing from suffering the same fate, a group of well-connected sportsmen, industrialists, and captains of finance formed The Jockey Club—with a capital *T*—as part of an effort to organize and regulate the sport and to fend off reformers and opponents of racing. (Capitalizing *The* emphasized the group's lofty ambitions and distinguished it from various local jockey clubs, but most newspapers used a lowercase *t* when reporting the club's doings. The *New York Times* was an exception, but even that paper's use of the capital *T* waxed and waned through the twentieth century before settling on lowercase by the 1990s.) When a new state constitution in New York that prohibited "pool selling, bookmaking, or any other kind of gambling" was adopted in 1895, Jockey Club members helped to convince legislators to pass confusingly worded legislation, labeled the Percy-Gray law, that limited any penalty for betting on horse racing to forfeiture of the amount wagered and created a state racing commission to oversee the sport in collaboration with The Jockey Club. Gambling on horses would still be technically illegal, but there would be no criminal consequence as long as bets were made orally. A disgruntled bettor could try to recover his losses in civil court under the new law, but without written records, redress would be difficult to achieve. Gambling was effectively given a green light, and a golden age for New York racing ensued.[10]

One of the Jockey Club's founding members, financier August Belmont II, would helm the entity for nearly three decades, including some of American horse racing's most pivotal years. The club would establish rules, manage racing calendars, punish cheaters, and issue licenses to trainers and jockeys for New York tracks and other Eastern racing associations that consented to be governed. Those that rejected oversight were deemed outlaw tracks. Horses that raced on outlaw tracks could be banned from officially sanctioned venues, as could their owners, trainers, and jockeys.

Though Weir maintained that he had set foot on an unsanctioned northern Virginia racecourse only to pay a debt, The Jockey Club determined that he had run a horse there and denied his licensure for several years. Forced to race at tracks outside the club's purview, Weir thrived at small meets in Maryland and Virginia, earning the nickname King of the Outlaw Trainers before being reinstated at the turn of the century. Back in the good graces of organized racing, Weir would make Brooklyn his training base. He had cut his teeth at some seedy tracks but was broadly respected as a meticulous trainer. In time, the brushes with regulators had been forgotten to an extent that the *Daily Racing Form* could assert his reputation for integrity had "always been above reproach."[11]

Weir landed one of the most important clients of his career, Frank Farrell, in time for the start of the 1903 racing season, shortly before Farrell bought the Baltimore Orioles baseball club and moved it to New York City. (He would call the team the Highlanders but would later change the name to Yankees.) Farrell's fortune had roots in a multimillion-dollar syndicate of illegal offtrack betting parlors called *poolrooms*, where gamblers could bet on horse races from across the country. His operation was protected by his business partner—the New York City chief of police—and the Tammany Hall political machine. Weir's stable would soon be filled with stakes-caliber horses. But it was a speedball named Roseben that made the trainer a household name in the American sports world. The massive gelding, a future Hall of Famer, earned the nickname Big Train before it became more famously attached to Washington Senators pitcher Walter Johnson. Roseben ran in the colors of Davy C. Johnson, an associate of Frank Farrell's and one of the last of

August Belmont II (1853–1924) was a founding member of The Jockey Club and chaired the organization for nearly three decades, including some of the most pivotal years in American Thoroughbred racing. (Library of Congress)

a generation of legendary Gilded Age gamblers who earned national celebrity for their capacity to calmly win or lose fabulous amounts of money in mere minutes. In 1906, Roseben shattered the American record for seven furlongs at Belmont Park. His time of 1:22 would not be bettered anywhere on the continent for more than forty years. And the Belmont track record would last until 1957. On retirement at age eight, Roseben was widely considered the greatest American sprinter of all time, and Frank Weir was credited with having kept the Big Train rolling through various ailments and injuries.[12]

With half a dozen tracks in the metropolitan area, New York was the center of American horse racing at the dawn of the twentieth century, and Weir was a major player hitting his professional stride. The *New York Sun* called him "one of the most important factors on the Eastern turf" and "one of the best trainers in the profession." But in June 1908, Progressive Republican governor Charles Evans Hughes signed a series of legislation labeled the Hart-Agnew bills, closing the loopholes created by the Percy-Gray law and putting the New York racing world on notice that gambling would no longer be tolerated. Hughes had narrowly defeated two-term congressman William Randolph Hearst, whose wealth and public profile had facilitated a pivot into politics as a champion of the working class, to win the New York governorship with extensive support from President Theodore Roosevelt. Roosevelt privately regarded Hearst as "the most potent single influence for evil in America" and had sent US secretary of state Elihu Root to campaign against the candidate in the waning days of the election. In a scathing speech, Root blamed Hearst for the assassination of William McKinley that had put Roosevelt in the White House, implying that an editorial published in Hearst papers had inspired the president's killer. While he had equivocated on the issue during the campaign, as governor, Hughes called racetrack gambling "evil" and promised that its abolition would save "thousands of men who are now going to their ruin."[13]

New York racing struggled to survive amid new restrictions, with gamblers furtively plying their trade under the heavy scrutiny of undercover police, and many leading American owners, trainers, and jockeys decamped to Europe. Some 1,500 horses were sent to England and France, where racing was not under regulatory fire. Stud farms in South America scooped up American broodmares and stallions at discount prices, and the bottom fell out of American Thoroughbred yearling markets. That autumn, after Election Day, so that he and his employees could cast pro-racing votes, Weir

OWNER AND TRAINER FRANK D. WEIR,
One of the Best Known Horsemen Before the American Public.

Frank Weir gained national fame for his work with Roseben, a giant, record-smashing gelding nicknamed "the Big Train," widely considered the best sprinter ever to race in America on his retirement in 1909. (*Oakland Tribune*, February 14, 1909)

Charles Evans Hughes's win in the 1906 New York gubernatorial election over publishing magnate William Randolph Hearst would have dire consequences for horse racing in the Empire State. (Library of Congress)

headed West. He settled in at the racetrack in Emeryville, near Oakland, and occasionally shipped a horse to the old Santa Anita track outside Los Angeles.

California had a long history of quality racing and breeding in the decades that followed the gold rush, supported by wealthy sportsmen like Lucky Baldwin, James Ben Ali Haggin, and his mining partner George Hearst (William Randolph Hearst's father). George was the primary financier of the Bay View Park racetrack in San Francisco, which opened in 1863. In 1890, he raced the top three-year-old in America (a colt named Tournament) while serving in the US Senate. California's other senator at that time, Leland Stanford, also helped to build a racetrack and was a major breeder of Standardbreds at his Palo Alto Stud. But political winds had shifted, and an antigambling bill under consideration in the state legislature, modeled on New York's Hart-Agnew law, cast a shadow of uncertainty over racing in the Golden State in 1909. Activists insisted that if California did not join the growing number of Eastern jurisdictions proscribing wagering, "the crooks and criminals who infest California like so many parasites" and "the racetrack gamblers who defile the state with their presence and debauch it with their infamy" would continue to move West in search of racing opportunities.[14]

When the Walker-Otis antigambling bill was enacted in California, Weir returned to Brooklyn. But further restrictive legislation in New York, passed in 1910, subjected racing officials to criminal liability, including imprisonment, should anyone be caught gambling at a racetrack. Track owners were unwilling to risk jail time, and the sport was shut down completely in the Empire State as challenges to the legislation wound through the courts. Weir lost his major clients during the blackout, but he persevered, racing in Canada, Kentucky, and Maryland. His income fell to a fraction of what it had been only a few years earlier, though he remained an avid bicyclist and photographer as he struggled to find horses to train and venues at which to race them.

In September 1912, Weir had a small stable of horses at the Kentucky Association track in Lexington, one of the few places in America where racing's supporters had managed to fend off efforts to end the sport. He was planning to take a string to Juárez and needed some new clients. Ed Applegate, once called "the most powerful racing magnate west of the Alleghenies, if not in America," was among the prominent horsemen in town for the late-summer meet and was looking to help his son Ham buy some racing prospects. Applegate had already distinguished himself as a racehorse owner, gambler, and racetrack operator. He had raced some capable runners but never a superstar. Their acquisition of the yearling they would name Old Rosebud would reinvigorate Frank Weir's career and take the Applegates on quite a ride.[15]

Born in Georgetown, Kentucky, in 1851, William Edward Applegate moved with his parents and siblings at the start of the Civil War to Mississippi, where his father took a job in the Confederacy's commissary department. After the war, Ed, as he was known to friends, finished his education at Georgetown College before the family moved to Louisville, where his father established a wholesale whiskey operation, Applegate & Sons. Ed began his professional career in the family business, and he and his wife, Bettie, would raise five children in Louisville, eventually residing in a stately Victorian house on Louisville's fashionable Third Street. He and his brother would expand the whiskey concern to include—in the names of various partnerships—rectifying facilities, a distributorship, and distilleries that would produce popular bourbon brands including Beechwood and Old Rosebud. The booze trade was big business—by one metric, the fifth largest American industry—but it was under threat from temperance advocates whose reform campaigns often overlapped with other Progressive causes. By 1913, "dry" counties would make up nearly half the geographical territory of the United States, thanks to the enduring efforts of groups like the Anti-Saloon League and the Woman's Christian Temperance Union that believed the elimination of alcohol could ameliorate poverty and other societal ills.[16]

Applegate demonstrated an early knack for commerce, but long workdays took a toll on his health. To tackle what Ed called chronic dyspepsia, a physician recommended that he spend more time outdoors and suggested horse racing as a beneficial amusement. That such a specific prescription seemed to be acquired with some regularity by sportsmen of that era might cause one to wonder whether following doctors' orders wasn't merely a convenient justification for engaging in a lifestyle that they were already drawn toward, but Applegate enjoyed the camaraderie and exhilaration of the racetrack and soon jumped into racehorse ownership. After achieving some early success in his new hobby, he surmised that there was more money to be made in booking bets than in owning racehorses. Within three years of his first foray into the sport, he had become a professional bookmaker, laying odds at race meets across the country. Soon he would control one of the largest gambling coalitions in America. Somewhere along the way, he acquired the nickname "Colonel."[17]

Some attributed the moniker to the brigade of associates that accompanied Applegate around the racing world, but it was a title utilized by many Kentuckians. Some colonels had their honorary title bestowed on them by a Kentucky governor, a tradition dating to the early nineteenth century. Most famously, Harland Sanders would receive a colonelship in recognition of his recipe for tasty fried chicken. Martin J. "Matt" Winn was made a Kentucky colonel soon after assuming the management of Churchill Downs, while serving on a local board of public safety. Those who used the title to its greatest advantage included men who had succeeded in less genteel corners of commerce, like booze and gambling. The label could connote a level of trustworthiness or respectability, paradoxically marking its holder as both an outsider and someone the monied classes could safely do business with—an indication that the bearer of the label was a "good guy," despite involvement in potentially unsavory trade. Colonel Applegate would become a respected member of Louisville's business community, serving as a director of several companies and earning a spot on the city's Board of Trade.

With a reputation for a composed demeanor, Applegate was, according to one newspaper, "as suave and gentle-spoken as a woman." Dexterity with numbers and a nose for business helped make the Colonel one of the most prosperous bookmakers in America, earning him recognition as king of the Western turf at a time when the line of demarcation between East and West was roughly the Hudson River. (That he would also later be labeled "the most prominent and influential of all southern horsemen" serves as further testament both to Applegate's stature in racing circles and to Kentucky's geographical ambiguity at that time.) After years of paying racetrack owners for license to ply his trade on their grounds, Applegate found it expedient to acquire the venues. Soon he would be one of the most prominent owners of racetracks in the United States while maintaining his lucrative gambling operations. As part of assorted syndicates, Applegate would control substantial interests in several racing sites, including Cincinnati's Oakley racetrack; Latonia, just across the Ohio River in northern Kentucky; and Churchill Downs in Louisville. His partners in these enterprises also tended to have deep roots in bookmaking and poolrooms.[18]

Mingling the pursuit of gambling profits with the administration of the races themselves risked the appearance of shadiness, the kind of optics that anti-racing reformers pounced on, but it made good business sense. By the turn of the century, the Colonel was involved in nearly every aspect of the Thoroughbred racing industry, including a partnership with Lexington horseman Charles McMeekin in a breeding farm called Oakwood, on Clays Mill Pike in Lexington. In the tradition of the family business where he had gotten his start, Applegate tried to involve his sons in his professional affairs. The Colonel's oldest was the likeliest heir to a budding racing empire. William Edward "Willie" Applegate Jr. followed his father into the racetrack life and gained a reputation as a fearless bookmaker and a charming character. He lacked his father's conservative business sensibility, however, and was apt to plow bookmaking profits into riskier enterprises, including theatrical productions.

In September 1898, under accusation of having passed bad checks, Willie fled to Europe. He left sizable debts to gamblers that his father could not afford to leave unpaid. Then twenty-three years old, he returned to the States a few months later with a sixteen-year-old bride. Mabel Howe played music hall dancer Kissie Fitzgarter in the New York and London productions of *The Belle of New York*, about the "misfortunes of a good hearted but weak young man who wastes his substance in riotous living and is disinherited by his father" before finding forgiveness and salvation in love and marriage.

Willie would eventually abandon the turf and open a bookstore in New Orleans.[19]

If the Colonel had a true protégé, it was not one of his children but the most famous young gambler in America, Charles "Riley" Grannan. A native of Paris, Kentucky, Grannan began his professional life selling programs at racetracks and then working as a bellhop and elevator operator at hotels popular with racing crowds in New Orleans and Cincinnati. A series of big scores at the bookmakers' expense won the wunderkind a national reputation as one of the most talented and fearless horseplayers in America while still a teenager. Colonel Applegate recruited him into a bookmaking partnership before Grannan went on his own, winning and losing several fortunes on both sides of the Atlantic. After a run of hard luck, he landed in the boomtown of Rawhide, Nevada, where he planned to open a gambling house. But he contracted a cold, developed pneumonia, and died, broke, at the age of thirty-seven. Applegate had loved him like a son. With Willie focusing on artistic endeavors, the Colonel's second son, Hamilton Clarke "Ham" Applegate, would become a dependable professional associate, though he would never possess Grannan's acuity or flair.[20]

Ham grew up in material comfort, if not opulent splendor. After finishing his education at Louisville's Male High School and the Michigan Military Academy, he joined the family whiskey business. A lifelong bachelor, Ham had dabbled in racehorse ownership as a young man, without much success. In the fall of 1912, he sought his father's assistance in selecting some racing prospects, hoping to change his luck. The Colonel suggested that Ham focus on fillies, believing that American racing had reached its ebb and that young female stock would have strong residual value as breeding markets rebounded.[21]

The Applegates connected with trainer Frank Weir, who purchased a small group of yearlings from Lexington breeder John E. Madden, the most accomplished American horseman of his era. The price was three thousand dollars for the lot. Madden's maxim, "better to sell and repent than to keep and repent," served him well throughout a legendary career in racing and breeding, but if he were ever inclined to lament a deal, it might have been this one. A couple of the fillies would prove to be stakes caliber, but the star of the bunch was Old Rosebud, named after one of the family's signature whiskey brands. He would race under the banner of H. C. Applegate & Co., with Weir retaining an interest. What portion, if any, that Colonel Applegate owned was never made public. But the press would tend to speak to the Colonel, rather than to Ham, when they sought news about Rosebud.[22]

Old Rosebud was bred for speed. His sire was the remarkably fast, but fragile, young stallion named Uncle. Rosebud's dam, Ivory Bells, by 1878 Kentucky Derby runner-up Himyar, had a brief and relatively unexceptional racing career despite showing some precocity in winning a race at Brighton Beach in Brooklyn as a two-year-old. It was Old Rosebud's maternal grandmother that gave the buyers a reason to think he might be more than an early sprinter. Ida Pickwick, "the Queen of the West," winner of forty-four races and nearly fifty thousand dollars, was among the top American racemares of the late nineteenth century. She won the Latonia and St. Louis Oaks as a three-year-old, in 1891, and continued to race at the highest levels at six, when she equaled an American record for a mile and three-sixteenths. She could run fast and far, and she could carry weight. She was also resilient, racing into her nine-year-old season before being retired with a ruptured tendon. After her racing career was finished, Ida Pickwick returned to her birthplace, Avondale Stud, the Tennessee nursery of E. S. Gardner, who had made a pile of money providing race results via telegraph to offtrack betting sites. After Gardner died, Madden bought the Queen of the West and shipped her to his state-of-the-art Hamburg Place farm near Lexington. As a condition of the sale, the Gardner estate asked the Kentucky horseman to take several other horses, including Ida's daughter—Old Rosebud's mother, Ivory Bells.[23]

Born in March 1911 at Hamburg, Old Rosebud spent his first months in spacious, verdant bluegrass pastures. Madden's level of devotion to his own physical health and fitness bordered on eccentric for its time, but his detailed regimen for raising horses at Hamburg was cutting-edge and would produce five Kentucky Derby champions among scores of stakes winners. There was no better place for a young horse to grow and develop.[24]

Following his auspicious introduction to racing in Mexico, Old Rosebud returned to his native Kentucky the last week of March to journalistic fanfare, despite some question as to how formidable his competition at Terrazas Park had been. Ham Applegate confidently declared that his gelding would be targeting the 1914 Kentucky Derby, more than thirteen months away. Rosebud notched a series of useful workouts at Churchill Downs before the Weir stable decamped to Lexington for the start of the April meet there. After Old Rosebud's sharp three-furlong, thirty-five-second breeze over the

Kentucky Association track, Weir determined his charge was fit to race and entered the horse in the Idle Hour Stakes, where he would have a chance to validate early accolades.

Another two-year-old son of Uncle, Little Nephew, had won his first start by five widening lengths on a damp and chilly opening day at the Lexington track, announcing himself as a leading candidate to challenge Old Rosebud for local juvenile supremacy. Owner Michael B. Gruber was a grocer in south Louisville. Long a fan of horse racing, he had only recently ventured into racehorse ownership with a six-hundred-dollar purchase from Little Nephew's breeder, John Madden. The gelding's trainer was Elza Brown, one of a rapidly diminishing number of Black trainers in early twentieth-century America. Calcifying Jim Crow laws, endorsed by the US Supreme Court in its 1896 *Plessy v. Ferguson* decision, gave state sanction to an environment in which intimidation and discrimination kept Black horsemen in more menial roles at the racetrack. Some Black jockeys and trainers found better opportunities overseas in the early twentieth century, while others left horse racing entirely as gambling bans drastically contracted the sport.[25]

Led by Little Nephew and Old Rosebud, Uncle's first crop of runners was off to a flying start, with six winners from his first six starters. Their early success recalled Uncle's own precocity, though time would tell whether the stallion's offspring would be more durable than he had been. Acquired by John Madden as a yearling in 1906 and raced by that wizard of the turf as a two-year-old, the son of British imported stallion Star Shoot was beaten by two noses at Belmont Park in his debut, then reeled off three consecutive wins, in which he demonstrated breathtaking speed. Four days before a showdown against Jockey Club vice-chair James R. Keene's undefeated colt Colin in the Saratoga Special, Madden cashed in, selling Uncle to trainer Sam Hildreth for a reported thirty thousand dollars. The Special became a match race when all other entries withdrew from the ten-thousand-dollar contest, seeing little chance of avoiding embarrassment. The pair raced neck and neck into the homestretch before Colin finally prevailed by a length. Colin would finish his career with fifteen wins in fifteen starts, earning a place on even short lists of the greatest runners in the history of American racing.

Hildreth, who topped the American trainers' earnings list nine times in his extraordinary career—and, incidentally, had worked for Frank Weir as a teenager in Illinois—called Uncle "unquestionably the fastest horse I ever saddled." The colt went lame following a workout a few days after his loss to

Colin but returned to the races that fall, scoring a series of stakes wins in New York. Soon after arriving at his winter quarters in California, Uncle injured his foot. Hildreth tried to get him fixed up, but the colt hurt himself again while training toward an appearance in the Withers Stakes the following May, where he was to have a chance at redemption against Colin. "The fact of the matter," Hildreth explained, "was that Uncle was such a rapid-going horse it was impossible to train him successfully. This can be understood better when I say that his speed was so great that he actually tore away ligaments and fractured small bones, which eventually caused him to break down hopelessly and forced his retirement."[26]

Conceding defeat on the rehabilitation project, Hildreth sold the colt for stallion duty to piano manufacturer Charles Kohler, with the stipulation that he would not be raced again. Uncle began his new career at Kohler's Ramapo Stud in New Jersey in 1910, the year of Old Rosebud's conception, when

Old Rosebud's sire, the speedy but fragile Uncle, "ran so fast you couldn't see his legs," according to Kentucky Derby–winning jockey and widely respected horseman William Walker. (Keeneland Library Cook Collection)

Madden sent more than a dozen mares to be bred to the new stallion. The following year, in response to the continued decline and uncertain future of American racing, Kohler sent Uncle to France.

In addition to their common paternity, Old Rosebud and Little Nephew shared the experience of having been castrated. They were but two of an abnormally large number of top-class geldings from that era, a phenomenon at least partially attributable to gambling bans. Geldings were easier to care for and train, and castrating a young colt allowed growth plates in his legs to remain open longer, giving undersized animals more time to develop. With many of the best American racehorses being sent to Europe, owning a gelding that could be more competitive in the shrinking pool of American racing often made more sense than preserving a horse's chance to become a stallion when there was no guarantee that a viable Thoroughbred market would even exist in a few years.

In an era filled with outstanding geldings, none would reach greater heights than Old Rosebud under Frank Weir's care. And no horse would be a sterner foe in his first year of racing than Little Nephew.

2

Freak

Pleasant springtime weather greeted a buoyant crowd at the Kentucky Association track when Old Rosebud and Little Nephew faced off for the first time. Named for the Lexington farm of Edward R. Bradley, one of the great Thoroughbred breeders of the twentieth century and proprietor of a luxurious, illegal Palm Beach casino, the Idle Hour was Kentucky's first stakes race of the year for two-year-olds, a four-and-a-half-furlong sprint for a $1,500 purse. It would live up to its billing as the featured event on the Thursday afternoon program.

On the strength of his reputation burnished at Juárez, Old Rosebud was a heavy favorite at odds of 1–2. Wearing the Applegates' white silks with blue sleeves, Johnny McCabe hurried his mount away from the barrier at the starter's signal. Little Nephew, off a step slowly beneath rising-star jockey Johnny Loftus, skimmed along the rail to poke a head in front of Rosebud in the opening yards. The two sons of Uncle soon left the rest of the nine-horse field far in the distance. Loftus and Little Nephew maintained a narrow lead into the turn, but McCabe sent Rosebud surging on the outside to put daylight between him and his opponent entering the homestretch. With an eighth of a mile to the finish, it appeared that Rosebud was primed to extend the advantage and win easily, but the inexperienced McCabe imprudently eased up on his horse and chanced a glance over his shoulder. Loftus was not ready to concede. By the time McCabe regained his focus, Loftus had Little Nephew rolling. The cacophony emanating from the grandstand crowd intensified as Little Nephew squeaked by Old Rosebud in the final strides to win by a short head. The press pinned the loss on McCabe, calling his riding overconfident and careless.

The young rider was still adjusting to the scrutiny of piloting a well-regarded runner, but he had come a long way in his short time in the saddle. McCabe had quit school at fourteen and taken a job as a delivery boy for a Brooklyn grocer. One of the stops on his route was a cigar store owned by a former jockey. The proprietor noticed McCabe's dexterity in handling the horse pulling his wagon and suggested that the kid might make a good rider, given his small size—under five feet tall and less than eighty pounds. Soon McCabe was working on the local racetracks in exchange for room and board. Within a couple of years, he was an apprentice jockey. He signed a contract with Weir and rode his first winner at Brooklyn's Sheepshead Bay in 1910. While McCabe clearly had ability, he still had much to learn.[1]

With Kentucky racing moving to Louisville, Weir eyed a shot at redemption against Little Nephew in the Bashford Manor Stakes at Churchill Downs, but a sharp four-furlong work told the trainer that Old Rosebud needed a race sooner. Weir entered him in a four-and-a-half-furlong allowance race, where he would meet another well-regarded two-year-old gelding. Roamer had won his debut at Lexington by five emphatic lengths against a good field that included a future Latonia Derby winner. His owners, the Clay brothers from Runnymede Farm near Paris, Kentucky, thought they might have a special horse. The quick, compact Roamer was the genetic result of a mating at Runnymede between a blind mare named Rose Tree II and Knight Errant, a stallion who also served as a teaser—a horse that breeders use to see if their mare is receptive to masculine overtures and ready to be bred. Runnymede's top sire, Star Shoot, was also blind, making him an unattractive option to breed with the sightless mare. A legend of Knight Errant jumping a paddock fence in amorous pursuit of Rose Tree would eventually attach to the gelding and enhance his popularity, though it seems to have little basis in fact.[2]

With McCabe serving a five-day suspension for failing to maintain a straight course in the stretch run of a race earlier in the week, Charley Peak reteamed with Rosebud for the two-year-old sprint on the Clark Handicap undercard. Only the Kentucky Derby drew a larger crowd at Churchill Downs that spring. Peak sent the 2–5 favorite straight to the lead on the track made heavy by rain and was thoroughly in command after a quarter mile. Roamer struggled to stay within sight of the leader on the turn, and Old Rosebud sailed on to a six-length win. It was another five lengths back to

Johnny McCabe was a talented but inexperienced jockey when he entered the national limelight with Old Rosebud in 1913. (Keeneland Library Cook Collection)

E. R. Bradley's Brave Cunarder, a colt that would finish second in the Preakness the following year. The next horse under the wire was a dozen lengths farther behind. Rosebud's dominant display gave the Weir barn reason for optimism headed into the rematch with Little Nephew two days later.

The marquee matchup attracted a large Monday crowd that would see Rosebud on another short end of a dramatic stretch duel. Johnny Loftus secured good early position aboard Little Nephew on the inside of a drying Churchill Downs racing surface, while Old Rosebud was briefly shuffled back. Though McCabe hustled his horse toward the leader in the opening furlong, Loftus forced the young rider wide on the turn. Rosebud ground his way to Little Nephew's shoulder with an eighth of a mile to the wire, but Loftus out-finished the young jockey in the final yards to post a near-record time of fifty-three seconds flat. E. R. Bradley's Black Toney, who would sire five champions, three Hall of Fame inductees, and two Kentucky Derby winners, was ten lengths back in third.

Originally from Chicago, Johnny Loftus had decided he wanted to be a jockey as a young teenager. Despite some indication that he would soon become too tall, he rode his first winner in 1909 at age sixteen. In a career that would barely last a decade, Loftus rode some of the most renowned horses of the era on his way to induction into Thoroughbred racing's Hall of Fame. His aptitude and dedication were obvious from the outset. "He has the natural interest in a horse," noted one of the trainers Loftus rode for early in his career, "and he'd sleep [in the stall] with one if I would let him."[3]

Little Nephew's talent was indisputable, and his owner was fielding offers as high as twenty thousand dollars to purchase the gelding. But the question of which was the fastest son of Uncle was hardly settled. "Loftus outgeneraled and outrode little McCabe and virtually won the race for Mr. Gruber," the *Louisville Courier-Journal* reported after the Bashford Manor. The *Daily Racing Form* flatly declared that "with riders reversed Old Rosebud would have been the victor."[4]

Four days later, Old Rosebud was back for a four-and-a-half-furlong allowance race on a muddy Churchill Downs track against a field of seven that included Brave Cunarder and a Tennessee-bred first-time starter named Hodge. Rosebud relished the heavy going and returned to winning ways as the odds-on favorite. He rushed to a ten-length lead in the first quarter and maintained the margin through the finish even as he was pulled to a canter through the final hundred yards.

Weir had forged a fast bond with the animal he called "old Buddy." The trainer had a lump of sugar for him, win or lose. "He always looks for it after a race," Weir told a reporter, "and if it was $100 a pound, he would get it. I always put two lumps in my pocket. He gets one, I get the other. We dine together." Weir even reportedly indulged the horse's taste for pastries, beer, and chewing tobacco on occasion. His humanlike characteristics and gentle demeanor helped endear him to a growing band of fans and admirers.[5]

At the conclusion of the Churchill meet, Kentucky racing shifted three miles south to Douglas Park, a former trotting track that had reached a cooperative arrangement with Churchill Downs in 1907. Continuing an ambitious schedule, Weir entered Rosebud in a five-furlong allowance three days after his last win. Despite threatening weather and occasional showers, ten thousand fans filled the spacious grandstand and lush lawns. A special train brought racegoers from Lexington for the day. The main event was the first running of the ten-thousand-dollar Kentucky Handicap, which organizers hoped would become one of America's great races for older horses. But no performance on the day was more impressive than Old Rosebud's.[6]

With McCabe again in the saddle, Rosebud jumped to a quick lead as the 1–4 favorite and was never threatened. Previously unbeaten Vandergrift gave chase early but was six lengths back at the finish. Black Toney gained ground in the stretch to take third, three lengths behind the runner-up. McCabe eased his mount before the wire, but the effort was still enough to set a new track record. Reporters began to speculate about how much the Weir trainee might be worth. Prompted for an asking price, Ham conceded that he had not received any formal offers. He declined to provide a specific number at which he might be willing to sell, but he did say that the twenty thousand dollars Gruber had rejected for Little Nephew would not be enough.[7]

Playing up the burgeoning rivalry between Old Rosebud and Little Nephew, Douglas Park officials organized a special Saturday afternoon event pitting the two gelded sons of Uncle and the impressive winner of the Breeders' Futurity at Lexington, Imperator, owned by future US senator Johnson N. Camden, in a one-thousand-dollar five-furlong sprint. Ten thousand spectators showed up to witness the clash of two-year-old titans and made Little Nephew the 7–5 favorite. At 11–5, Rosebud was the long shot of the trio. Before the race, track stewards spoke to McCabe, Loftus, and Imperator's jockey, Phil Musgrave, who would have his license suspended by the Jockey

Club later that year, emphasizing that there should be no rough riding. The jockeys had a collective reputation for aggressive tactics, but they assured officials it would be a cleanly run race. The three contestants ran necks apart in the early going, with Little Nephew and Johnny Loftus staked to a short lead on the rail. After a quick opening quarter, Little Nephew and Old Rosebud began to distance themselves from Imperator. Rosebud clung to Little Nephew's flank as the pair rounded the final turn. Entering the stretch, Rosebud bore down on his adversary until the two were eyeball to eyeball. When McCabe urged him forward, Rosebud slid past Little Nephew and flew under the wire four lengths in front. It was the fastest five furlongs ever run in Kentucky, 58⅘ seconds.[8]

Little Nephew came out of the race well. Three days later, he posted a three-furlong workout in :35⅘, convincing his trainer that he deserved another crack at Old Rosebud, in a five-furlong allowance on a fast Douglas Park track. Johnny Loftus was off all his mounts that day due to illness, which one report attributed to fallout from the jockey's habit of "flipping"—forcing himself to throw up to maintain riding weight. Loftus's replacement, Merritt "Happy" Buxton, employed a new strategy and pushed his horse right from the start. He opened a sizable lead, forcing Rosebud out of his comfort zone, but Little Nephew couldn't maintain the lively pace. Old Rosebud began rolling on the turn and reeled in the front-running target in the homestretch to win by a widening length, clipping another fifth of a second off his track record.

Roamer was eight lengths farther back in third. At the start of the season, his owners had thought they had a budding superstar. Subsequent performances would eventually validate the early evaluation and land Roamer in American horse racing's Hall of Fame. But his handlers were sobered by the second consecutive flogging he had received from Old Rosebud and decided to send him to New York to get out from the Applegate gelding's shadow and possibly find him a new owner.[9]

No horse had ever run consecutive sub-fifty-nine-second races in less than a week. Old Rosebud would try to extend the streak in the Spring Trial Stakes. His back-to-back wins had seemed to settle any debate as to the relative merits of Rosebud and Little Nephew. But the fat $3,700 purse made the Spring Trial the third most valuable race for two-year-olds in Kentucky that year, trailing only the Breeders' Futurity in Lexington and the Cincinnati Trophy at Latonia. It was more than sufficient to entice Little Nephew's people to give him one more stab at the Weir trainee, three days after the latest trouncing.

Heavy rain left parts of Louisville soaked the morning of the Spring Trial. Threatening skies loomed over Douglas Park for most of the day, but the showers held off. Another huge Saturday crowd filled the grounds for a last look at a rising star on the closing day of Louisville's spring racing season. The track was again fast, and Rosebud again lowered the local record, posting the quickest five-furlong time by any two-year-old on an American oval. McCabe took control of the race from the start aboard the odds-on favorite. Breaking from the outside, he settled his mount on the lead and never allowed Little Nephew, with Johnny Loftus back in the stirrups, to advance past his hip. Old Rosebud extended the margin to two comfortable lengths in the stretch while McCabe sat still. Little Nephew gave chase but could not close the gap. Imperator was a dozen lengths back in third.

Rosebud's superiority over his adversary was clear. Owner Michael Gruber and trainer Elza Brown determined that it was time to find Little Nephew some softer competition. Their gelding was soon on a train to Canada. Gruber told the press that he hoped to bring him back for another showdown with Old Rosebud in the Cincinnati Trophy over the Fourth of July weekend, assuming things went well up North. The grocer was still not prepared to concede the two-year-old championship to anyone.[10]

Following Rosebud's unprecedented run of success, whispers concerning a possible sale of the Applegates' speedy youngster grew louder. The *Daily Racing Form* reported that his owners had agreed on thirty thousand dollars for an asking price. Leading trainer Mose Goldblatt was intrigued, calling Old Rosebud "one of the greatest two-year-olds that ever looked through a bridle."[11]

As the ultimately fruitless discussions of a deal continued, racing in Kentucky moved to Latonia for the start of the summer meet at one of the finest facilities in America. With Old Rosebud as a marketable attraction, officials there were optimistic for a successful racing season despite recent labor strikes and a devastating flood in the Cincinnati area. Heavy showers soaked the track before the day's first race, but thousands showed up to witness Rosebud's appearance in the $3,500 Harold Stakes, a five-furlong local prep for the Cincinnati Trophy. A six-horse field shrank to three after defections of the mud-averse. As he had in the past, Rosebud relished the boggy conditions and was never seriously threatened. He casually dispatched a couple of mild early challenges and splashed along to a five-length win.

Weir toyed with the idea of giving Rosebud another start or two before the Cincinnati Trophy but decided to train him up to the race. Perhaps a three-day suspension earned by Johnny McCabe for misbehavior at the starting post made that decision easier. Meanwhile, Little Nephew was thriving in Canada, notching three consecutive wins. Jockey Killingsworth—known to racing fans only by his surname and described by the *Courier-Journal* as "one of the few colored boys now riding"—had replaced Johnny Loftus as the gelding's regular rider. As late as July 1, Latonia officials expected to see Gruber's two-year-old in the six-furlong Cincinnati Trophy, but trainer Elza Brown would keep his gelding abroad until the start of the Saratoga meet.[12]

Even without Little Nephew, anticipation for the six-thousand-dollar race was high. Track officials expected record holiday crowds, and railroads offered special rates to attract fans from Louisville, Chicago, and St. Louis. Despite ideal weather, a perfect racing surface, and a stout purse, Old Rosebud scared off much of the competition. Only three horses lined up to face

Little Nephew, with trainer Elza Brown and jockey Killingsworth, was the only horse to defeat Old Rosebud as a two-year-old in 1913. (Keeneland Library Hemment Collection)

him, and Rosebud was an overwhelming 1–4 favorite against the reduced, middling field. In the paddock before the race, one turfman muttered the ultimate racetrack compliment about the Applegate gelding: "He is simply a freak horse." Minutes later, the Bud would again exceed lofty expectations.[13]

Old Rosebud broke a step slowly, but McCabe gathered him quickly, and the pair zipped along the rail to seize the lead before the equine quartet had traveled a furlong. Rosebud soon opened an eight-length lead, finishing the first half mile in :46⅖. He maintained the margin into the stretch before McCabe, glancing over his shoulder and seeing no one, throttled down. Old Rosebud glided to the finish six lengths ahead of his closest foe and could have won by twice that margin. McCabe, who had taken his share of public criticism for some of his rides on Old Rosebud, received a five-hundred-dollar gratuity from Ham and Weir after the race in recognition of his contributions to what was becoming a historic season for the star of the stable.

It was another gaudy performance, impressing even longtime racetrackers, including George Long, master of Bashford Manor Stud in Louisville and owner of one of the horses thumped by Old Rosebud. "He takes a rival by the head and runs him into the ground, and then comes on to win as he pleases," the breeder of three Kentucky Derby winners said after the race. "He seems to have unlimited powers as a racehorse and acts like a horse that is absolutely unbeatable when in his best condition." In articulating what made Rosebud such an efficient runner, a reporter for the *Courier-Journal* pointed to the gelding's "superb action," explaining, "When at full speed he runs like a piece of the most highly improved machinery, there being no friction whatever in his way of going. He is undoubtedly the champion 2-year-old of 1913, and if he meets with no ill-luck there is no reason to prevent him from also being the champion 3-year-old next season." A Texas turf writer who had seen the gelding in Juárez went even further in his praise, noting that Rosebud appeared destined to become "the greatest thoroughbred of recent years" and "one of the most sensational performers that ever pranced to the post on a race course throughout the world."[14]

Rosebud was the best two-year-old anyone had seen in Kentucky in quite some time, but there were plenty of scoffers in New York who still saw the Bluegrass State as part of the American backwater. They would reserve judgment on the gelding's greatness until after he had faced competition from top Eastern stables. Racing had returned to the Empire State only a few weeks earlier, following a favorable ruling from a New York appellate court that determined the state's antigambling statute only forbade organized bookmaking and was unenforceable as to casual bets between individuals. Two weeks after his resounding score in the Cincinnati Trophy, Old Rosebud was settling in at Saratoga, where he would have the chance to quiet the critics and substantiate his early success in front of the sport's nobility.

The quaint Victorian resort town of Saratoga Springs, in the Adirondack foothills of Upstate New York, had drawn vacationers since the early nineteenth century. Racing enthusiasts had been flocking since 1863, when former bare-knuckle boxing champion and underworld kingpin John Morrissey revived the sport there, in part to attract gamblers to his seasonal casino operation. In the summer of 1913, streets and sidewalks teemed with tourists eager to welcome horse racing back to one of its most picturesque settings after a nearly three-year hiatus. The release of pent-up demand was palpable on shop floors, in hotel lobbies, and on the town's main thoroughfare. Trains filled with horsemen, gamblers, and various hangers-on steamed into town from across the region. "Saratoga is again looking something like itself," the *New York Evening Telegram* happily reported. "Never did the villagers exhibit such jubilant feelings."[15]

Old Rosebud seemed to relish his new surroundings and was working well in the cool mornings. Racing fans clambered to get a glimpse of the ballyhooed runner. Not all were convinced of his invincibility, however. August Belmont's strapping gelding Stromboli was among the best of a deep group of New York–based two-year-olds expected to provide Old Rosebud a stern test. Young rider Tommy McTaggert, who had guided the Jockey Club chairman's fleet runner to a pair of wins in New York that summer, cheekily told Weir, "Don't bet too much on Old Rosebud to beat Stromboli, for Mr. Belmont's gelding can fly."[16]

But Weir changed a few minds when Old Rosebud worked three furlongs in :33⅘. One witness was dumbfounded by what he saw. Tom Healey had trained for Richard T. Wilson, president of the Saratoga racing association, for years and would later earn acclaim for his handling of five winners of the Preakness Stakes and all-time greats like Equipoise. The future Hall of Famer told Weir that he could not recall a two-year-old ever going much quicker than :36 at Saratoga and then spent the next fifteen minutes staring at Old Rosebud in disbelief as the gelding cooled out.[17]

Despite his blossoming fame, some journalists still evinced confusion over how to classify the gelding, given his anatomical condition. A writer for the *New York Sun* praised the extraordinary workout, referring to Old Rosebud as "she" and telling readers that the filly would make her New York debut in the Flash Stakes on opening day at Saratoga. Perhaps the error was an inadvertent one committed by an inexperienced scribe, but there were plenty of sportswriters who were unsure how to categorize geldings at a time when gender-related issues were becoming hot political topics.[18]

Months earlier, in Washington, DC, thousands of advocates for women's voting rights marched down Pennsylvania Avenue in protest of what the National American Woman Suffrage Association called "the present political organization of society, from which women are excluded." Some of the activists brazenly rode horses astride, rather than sidesaddle, flouting the norms of polite society. A crowd as large as 100,000, many in town for Woodrow Wilson's presidential inauguration, lined the parade route to heckle, kick, spit on, and impede the procession. When hopelessly outnumbered police proved incapable of controlling the biggest gathering ever seen in the capital, mounted patrolmen were summoned to clear a path. Ambulance drivers had a tough time navigating the hostile masses as they shuttled more than a hundred injured people to the hospital.[19]

The scene at Saratoga was far more tranquil, but not without its own tension, on opening day. The Saturday sky was sunny and the air cool, as if the start of the meet and the attendant carnival atmosphere had received divine approval. Shortly after noon, a New York turf writer observed the spectacle as racegoers made their way from Broadway hotels, past the shuttered casino once presided over by John Morrissey, and out Union Avenue to the track. He admired the "countless surreys and gliding automobiles in one long, gay parade," noting that Saratoga "looked like old times, and everybody seemed happy and contented." A correspondent for the *Louisville Courier-Journal* reported a pervasive "spirit of conviviality" among the patrons, "a feeling that racing would live no matter what the conditions should be."[20]

Lest anyone get the wrong idea that all was completely back to normal at the stately racetrack, a conspicuous law enforcement contingent, including the sheriff, the district attorney, and a squadron of Pinkerton agents, was on hand to apprehend anyone foolish enough to conduct their betting in an obvious manner. The president of the New York Law and Order League also promised to be on the lookout for criminality. The police presence was a deterrent to would-be delinquents, but it was also a symbolic gesture aimed to placate any antigambling scolds who might be checking to make sure the Hart-Agnew law—as most recently interpreted by New York's highest court—was being strictly applied. Bets among friends were permitted, but no money could change hands, and no evidence of recordkeeping or solicitation of wagers from the public would be allowed. The head of the sizable security detail at the track addressed gamblers before the first race. He promised that anyone caught breaking the law would face a lifetime ban from all organized racetracks.[21]

The grounds were swarming with patrons long before the first race. Newspapers noted that half the crowd was female and that the festively clad women added touches of color against the backdrop of the men's conservative suits. How evil could horse racing be, the writers seemed to be asking their readers, with so many respectable-looking women in attendance? Horsemen and gamblers shared gossip and tips in the shaded paddock area. The Saratoga Handicap was the nominally featured race, but all the talk was of Old Rosebud.[22]

The crowd of ten thousand cheered gratefully as an otherwise unnoteworthy field of horses filed onto the track for the day's first contest, a cheap selling race for two-year-olds. The equine procession symbolized the survival of a sport that had been an integral part of the local culture and economy for decades. Those who wondered whether Old Rosebud could sustain his prior success would have to wait only until the third race, the fortieth running of the five-and-a-half-furlong Flash Stakes. Frank Weir was hounded by new fans and old friends who wanted to know just how good his celebrated gelding was. His canned answer was, "You'll see." If the trainer wanted to add a bit of levity to an encounter, he would add of his horse, "I wish he was a bit bigger."[23]

At the conclusion of the second race, hundreds hurried to the saddling area to have a look at the young phenom. Rosebud seemed unfazed by the hubbub, standing "docile as a lamb," according to a New York journalist. Among the throng was his breeder, John E. Madden. "He's a racing machine, that's all," Madden told a bystander. "The only bad point I see about him is that I sold him." As he stroked his chin and strolled around the horse to examine him from all sides, Madden added, "If Applegate isn't satisfied with the bargain, I'll return his money. I don't think they'll beat him today."[24]

Under the conditions of the race, Old Rosebud would carry 124 pounds, a dozen more than August Belmont's pair of promising juveniles, Stromboli and Flittergold. Many thought the former to be among the best two-year-olds in New York, and the latter was a full brother to Fair Play, who would later sire the immortal Man o' War. They had been pointed toward the race for months. Harry Payne Whitney's gelding Black Broom would tote only 109, as would Bradley's Choice, owned by E. R. Bradley. Bettors were getting odds of 3–5 on Old Rosebud—unofficially, of course.

As had become his habit and his preference, Rosebud broke sharply and was in control of the race within fifty yards. The Belmont-owned pair also showed early speed, but they were three lengths back of the pacesetter after a furlong. Rosebud was running well within himself beneath Johnny McCabe as he zipped through three-eighths in :34⅗. Entering the homestretch, he was two lengths ahead of Stromboli. McCabe peeked over his shoulder, but this time there was no Little Nephew looming. With no target to chase, Rosebud started to drift toward the middle of the track. Tommy McTaggert had Stromboli full out. But when McCabe shook his reins and smooched to his mount, Rosebud skipped away to a convincing win.

With a win in the 1913 Flash Stakes at Saratoga, Old Rosebud and Johnny McCabe showed they could compete against top New York competition. (Keeneland Library Cook Collection)

Doubters were becoming believers. The *New York Sun* called Old Rosebud "a racing machine par excellence." Prominent East Coast trainer Simon Healy gushed, "He's a wonder. Everything we've heard about him is true. Yes indeed, I want to see the horse that's going to trim him." Columnists were left to look to the past for comparisons, some landing on the unforgettable Colin's brilliant speed as the closest they had seen to Old Rosebud's.[25]

Even the once-maligned Johnny McCabe caught a few rays of the commendation being heaped on his mount, though his treatment in the press had risen only from outright criticism to faint praise. "Instances are not infrequent that a great 2-year-old like Old Rosebud has brought into prominence a rider with previously little reputation as a star," the *Courier-Journal* noted. "In all his races but two, the Louisville-owned crack has been ridden by J. McCabe, a rider who is fast coming to the front, it is true, but is far from a finished saddle artist. . . . Other similar instances could be cited which would as fully illustrate the truth of the old saying that 'it is the good horse that makes the good rider.'"[26]

Three days after his resounding score in the Flash, Rosebud's status was indirectly enhanced when his erstwhile rival Little Nephew won a juvenile handicap at Saratoga, spotting weight to a strong field that included Roamer and Black Toney. The following Saturday, Roamer's triumph in the Saratoga Special further flattered Old Rosebud. It was Roamer's first win, in his second start, for new owner Andrew Miller. The Saratoga Association secretary-treasurer, Jockey Club steward, cofounder of *Life* magazine, and, incidentally, Harvard classmate of Theodore Roosevelt had recently acquired the gelding from his Kentucky breeders for a reported $3,500 after they had become disheartened by the drubbings Roamer had taken from Old Rosebud in Kentucky.

Just when it appeared that geldings from the Bluegrass State were poised to sweep all the major races for two-year-old males at the meet, an Eastern hope emerged in industrial heir and New York racing stalwart Harry Payne Whitney's colt Pennant. The Kentucky-bred son of Peter Pan equaled a Saratoga track record for five and a half furlongs in his first career start, on August 12 for trainer James Rowe, beating Stromboli by two persuasive lengths. New York turf writers pegged Pennant as the next American superhorse and suggested that calls to anoint Old Rosebud two-year-old champion might have been premature.[27]

The Rosebud camp did not give that seed of doubt much time to sprout. The day after Pennant's flashy debut, Old Rosebud captured the six-furlong United

States Hotel Stakes, proving to any remaining agnostics that he could concede weight to Eastern competition and carry his speed at least three-quarters of a mile. Old Rosebud was the center of attention under cloudy skies at the Saratoga saddling area before the race. One journalist described him as looking "as cool and collected as an old stagehand." While his trainer and groom finished prerace preparations, Old Rosebud "simply looked around at the trees and shrubs and the people, and when McCabe came along to ride him, he turned his eye on him and sort of winked in recognition." Before the march to the starting gate, McCabe briskly galloped the gelding a quarter mile in front of the grandstand, to the delight of the spectators.[28]

Let off at odds of 1–6 against an overmatched six-horse field that included a couple of stakes winners, Rosebud established a lead in the first few strides after some fractiousness at the start, skittered an opening furlong in eleven seconds, and controlled the race the rest of the way, with McCabe keeping his horse under a snug hold through the stretch. His three-length victory was a more workmanlike performance than Rosebud had displayed

Old Rosebud, with jockey Johnny McCabe, winning the 1913 US Hotel Stakes at Saratoga to finish his two-year-old season with a record of twelve wins in fourteen starts. (Keeneland Library Hemment Collection)

in his spectacular Saratoga unveiling, and prerace misbehavior earned him a spot on the starter's schooling list. Still, the Bud's early speed was undeniably impressive, and his ninth consecutive win quieted the early hype surrounding horse-of-the-hour Pennant.

Even a veteran observer like Ed Cole, turf editor for the *New York Evening Telegram*, was awestruck. Labeling Rosebud the "Western wonder" and comparing him to a skillful lightweight wrestler, Cole wrote, "Were he to be trotted out with a batch of horses unclipped and unshod he would be about the last one to be picked out as a racehorse. [But] when he extends himself in a race it reminds one of a little mouse scampering off to its hole to get out of sight."[29]

Easterners' confidence that Pennant would knock Rosebud from his perch atop the juvenile division had been dampened by Rosebud's latest victory. Still, Saratoga officials sought to squeeze all the juice they could from the Weir trainee's popularity and capitalize on any lingering doubts that he could beat all comers. They floated the idea of a special Labor Day race that could decide the issue on the racetrack. Invitees would include Old Rosebud, Little Nephew, Pennant, and Stromboli. Little Nephew's wins in the Sanford Memorial Stakes and Adirondack Handicap further whetted appetites for such a showdown. But it was not to be. Pennant exited his win in the Futurity (held on August 30 at Saratoga that year due to a limited New York racing schedule) with sore shins, ending his racing season. And whispers from the backstretch intimated that Old Rosebud was not right. The gelding had looked uncharacteristically dull in a six-furlong work a week earlier, leaving railbirds to speculate that something was amiss. Perhaps casting an eye toward potential buyers, Weir publicly insisted that his horse was "never sounder in limb and wind than he is today."[30]

At the close of the Saratoga meet, Old Rosebud accompanied the rest of Weir's stable to Kentucky. After the fall racing season there, the trainer brought his star pupil to John D. Carr's farm six miles northwest of downtown Lexington, where he would enjoy some downtime, turned out in a paddock, while most of the string went to Mexico for the winter. "I have decided not to take him with me to Juárez," Weir told a local reporter. "I disliked leaving the gelding. However, he is in good hands and several other horses will be left with him. Barring illness, Old Rosebud will develop into a great three-year-old. I have not asked him to do any work since the Saratoga meeting. I am glad I gave him a rest."[31]

Protestations to the contrary notwithstanding, Weir would later acknowledge that the two-year-old had in fact bowed a tendon. "Old Rosebud pulled up lame that year, but I never told anybody about it, and it was never mentioned in print," he admitted years later. Weir would also later disclose that he had advised Colonel Applegate to sell the gelding over the winter if they could get a good price for him.[32]

At the conclusion of the Eastern racing season, the *Daily Racing Form* named Old Rosebud its champion two-year-old. The choice was hardly a surprise, given his remarkable record in 1913—twelve wins and two second-place finishes in fourteen starts, with earnings of $19,057, tops among all North American runners. Frank Weir was among the cavalcade of American horsemen and horses making its way to Juárez when he learned of Old Rosebud's championship honors.[33]

Racing officials there were doing their best to reassure Americans that the meet would be unaffected by recent violence. Francisco Madero had been elected president months after his forces seized Juárez in 1911. His moderate government frightened the oligarchs but failed to satisfy the revolutionaries. He was removed from power and assassinated in a military coup two weeks after Old Rosebud's debut win in the Yucatan Stakes. General Victoriano Huerta took control of the Mexican government and was immediately opposed by former Madero supporters. Incoming American president Woodrow Wilson, a progressive Democrat with more interest in domestic reform than foreign policy, was critical of Huerta's seizure of power and refused to recognize the regime, which he called a "government of butchers." Huerta's strongarm tactics offended Wilson's idealism, but protection of American business interests would be the primary focus of US relations with Mexico for the rest of the tumultuous decade.[34]

Disparate revolutionary factions would find common cause in seeking Huerta's ouster. Locally influential warlords, including Pancho Villa, began to wrest regional strongholds from federal control. In the early morning of November 15, 1913, Villa and two thousand of his Division del Norte troops snuck into Huerta-held Juárez aboard a hijacked coal train. Despite heavy fighting near the racetrack and a barrage of bullets and artillery shells whizzing overhead, no horses, handlers, or racetrack property was harmed. When the dust settled, Villa was in possession of the city and would soon control all of Chihuahua. He announced that he looked forward to the racing season, scheduled to begin Thanksgiving Day. Alberto Terrazas, founding president of the Juárez Jockey Club, had resigned from the post, but he remained a supporter of the venture. Terrazas was a backer of Huerta and had commanded troops against the revolutionaries. He was not on friendly terms with Villa, who would soon kidnap Terrazas's brother. With Villa dominating the region, Terrazas fled to the United States, and the Juárez Jockey Club dropped his name from the racetrack. Hearst associate Jack Follansbee would assume the presidency of the association.[35]

Villa and his staff attended the opening of the Juárez races, where they were greeted warmly by Mexicans and Americans. The general maintained a cordial relationship with track leadership. "Of all the Mexican leaders, I knew the picturesque Villa best of all," Matt Winn fondly recalled. "Although he was known as a ruthless man, and a cold-blooded killer, he gave us no trouble." Villa was constantly seeking funding for his revolutionary endeavors, but he never directly threatened horsemen or the racetrack. Instead, he would offhandedly point out something that his men needed, like new uniforms. Track officials would take the hint, and racing would continue undisturbed. Winn recalled one instance when hay began to disappear from the track's stables. He asked for a meeting with Villa and explained the situation. The next day, posters plastered around town stated in Spanish, "Anyone who molests Colonel Winn, or any of the property of the Juárez race track, will be shot. [Signed,] VILLA."[36]

While the racing in Juárez proceeded without him, Old Rosebud wintered comfortably in Kentucky. In late December, Weir received a glowing report from John D. Carr; the trainer could begin to chart a path to the Kentucky Derby, and Rosebud would be ready to start galloping in January. Shortly after the new year, Weir's assistant Harry "Mack" McLaughlin put the rested gelding on a train to Louisville, where McLaughlin would look after him until Weir's return from Mexico.

Old Rosebud had resumed light training at Douglas Park when Weir arrived in Louisville at the end of March. The three-year-old had filled out nicely over the winter. While still on the small side, he could no longer be described as freakishly undersized. Rosebud garnered steady, if lukewarm, backing in winter-book betting on the Kentucky Derby, still six weeks away. He was perhaps the most accomplished pre-Derby favorite in the history of the race, but many questioned whether he would be able to carry his brilliant

Revolutionary bandit Pancho Villa attended the opening of the 1913–1914 race meet at Juárez. "Although he was known as a ruthless man, and a cold-blooded killer, he gave us no trouble," Matt Winn recalled. (Library of Congress)

speed the Derby's mile-and-a-quarter distance. "There seems to be a suspicion that Old Rosebud is not cut out for a Derby horse and will not like the route," the *Daily Racing Form* reported in mid-March. And though no one had seemed bothered by Rosebud's lack of testicles as a two-year-old, some skeptics now seized on his status as a gelding, wondering whether he would have the grit to win such a long race so early in the season. "There has been some objection to Old Rosebud because he is a gelding," the *Racing Form* noted, citing several disappointing performances by prominent geldings in the Kentucky Derby over the years. Three geldings had won the Derby, but none had done so in more than a quarter century. More recently, the Weir-trained gelding Roseben had proved himself to be the fastest horse in America, but he had rarely been asked to run farther than seven furlongs and had never won a race longer than a mile. Veteran turfmen certainly knew that Rosebud's anatomy would not prevent him from winning the Kentucky Derby. But pockets of misguided skepticism reflected broader American trepidation about declining masculinity in an increasingly urban, mechanized, and technocratic society.[37]

Teddy Roosevelt, still a force in American politics after failing to earn a return to the White House in the 1912 presidential election, had first won national fame with the Rough Riders in the Spanish-American War. He rode that celebrity, and a hypermasculine, super-energetic public persona, to the New York governorship in 1898 and was selected as President William McKinley's running mate two years later. Roosevelt had been a sickly child but later relished exercise and adventure, becoming an avid outdoorsman, boxer, and equestrian as a young man. He advocated "the life of toil and effort, of labor and strife" as a path to the "highest form of success which comes, not to the man who desires mere easy peace, but to the man who does not shrink from danger." He thought that those principles should be applied not just by individuals but also on the international stage. "No nation can achieve real greatness," Roosevelt wrote, "if its people are not both essentially moral and essentially manly."[38]

Roosevelt would ascend to the presidency when McKinley succumbed to wounds inflicted by an assassin's bullet at the 1901 World's Fair in Buffalo. Days earlier, Roosevelt had told a Minnesota audience, "The men who, with ax in the forest and pick in the mountains and plow on the prairies, pushed to completion the dominion of our people over the American wilderness have given the definite shape to our nation [and] make up the essential manliness of the American character." A perceived crisis of American virility at the turn of the century would coincide with the United States' lurch toward a place among the great Western imperial powers at the height of social Darwinism's "survival of the fittest" attitudes.[39]

Roosevelt's decision to run for president in 1912 under the Progressive Party banner against his former vice president and handpicked successor—the incumbent William Howard Taft—and Democratic nominee Woodrow Wilson caused a split in the Republican Party and essentially handed the election to Wilson. While Wilson was not the jingoistic saber rattler that Roosevelt was, the former college professor, Princeton University president, and son of a Presbyterian minister had a quiet confidence in his ability to shape the nation, and the world, for the better. He believed that God had ordained his rise to power and governed accordingly. Wilson pursued an aggressive Progressive domestic agenda early in his presidency, signing bills into law that established the Federal Reserve System, reduced tariffs, strengthened

Woodrow Wilson brought a sense of moral purpose and Progressive idealism to the White House in 1913. His administration would support and enact countless reform measures during his two terms in office, but horse racing would avoid federal scrutiny. (Library of Congress)

antitrust rules, regulated child labor, implemented federal income and estate taxes, and created the National Parks Service. Early in his political career, Wilson's knowledge of, and interest in, international relations was limited. "It would be the irony of fate," Wilson noted prior to assuming the presidency, "if my administration had to deal chiefly with foreign affairs." But when fate required him to navigate some of the stickiest geopolitics ever faced by an American president, he built on Roosevelt's big-stick diplomacy and Taft's dollar diplomacy in crafting a "moral diplomacy," which he hoped would spread democracy and hinder European imperialism. He would cite principled justifications for American military interventions in Latin America and, most consequentially, in Europe.[40]

An early opportunity for Wilson to apply his moral diplomacy emerged in the spring of 1914, when a small, unarmed crew from the USS *Dolphin* came ashore for supplies at Tampico, a thriving port serving a nascent American and European oil industry on Mexico's east coast. Several American sailors were arrested by a Mexican official for loading fuel at a restricted dock. After an hour of detention, the seamen were released with an informal apology. The commander of the US ships in the region felt that his nation's dignity had been besmirched and demanded a proper *mea culpa*, including a twenty-one-gun salute to the American flag. As the two nations haggled over logistics concerning reciprocal homage to be paid, Wilson sent seven battleships to the Mexican coast. When American intelligence reported that a German shipment of fifteen million rounds of (American-made) ammunition would soon arrive in Veracruz, Wilson ordered US forces to take control of the port to prevent delivery to Huerta's forces. "I have no enthusiasm for War," Wilson said, "but I have enthusiasm for justice and for the dignity of the United States." Nineteen Americans and more than one hundred Mexicans were killed in the fighting. After enduring a string of military losses to rebels farther north, Huerta would resign the Mexican presidency in July, and revolutionary factions again clambered to fill the power void.[41]

3

Roses

Frank Weir heard the naysayers but was confident that Old Rosebud would be ready for the Derby. With horse racing in New York still recovering from its two-and-a-half-year shutdown, and the sport eliminated or severely curtailed in all but a few American jurisdictions, fans eagerly awaited the rare treat of a big-time event. The possibility that Old Rosebud might prove to be a true superstar only amplified the anticipation. With a heightened purse of ten thousand dollars—double the previous year's prize money and the largest in the forty-year history of the race—local and national interest in the Derby had never been higher.

Widespread coverage of the lead-up to the race in the sports pages of American newspapers surely pleased Colonel Applegate and the rest of the Churchill Downs ownership. National attention paid to the 1914 Derby served as proof that their vision for returning the once-great race to the top of American racing's hierarchy was coming to fruition. The Kentucky Derby had arrived with great fanfare in 1875, on the first day of racing at the Louisville Jockey Club and Driving Park Association track that would eventually be known as Churchill Downs. The morning of the first running, a local newspaper confidently declared that the Derby was "destined to become the great race of this country" and called for it to be observed as a local holiday. "For one day let us lay aside business cares, get away from the counting-room," the *Louisville Commercial* implored,

> and spend an afternoon in the cool, fresh air of the country. It will make us feel better and happier. St. Louis has her fair days, New

Orleans and Memphis their Mardigras. Let Louisville have her "Derby Day." Inaugurate such a custom, and that day will see thousands of strangers in the city. In England "Derby Day" is the greatest of all days, and it can be made the same here if everybody will just say so.[1]

Track founder Meriwether Lewis Clark had predicted that someday a winner of the Kentucky Derby would be worth more than the farm where it was raised. As ludicrous as the statement may have seemed at the time, it proved to be accurate. In its early years, the Kentucky Derby, then contested at a mile and a half, was heartily supported by the Kentucky racing community and attracted attention from the national sporting press. It attracted runners from the top local and regional stables as well as an occasional entry from leading national turfmen like William B. Astor Jr., Pierre Lorillard IV, the Dwyer Brothers, Lucky Baldwin, and lawyer–turned–mining tycoon James Ben Ali Haggin. In 1886, Haggin became frustrated at his inability to get a bet down on his colt, Ben Ali, in the Derby due to contract disputes between bookmakers and the person who controlled the betting privileges at Churchill Downs. Haggin removed his stable from the track in protest, and Ben Ali would be his last Derby starter. Though the significance of the kerfuffle may have been exaggerated by later historians, most leading Eastern stables would stay away from the Derby for more than a quarter century.

By the 1890s, thanks to financial mismanagement of the racetrack, increased competition within a growing sport, flagging support from the Louisville business community, and an emphasis on speed over stamina in American racing and breeding, the Derby had degenerated to a derisory condition described by a local writer as "greatness in decay." In May 1894, the *Chicago Tribune* declared that "the race amounts to but little except . . . the memories that cling about it." The underfunded Derby had become a relic of a bygone era. It was too long a race, too early in the season, and contested for too little money to attract top contestants.[2]

Colonel Applegate and his partners, all heavily involved in ownership of offtrack betting parlors, acquired the racetrack from Clark and his fellow shareholders in the autumn of 1894. Applegate's group rechristened the entity the New Louisville Jockey Club (NLJC). They constructed a new grandstand, adorned by the now-famous twin spires, on the opposite side of the track from the original and reduced the Derby's distance to a mile and a quarter in hopes of attracting fuller fields and more gambling. To shore up the track's finances, they enhanced the betting facilities and suspended a free-admission infield policy that had allowed everyone a chance to witness the Derby spectacle.

Facing pressure from social reformers who wanted to end gambling on racing, if not halt the sport altogether, and with the Derby still mired in small fields and general apathy, Applegate orchestrated a managerial shake-up at the NLJC in 1902. Though the move was made largely for optics, the new leadership would better position the track to survive Progressive Era reform and put the Kentucky Derby on a path toward becoming one of the most iconic sporting events in the world. And while he would no longer be listed among the club's officers, Applegate quietly maintained a controlling ownership interest.[3]

The New Louisville Jockey Club built a new grandstand, topped with now-iconic twin spires, on taking control of the track in 1894. (Library of Congress)

The Colonel had made his mark in all facets of the racing business in the late nineteenth century, but the steps he took toward growing the fan base and bringing the Louisville swells back to the races would be his most enduring legacy. Charlie Grainger, the mayor of Louisville, was named president of the NLJC. Applegate's son Ham, then twenty-three years old, was installed as board secretary and would later become treasurer of the association. But the most significant addition to the Churchill Downs management team was Matt Winn, the son of an Irish immigrant grocer and saloon keeper, who would become vice president and general manager of the revamped operation. Winn had been a merchant tailor with a broad clientele that included some of the city's most influential citizens, including Applegate, and was well connected in the city's various social circles. His skill in cultivating relationships with sportswriters would prove invaluable in the Derby's growth over the coming decades. As he took on broader roles and responsibilities in American horse racing, the nation's scribes could always count on Winn for free Derby tickets, a convivial drink, and a dose of his Southern charm.

The new management team wanted to market Churchill Downs to a wider range of sports fans, including local high society, and to broaden horse racing's appeal beyond those who saw it as merely a medium of gambling. Though wagering was indispensable to the track's financial sustainability, the NLJC knew that for the sport to survive in Louisville it would need support from the community beyond hardcore bettors. Track leadership also wanted to entice the top national stables to run in their major races, especially the Derby. In pursuit of those ends, the NLJC built a fancy clubhouse with a wide, two-story, rounded veranda that resembled the deck of a riverboat and evoked a romanticized vision of the Old South, a connotation that would be a crucial component of the Derby's phenomenal growth and persistent cultural relevance in the years to come. They would also return the free infield. But the most enduring contribution to horse racing made by the new management would be the reintroduction of pari-mutuel betting to American racetracks.

Antigambling zealots and political rivals, including new Louisville mayor "Honest Jim" Grinstead, with various axes to grind against Churchill Downs and the horse-racing industry—including a political feud with track president Grainger—tried to put the NLJC out of business in 1908 by strictly enforcing an old statute that the crusaders believed prohibited bookmakers from taking bets on horse racing in Kentucky. But track management thwarted those efforts by dusting off some pari-mutuel machines that had

Matt Winn (*right*) would help the Kentucky Derby become an iconic piece of American culture. On the left is New York grocery magnate and racetrack owner James Butler. (Keeneland Library Hemment Collection)

After a managerial shake-up in 1902, the New Louisville Jockey Club added a fancy clubhouse as part of an effort to attract a broader clientele to its racetrack. (Photographic Archive, P_00408, Special Collections, University of Louisville, Louisville, Kentucky)

been introduced decades earlier and discontinued before the turn of the century. When bookmakers ran the betting, the public might have reason to believe that the "house" could prefer one result over another, especially when the bookies owned racing stables or, in some cases, even the racetrack itself. But under the pari-mutuel system, odds were based on the amount of money bet on each horse. The racetrack took a percentage of each bet placed and thus had no reason to favor any particular outcome. This antiseptic form of gambling reduced the incentive to cheat and the likelihood of an appearance of chicanery, thereby blunting a good portion of reformers' criticisms of the sport. Kentucky's highest court would soon confirm that the machines did not violate Kentucky law.[4]

The transition to pari-mutuel wagering, done by necessity, not only stymied racing's opponents in Kentucky but also helped to reinvigorate national interest in the Derby. It would soon become the predominant form of betting on American horse racing. In 1913, bettors who chanced the new minimum wager of two dollars on Donerail to win the Derby at odds of 91–1 cashed $184.90 tickets through the pari-mutuel system. Newspaper coverage of the astonishing payout gave the Derby and the still relatively novel form of gambling some helpful publicity. The following year, as Old Rosebud prepared to return for his three-year-old season and a shot at the 1914 Derby, applications for the most expensive seats arrived from across the country, many tourists planning their first trip to Louisville. Churchill Downs and its signature event were returning to national relevance.

Having conquered the best of his generation as a two-year-old, Old Rosebud was a burgeoning national star. And his presence atop the list of Derby hopefuls further legitimized the race in the eyes of Easterners who had witnessed, or at least read about, his remarkable exploits as a two-year-old. Most knowledgeable racing fans believed Rosebud to be the deserving favorite, but there was plenty of talent among the other contenders. Owners without a Derby horse frantically sought to add one to their stable, but it was a seller's market. With supply tight and demand high, prices for top three-year-olds reached unprecedented levels.

The Applegates were not coy about their willingness to part with Old Rosebud. Given the glut of buyers and the paucity of sellers, some speculated that a price of $40,000 or $50,000 might be attainable. Perhaps equivalent to $1.5 million in twenty-first-century purchasing power, it was an enormous sum for a gelding that had never raced beyond six furlongs. Jockey Johnny McCabe was aboard Old Rosebud for well-attended morning gallops at Douglas Park. In the afternoons, Weir would show off his equine luminary to visitors gathered at his stable near the venue's main entrance.

Little Nephew had injured his hock over the winter and was not expected to make the Derby. But owner-trainer Kay Spence's strapping Tennessee-bred gelding Hodge, who had made a name for himself in Juárez over the winter, had impressed in the mornings at Churchill Downs and was looking like a viable contender. Neither he nor Rosebud was fully cranked up yet, but each drew crowds of spectators for their morning exercise and plenty of interest from would-be buyers salivating at the Derby's enhanced purse. One of the serious shoppers was Jefferson Livingston, a Cincinnati native who had made a fortune in ketchup manufacturing before diversifying his business interests.

The condiment king never missed a Kentucky Derby and wanted a competitive candidate for his stable. He wired a proposal to the Applegates from New York offering thirty thousand dollars for Old Rosebud, provided the gelding could pass an inspection conducted by Livingston's agent, the renowned Kentucky horseman, salesman, and raconteur Colonel Phil T. Chinn. Rosebud's ownership responded quickly, via telegram: "Would breeze him for you or Mr. Chinn and will sell him to you subject to examination by any veterinarian. Our price for the horse is $40,000, and we consider him cheap at that price. We are confident no horse can beat him."[5]

It took Livingston several moments to catch his breath after reading the counteroffer. "I would like to have Old Rosebud run in my colors for the Derby," Livingston told a reporter, "and I know he is a good horse, for I saw him win several stakes in his two-year-old form. But when you make a liberal offer and $10,000 is tacked on to the price at one clip, it causes you to hesitate. If Old Rosebud were a stallion he might be worth the money, but $40,000 looks like a high figure for a gelding in these days of racing."[6]

Despite the grousing, Chinn was at Douglas Park two days later to inspect the gelding and watch him gallop on Livingston's behalf. "A horse to win the Kentucky Derby is what Mr. Livingston wants," said Chinn, "and I am hoping that he will wind up with the winner." After Rosebud cruised around the one-mile oval under a tight hold from McCabe, looking every bit of a champion, Chinn conceded that the horse was handsomer than he had expected and that the workout was visually impressive. He upped Livingston's offer to thirty-five thousand dollars, which would have been the highest price for a three-year-old gelding in the history of American racing. But when Rosebud's owners held firm on their price, Chinn ended the negotiations.[7]

The Kentucky equine community was taken aback at the Applegates' brazenness in declining such a sizable amount of money. "I do hope that no ill-luck will attend Old Rosebud," said a veteran Derby-winning trainer, "but there is a jinx that generally follows the refusal of large sums for racehorses. I have had it happen to me a number of times. Racehorses are mighty perishable property, especially when it comes to $40,000 geldings."[8]

The staff at the Weir stable was surprised and relieved when they learned that Rosebud would remain in their care. They had become resigned to the idea that he would surely be sold, given the fabulous amounts of money being discussed—more than they would likely earn in a lifetime of work. Instead, Weir was left to plot a course to the Derby, slated for May 9. The trainer was not overly concerned about getting a longer race into his horse beforehand, and training up to the Derby was still an option. Weir was confident that he could build the gelding's endurance in his morning works and that his early speed would be enough to subdue any competition, even at ten furlongs. By the third week in April, Weir had shipped Old Rosebud to Lexington for the start of the Kentucky Association spring meet. There would be an assortment of races for his horse there, and Weir would be able to personally oversee his morning training.

Old Rosebud was still the leading Derby prospect, but several three-year-olds were emerging as legitimate challengers, including two fillies. Bronzewing, who would win the Ashland Oaks, Blue Grass Stakes, and Kentucky Oaks that spring, was performing well in morning breezes at Churchill Downs. And William Walker, former Kentucky Derby–winning jockey, had taken over training duties of the fleet filly Watermelon from owner John Madden. Walker, who also trained a few horses for Colonel Applegate over the years and was one of the most respected Black horsemen in the sport, had Watermelon working well. Few saw the Derby as a one-horse race, but Rosebud seemed to be improving with each workout, and his odds to wear the Derby winner's roses dipped accordingly. A few weeks earlier, he had been 5–1, but by late April, punters were getting only 7–2. Hodge was 8–1, and Watermelon could be had at 30–1.[9]

Rosebud was frisky and playful as he stepped off the train in Lexington. He joined the rest of Weir's eight-horse string in the same Kentucky Association barn that coincidentally had housed Derby winner Donerail the previous spring. Those who hadn't seen him since the previous summer were impressed with how well Rosebud had developed. Weir wanted to give the gelding a short work the day after his arrival, but the inside portion of the track was muddy and unsuitable for training. Word spread around town that he would be breezing in the afternoon, after the mud had dried. A large crowd gathered to watch him go three furlongs in :36⅕.[10]

Four days later, a steady Saturday afternoon rain kept less-hardy fans away and left the Lexington track several inches deep in mud for Old Rosebud's three-year-old debut in a one-mile allowance, two weeks before the Derby. Given his affinity for a sloppy surface, Rosebud was a 3–10 favorite against a stout field of three-year-olds that included Christophine, a filly that had set a North American record for a mile over the winter at Juárez; E. R.

Bradley's Black Toney; and Surprising, a striking gelding ridden by Charley Peak, who had largely recovered from injuries sustained in a fall from the saddle at Latonia the previous November that had left him with a fractured skull, a lacerated face, shattered ribs, and a broken arm.[11]

Johnny McCabe pushed Rosebud along at the spring of the barrier to secure a quick lead and was two lengths clear of Surprising after a speedy half mile. Rosebud stretched his advantage from there, running easily under a light hold. Peak's efforts to keep up with the front-runner had tired his mount, and Surprising would finish some seventeen lengths back, in fourth, which was still seven lengths better than Black Toney, who did not care for the mud. The fast filly Christophine finished gamely, passing tired horses in the stretch to take second place, still half a dozen lengths behind the winner. Rosebud coasted through the homestretch unchallenged, McCabe merely a passenger. On their return to the winner's circle, the jockey's jacket was soaked with rain but bore not a speck of mud.

The Rosebud camp was emboldened by the effort and began to discuss longer-term plans for major races later in the summer. But the immediate goal was still the Kentucky Derby, and the Bud was looking more like a deserving favorite every time he stepped on the track. His odds fell to 9–5 after another strong workout that week. The time was not remarkable, 2:13⅕ for ten furlongs, but muddy conditions on the inside half of the track had forced him to run near the outside fence. He fought McCabe much of the way around, begging to go faster. Witnesses knew that Old Rosebud was a fit racehorse that would last the Derby distance.

Jeff Livingston's trainer, Mose Goldblatt, had watched the work and immediately contacted the ketchup king with advice to resume negotiations for Rosebud's purchase. But Livingston's interest had cooled, and the gelding would remain in Weir's care. Although he was now fully convinced that Rosebud would win the Derby, Livingston simply could not justify shelling out that kind of money for a racehorse with no residual value as a stallion.[12]

Back in Louisville, Hodge was training up a storm. Eight days before the big event, he turned in what was called the fastest-ever pre-Derby work, completing the mile and a quarter in 2:05⅖. The *Nashville Tennessean* reported that the Tennessee-bred was "hard as nails" and primed for a big effort. Kay Spence, who began a life in horse racing on the Missouri fair circuit and would become one of the leading trainers in America, fielded questions from assembled reporters regarding rumors that various parties had made overtures to buy his gelding. "The best offer I have received is $15,000," said the veteran horseman. "I have stated that I am willing to part with Hodge for $20,000 but am not sure that I would not be making a foolish move in so doing. I will have no excuse to offer in the event he goes down in defeat. He has done everything that one could ask of a three-year-old and is in wonderful condition."[13]

A large crowd convened to witness Old Rosebud's last major pre-Derby work the next day. Old Rosebud strode onto the Lexington track shortly after seven o'clock, beneath Johnny McCabe. After a preliminary warm-up, the pair sped through fractions of :11$2/5$, :22$3/5$, :35, :46$3/5$, and :59$2/5$ before galloping out the mile and a quarter in 2:06$2/5$. It was a full second slower than Hodge's recent breeze in Louisville, but careful observers noted that Hodge had been all out to make his record-setting time. McCabe had won the Ashland Oaks the day before on Bronzewing and would again be aboard when the filly captured the Blue Grass Stakes five days later. The impressive feat caused some locals to call her the best filly they had seen in decades. But there was no question in McCabe's mind as to which was the superior of his regular mounts. Old Rosebud was the fastest horse the jockey had ever seen, and he was not concerned about any competition.[14]

The day before shipping to Louisville, Weir sent his gelding out between the fifth and sixth races at Lexington for an easy one-mile gallop, giving the assemblage a thrill. The track was not fast, and the time was irrelevant. The Bud was thriving. The Derby favorite arrived at Churchill Downs three days before the big race and had a solid leg stretcher at the Derby distance the following afternoon. He started slowly but picked up speed, traveling the last quarter in 23$4/5$ seconds. Old Rosebud was ready.[15]

Louisville was overfilled with visitors. Churchill Downs reported record-breaking advance ticket sales, and trains packed with Derbygoers from Chicago, New York, and Cincinnati filed into the Union and Central Stations, many pulling deluxe Pullman cars. Travelers without hotel reservations scrambled to find accommodations, and streetcar operators reported unprecedented traffic. If only the weather would cooperate; heavy rain on Thursday had dissipated to intermittent showers on Friday, but those lingered long into the night. All assumed that the track would be wet and slow for the Derby.[16]

As many as a dozen horses had been expected to start, but by Derby eve, scared of weather or of the prohibitive favorite, the field had been whittled to seven. As they had for weeks, Old Rosebud and Hodge received the most attention from the press and backing from gamblers. But they would face a group of genuine competitors: talented gelding Surprising would finish second (to Roamer) in the Travers that summer; Old Ben, owned by bookmaker W. G. Yanke, was a long shot; fleet filly Bronzewing won the Ashland Oaks and Blue Grass Stakes in Lexington in the span of five days and would soon add the Kentucky Oaks to her résumé; John Gund, the only colt in the bunch, had second-place finishes in the Breeders' Futurity and Blue Grass Stakes to his credit; and John Madden's filly Watermelon had impressed in morning workouts but was probably not quite yet fit for the distance.

The prospects for a good track on Derby Day had seemed slim only hours before, but racegoers awoke to clear skies and warm sunshine. The racing surface was still speckled with puddles, but the track superintendent equipped a crew of twenty-five men with sponges and buckets to sop up some of the excess moisture. By post time, the track was listed as fast, if still on the damp and slow side of perfection, and the pleasant weather drew larger than expected walk-up crowds. The Downs ran out of preprinted tickets and had to use a batch of old ones. Total attendance soared past thirty-five thousand, including some seven thousand who availed themselves of the free-admission infield policy that had been reinstated by Winn and company four years earlier. Organizers would call it the largest crowd ever to watch a horse race in Kentucky.[17]

The grounds were bustling long before the day's first race. By midafternoon, every stairway, walkway, and vantage point was filled. Cameramen scurried about as politicians, including the mayor, the governor, congressmen, and senators, made their glad-handing rounds. The track had implemented a ban on automobiles in the infield to thwart a cartel of entrepreneurs planning to charge a premium to pick up patrons downtown, convey them to the track, and secure front-row seats by forcing their way to the rail. Winn objected to the idea that someone besides Churchill Downs might profit from the free infield, whose purpose was to allow the multitudes access to the civic spectacle—and to enhance the visual experience of those in the expensive seats across the track. The presence of the swells and the masses, separated by the width of the racing surface, had been a defining feature of the Derby from the beginning.[18]

In the absence of motorcars, horse-drawn wagons dotted the infield, and spectators lined the inside rail from the quarter pole to the clubhouse turn.

On the other side of the homestretch, the lawns, terraces, and balconies were packed. Some found relief from the congestion on the grandstand roof. Bettors enduring long lines plowed more than a quarter-million dollars into the pari-mutuel system, a record handle for the track. Mounted police patrolled the infield, and detectives roamed the grounds watching for pickpockets.

Nearly half the patrons were women. Journalists devoted significant column space to describing fashionable ladies' colorful garb, implicitly reminding readers that horse racing was not just for (male) degenerates and lowlifes. A local reporter noted that "Kentucky beauty was the thoroughbred's only rival in the matter of interest. Milady had put on her most alluring apparel to make her part in the picture adequate." Coincidentally, Woodrow Wilson had earlier that day announced that Mother's Day would henceforth be a nationally observed holiday. In the clubhouse dining room, a confident Ham Applegate told a reporter that he was already plotting a summer schedule for Old Rosebud that would include a trip to Montreal for the International Derby at Dorval.[19]

Just before five o'clock, swarms of onlookers descended on the paddock to get a closer look at the Derby contestants. When the bugler made the call to the post, noise from the crowd subsided as trainers boosted jockeys into their saddles. Weir told McCabe to be aggressive if there was no pace up front.[20]

"Hurry back, Johnny," a young stable hand hollered as the seven-horse parade marched through the paddock gates toward the racetrack. Another railbird loudly predicted that Hodge's rider, Walter Taylor, would not let Rosebud have it easy on the front end. McCabe looked back at Taylor, and the pair exchanged genial smiles.[21]

The field received a warm salute from the grandstand crowd as the jockeys cantered their horses toward the starting line. They assumed their positions behind the barrier, with Old Ben on the rail. Watermelon was next to him, then John Gund, Bronzewing, and Surprising. Old Rosebud and Hodge rounded out the field. At the post less than two minutes, they were released to a good, even start. Rosebud broke on his toes and had distinguished himself from the pack after a few strides. Clear of the horses to his inside, McCabe eased him toward the rail. Hodge followed and secured a stalking position. The others were tightly bunched except for Bronzewing, who was slow to get rolling and was already five lengths behind the leader as the herd rumbled past the grandstand.

"They'll never catch Rosebud," someone shouted from the crowd as McCabe and his mount rolled into the clubhouse turn two lengths in front of Hodge. With the Bud under a snug hold, Hodge had cut into the front-runner's lead as the field entered the backstretch. A cry of "Old Rosebud is through, he's only a sprinter" pierced the din of the grandstand, but McCabe let out a notch on his reins, and Rosebud was flying into the far turn.[22]

Hodge was full out, but he was losing ground. On the final turn, he was six lengths behind Old Rosebud and four lengths ahead of John Gund, Surprising, and Old Ben, with Bronzewing making up ground behind them. Still with time to mount a final rally, Hodge dug in and appeared to be making some progress as he chased Rosebud into the stretch. But when McCabe tried to adjust his hands, the reins slipped through his fingers a couple of inches. Rosebud bounded ahead, fully extended. The race was over with a sixteenth of a mile to go. As McCabe and Rosebud floated toward the finish line, the jockey steadied his horse and chanced a quick look over his shoulder. The roar from the crowd was earsplitting.[23]

Old Rosebud's eight-length winning margin was a Derby record. When McCabe returned to the judges stand aboard a still-bouncy horse, no one could remember a louder ovation in the long history of Kentucky racing. But for a few spots of sweat and foam on his neck, the animated gelding gave no indication that he had just run the fastest ten furlongs in Churchill Downs history. The final time of 2:03⅖ would not be bettered for sixteen years.

Continuing a tradition that dated to 1896, Rosebud received a wreath of roses around his neck (the now-familiar floral blanket would not be introduced until the 1930s). Governor James B. McCreary, a former Confederate officer who had become moderately progressive amid shifting political winds, presented McCabe with a large bouquet. "I've been on some real racehorses in my day, but there were none of them like 'Old Rosie,'" the jockey told reporters in a heavy outer-borough accent. "He's got human intelligence. I don't believe there's a horse in the world that could have beaten him today." The victory marked a moment of redemption for the young rider. The press had not always been complimentary of McCabe, but turf writers called the jockey's Derby ride "wonderful" and "perfect." He received $750 from the owners as a token of their appreciation.[24]

Hodge's trainer, Kay Spence, was satisfied with his horse's runner-up effort: "Hodge can't beat him, but that is no disgrace, as no other horse in training has any chance with the Derby winner. I would not sell Hodge now for a dime less than I would have taken for him before his Derby race."[25]

Ham Applegate had watched the race from the back of an ice wagon in the infield, along with Frank Weir. When Rosebud rounded the final turn, Ham leaped off the wagon and scrambled toward the track, ignoring shouts from mounted police. The jubilant owner met horse and rider in front of the judges' stand after the rest of the field had staggered home. He told a reporter how happy he was to have failed in his earlier efforts to find a buyer for the gelding: "I think the colt [*sic*] the greatest seen in years, and he will easily, barring a mishap of course, win out the amount we originally priced him."[26]

Praise for Rosebud's performance was profuse from horsemen, fans, and journalists. "He ran as if he had wings," said W. O. Parmer, a prominent Tennessee breeder. "Old Rosebud is a freak. I never expected to live to see a three-year-old do a mile and a quarter in 2:03$\frac{2}{5}$ without trying." Albert Fall, US senator from the recently admitted state of New Mexico, told a reporter, "At first glance, he appears ungainly . . . [but] Old Rosebud, unless I make a mistake, will prove to be one of the greatest thoroughbreds the American turf has ever known." And the sports editor for the *Toronto Globe* declared, "One may go to the races for a generation without seeing duplicated what he showed in the way of speed." Screenwriter Herman J. Mankiewicz, who would win an Academy Award for Best Original Screenplay for his work on Orson Welles's masterpiece *Citizen Kane*, was among the untold numbers across the country who cashed bets on Old Rosebud, according to a Welles biographer who also claimed that the name of the iconic sled in the movie was inspired by the Derby winner.[27]

Concerns about Rosebud's stamina had seemingly been put to rest. There was little in his dominating Derby run to criticize—except that he had won too easily. "Those who hoped to see his gameness tested were not satisfied," a *Courier-Journal* columnist opined. "Whether Old Rosebud possesses courage is a question still unsettled." Rosebud had notched eleven consecutive wins against top competition, fourteen victories, and two second-place finishes in sixteen career starts. Half an hour after the race, the Derby champ was cooling out at the barn, nipping at his groom.[28]

As Old Rosebud returned to his morning routine in the days after the Derby, horsemen from surrounding stables would stop what they were doing when the horse of the hour passed. The Clark Handicap at Churchill the following

Saturday was an obvious option for a next start, but Colonel Applegate had publicly indicated his inclination to see the gelding compete against his own age group for as long as possible before taking on older horses. The Withers Stakes at a mile for three-year-olds at Belmont Park in New York would satisfy the Colonel's publicized preference.[29]

When Weir began to work his horse clockwise, the same direction races were then run at Belmont, it seemed that the decision had been made. Eleven days after the Derby, Old Rosebud breezed a mile the "wrong" way in 1:39⅖, the fastest time ever recorded for a right-handed drill at Churchill Downs. Two days later, he made an appearance for a light public workout between the second and third races. Johnny McCabe was aboard, decked out in the Applegate silks. Weir asked the jockey for another clockwise spin around the one-mile oval, with instructions not to let him go much faster than 1:43. McCabe kept his mount under a sung hold, but his unofficial time was 1:40 and change. To Weir's consternation, Rosebud's easy way of going had fooled the young rider. But the spectators were duly impressed and gave the gelding a hearty round of applause as he passed the wire.[30]

Despite all indications that he would be headed to Belmont, Weir remained publicly noncommittal. He hesitated to completely rule out a start in the Kentucky Handicap on opening day at Douglas Park, but he worried about the possibility of a large field in the ten-thousand-dollar contest and told a reporter that he feared an accident at the starting line or during the running of what was expected to be a competitive race. Perhaps Weir was overthinking. He was clearly burdened by the responsibility of keeping a superstar racehorse safe and sound.[31]

When a local newspaper reporter showed up at his barn with a photographer in tow, hoping to get an action shot of the Derby winner, Weir waved his arms and chased them away. "It's the worst luck in the world," Weir shouted. Undeterred, the intrepid journalists sought out Colonel Applegate for assistance. Applegate told them about a planned workout the day before Rosebud was scheduled to leave for New York. The reporters returned then and got their shot. The next day, the Bud was on a train for a start in the Withers, one of the most prestigious fixtures on the New York calendar. Several equine immortals had won the Withers since its first running in 1874, but few horses had entered the race with more fanfare than Old Rosebud.[32]

Rosebud was the star attraction for the Memorial Day weekend program at Belmont Park. More than twenty thousand spectators filled the grandstand

and lawns as crowded trains shuttled racegoers from Brooklyn and Manhattan. Thousands more flowed into the infield, opened free of charge by the Westchester Racing Association for the occasion, creating a festival atmosphere on a lovely late-spring afternoon. Some called it the largest and most socially diverse crowd at a New York track since the resumption of racing there. Many came to salute the Kentucky Derby winner, while others hoped to see him humbled. Food and drink vendors reported record business, and the tangle of automobiles in the parking area would take more than an hour to unravel on completion of the day's sport. Pro-racing journalists trumpeted the atmosphere as evidence that reports of New York racing's demise had been greatly exaggerated.[33]

Hundreds of eager fans flocked to the paddock to have a look at the heralded horse as the participants filed in to be saddled for the featured race. Many had never laid eyes on him before. Some were unimpressed by his modest stature. With many owners convinced that Rosebud was unbeatable, and Harry Payne Whitney's colt Pennant having yet to return to the track following his season-ending injury at Saratoga, it would be a field of only five, including Roamer, who had won at Belmont three days earlier in his seasonal debut. Long shots Gainer and Charlestonian seemed to be there in hopes of catching a small piece of the purse. Few of the surreptitious bookmakers would even quote a price on Old Rosebud. Those who did offered no better than 1–5. Bettors who liked Charlestonian could get 40– or 50–1. As the quintet stepped onto the track, the vast grandstand crowd saluted Old Rosebud and his outstanding record of success while infielders scampered toward the backstretch for a view of the start.

Whether it was the front bandages Rosebud was wearing or knowledge about the injury that had ended his two-year-old season, Roamer's trainer, Jack Goldsborough, later claimed to have been aware that Weir's gelding was "dickey on his leg." He instructed his rider to "go right after" the favorite. Johnny McCabe would acknowledge after the race that something about his horse did not feel quite right at the starting post. "He didn't lunge at the barrier as he did in his other races," the jockey said. Rosebud broke a step slower than usual but secured a short early lead, with Gainer and Roamer also forwardly placed. The 8–1 second choice, Superintendent, briefly threatened heading into the turn, at which point Rosebud bobbled for a jump or two and bore out, causing some to speculate that he had struck himself. As Superintendent fell back, Gainer moved up to the front-runner's flank.[34]

Rosebud seemed to be laboring. McCabe was sitting still, but real trouble became apparent as they turned into the homestretch. With Gainer looming on the outside, the crowd readied for a dramatic duel to the finish. But Rosebud carried Gainer very wide out of the turn and seemed to be headed for the outside fence. Cheers turned to shrieks and groans as spectators realized that something was amiss. McCabe managed to straighten his horse, but Rosebud was out of the race. Gainer recovered to take the lead before succumbing to a late-charging Charlestonian deep in the stretch to lose by a whisker. Roamer plodded steadily along on the rail to take third, while McCabe let his horse lope to the finish some sixteen lengths back as spectators stood gapemouthed, trying to process what they had witnessed. Murmured concern for Rosebud was supplemented by isolated yips of delight from the few who had some money on the winner.

A flummoxed Ham Applegate could provide little insight. "I saw the colt pulling up a little short with just a slight limping action," he told a reporter. "I knew something had happened to him when he could not get away from his field in the early stages of the race, and when Gainer went alongside of him it was a sure thing he was in some sort of trouble. I have not seen Mr. Weir, so I really do not know what the trouble is, and I hope it is not serious. But there is no question something hurt him soon after the start of the race."[35]

When Rosebud arrived back at the barn, Weir hoped that his horse had merely nicked himself, though there was no apparent wound. After cooling out, the back tendon on his left foreleg was badly swollen. The trainer said he would know more in the morning and declined to provide further information, leaving reporters to speculate wildly.[36]

Coverage of the Withers appearing in the Sunday newspapers contained all sorts of explanations for Rosebud's defeat. Some journalists supposed that Old Rosebud simply could not handle the New York competition. Or they blamed the unfamiliar clockwise direction of the race—ignoring his recent speedy right-handed works in Louisville. Other explanations were more simplistic. The *Nashville Banner* implied that the horse lacked heart, declaring that he had folded "like a jack-knife" and "quit like a lobster."[37]

By the time Ham arrived at the stable Sunday morning, accompanied by several friends, word had spread around the Belmont barnyard that Rosebud had, in fact, ruptured a tendon. Weir gave no public statement, but he informed Ham that their star would be taken out of training. The logistics of sending him back to Kentucky were discussed, but Weir decided that a long train ride might be too stressful. Instead, Rosebud would remain under his care in New York for the summer. The trainer put on a brave front, but the consensus at Belmont was that if the gelding was ever to see a starting gate again, it would not be for quite some time.

Weir had quietly hoped to have his star back to the races before the end of the 1914 season, and Rosebud joined the rest of the stable on a train to Saratoga at the conclusion of the downstate summer racing. But after a round of pin firing, a treatment dating to the Middle Ages in which an injured leg is stuck with a hot metal-tipped instrument to stimulate healing, the trainer decided he would not rush his horse. By late August, Rosebud was doing well enough to accompany the Weir string to the Kentucky Association track. At the conclusion of the Lexington meet, the convalescent gelding went to John D. Carr's farm in hopes that a regimen of rest and relaxation would yield the same results as it had the previous year. In late November, as Weir settled in at Juárez for the winter with a ten-horse stable, he received word from Carr that Rosebud had been putting on weight and was "hearty and rugged as a bear."[38]

The political situation in Mexico had further deteriorated. Venustiano Carranza, a wealthy cattle rancher and former governor of the northern Mexican state of Coahuila, had seized power in Mexico City following President Huerta's resignation that summer. But Carranza proved to be incapable of preserving the revolutionary coalition he had helped to organize in opposition to the previous regime. Soon Mexico would be mired in the deadliest stage of the bloodiest civil war in the history of the Americas, one that would claim nearly one in fifteen Mexican lives.[39]

President Wilson was initially inclined to back Pancho Villa, one of the key defectors from the Carranza alliance. Villa had become a favorite subject for American filmmakers, who depicted him as a Mexican Robin Hood in newsreels, documentaries, and fictional features. One of the most popular, *The Life of General Villa* (1914), produced by D. W. Griffith, was shot on location in Mexico. Villa himself was a paid participant and shared in the film's profits. American newspapers described brutal acts committed by the revolutionary's army, but they also helped to reinforce his heroic image, particularly in early stories written by reporters embedded with the general's troops, when Villa could be seen as a stabilizing influence in the region.

Pancho Villa initially received favorable portrayals from American reporters and film crews who traveled with the warlord. (Library of Congress)

The powerful Hearst media machine was a consistent advocate for American military intervention in Mexico. William Randolph Hearst had been an early supporter of Villa but would change his tune after the warlord's forces ransacked the Hearst family ranch in Mexico, expropriating some sixty thousand head of cattle, taking prisoner five Mexican employees, and killing an American bookkeeper. As Europe descended into continent-wide combat for the first time since the Napoleonic Era following the assassination of the heir to the Austro-Hungarian throne by a Serbian nationalist in June 1914, the American need for stability on its southern border and protection of US oil and mining interests in Mexico would become more acute.[40]

The Great War, as it was soon labeled, would be the deadliest struggle humankind had yet produced, pitting Germany and its confederates against the Allied Powers led by Great Britain, France, and Russia. European armies would dig a system of trenches stretching from the English Channel to the Swiss Alps that produced a long, horrific war of attrition on the Western Front. In four years of fighting, sixteen million people would die, and more than twenty million would be wounded, as innovations in weaponry, including tanks, warplanes, long-range artillery, poison gas, and machine guns, outpaced medical technology and facilitated human slaughter on an industrial scale. Soon after the start of hostilities, as German forces invaded Belgium and France, Woodrow Wilson insisted on preserving American neutrality. "There is such a thing as a man being too proud to fight," the president would declare. "There is such a thing as a nation being so right that it does not need to convince others by force that it is right."[41]

By the start of the racing season at Juárez in late November 1914, Wilson had pulled American troops from Veracruz after a seven-month occupation. Unwilling to declare official support for any faction in the messy Mexican conflict, American envoys assured Villa—still the predominant power broker in northern Mexico—that the evacuation was not intended to aid the Carranza-controlled government. Villa remained on friendly terms with the horsemen in Juárez and ordered his regimental band to provide musical entertainment for the opening of the race meet. Shortly after the new year, Villa and Gen. Hugh Scott, recently appointed chief of staff of the US Army, attended the races together following a conference in El Paso.[42]

Villa and Gen. Hugh Scott attend the races at Juárez in January 1914. (Library of Congress)

Old Rosebud was looking well when Weir returned to Kentucky in the spring of 1915. Soon, veterinarians deemed him ready for training. Weir brought the gelding to the Kentucky Association track in April to resume light exercise in hopes of a return to the races that summer. A rematch with Little Nephew, who was also nearing a return from injury, was even discussed. But Rosebud stopped suddenly during what was supposed to be an easy six-furlong breeze at Latonia early that summer and came up lame. It was the same leg but closer to the fetlock this time.[43]

Whispers that he was finished as a racehorse swirled through the barnyard, but Weir was hopeful that the problem might not be too serious. After a couple of weeks of rest and treatment, Rosebud was full of energy but still not ready to carry a rider. To allow him to exercise without putting unnecessary strain on the injured leg, Weir hitched him to a sulky—the two-wheeled carts used in Standardbred racing—and had his assistant drive Rosebud along the roads near the racetrack.[44]

Overseen by foreman Mack McLaughlin while Weir went East with a string for the summer, Old Rosebud's new training routine proved effective. The recuperating patient was a willing participant in the program, but he had not lost his competitive bent. While out for a spin one morning, according to one report, Rosebud zipped after a loose horse that was running freely down a paved road. He lost four shoes in the chase but refused to be pulled up until he had caught up to the escapee. By the end of the summer, there was talk of pointing the Bud toward a sprint stake at Churchill Downs. Though he would not be ready by the end of the Kentucky racing season, Weir decided to bring Rosebud to Juárez in November 1915. Fans and reporters looked forward to a possible showdown between the Applegate gelding and Pan Zareta, a speedy and durable racemare who had set a world record for five furlongs at Juárez the previous winter. But the political situation there was precarious, and some American horsemen were lingering in El Paso, hesitant to take their horses across the river for fear that Villa's troops might seize their stock as they prepared to evacuate in the face of Carranza's advancing army.[45]

Carrancistas had inflicted heavy damage on Villa's forces in the spring of 1915. Villa's cavalry attacks were no match for the barbed wire, trenches, and machine guns of Carranza's army, whose generals had been studying the battlefield tactics and equipment being used with deadly efficiency in Europe. Once the commander of more than forty thousand troops, Villa would be reduced to regional-jefe status in Chihuahua by the autumn. The Wilson administration acknowledged the shifting tides in offering official recognition of the Carranza regime and an embargo on arms shipments to anti-Carranza rebels in exchange for a promise to respect foreign lives and property in Mexico. The American government needed the Mexican situation to be resolved, lest Germany use the chaos to its advantage against the United States, which had yet to enter the Great War in Europe but was providing Germany's enemies with tons of food and supplies and billions in loans.

Villa was furious when he learned of Wilson's decision to passively back Carranza in the Mexican fighting. Speaking with a reporter for the *El Paso Morning Times*, the last interview the general would grant to an American newspaper, Villa remained committed to the revolutionary cause but admitted that he was exhausted. He expressed doubt that he would be able to oust Carranza from power but vowed to continue the fight. In October, the United States allowed Carranza to move troops through American territory to support a garrison at Agua Prieta, where Villa was mounting an attack, across the border from Douglas, Arizona. Due in part to the reinforcements, Villa suffered a devastating defeat.[46]

Fears that racing would be interrupted as Carranza took control of Juárez proved to be unfounded, and by late November, there were more American horses stabled at the track than there had been the previous year. Old Rosebud became mildly sick on the train from Kentucky to El Paso but recovered quickly, and Weir hoped to have him ready for a race in January. Rosebud attracted plenty of attention from well-wishers and tourists, often in the late mornings before his daily post-lunch nap. With Johnny McCabe exercising him, the gelding was regaining his old form. He posted the fastest six-furlong work of the young season soon after his arrival in Mexico. The following week, Weir told McCabe to push his horse, and he went a half mile in forty-seven seconds. As concerns about the ramifications of military upheaval receded, the grounds at the Juárez track had never looked better, and all were cautiously optimistic for a peaceful, prosperous winter of racing.

4

Miracle Horse

Old Rosebud's last reported work for 1915 was a quarter-mile tightener on November 22. Back at the barn after the breeze, he again showed signs of lameness. Veterinarians could prescribe only more rest. Weir did not publicize the injury and quietly accepted an offer to send the troubled gelding to his friend Wade McLemore's Texas ranch, thirty miles northeast of Abilene, a last pocket of greenish grass and mild topographical variance before hundreds of miles of flatter, less hospitable territory to the west. There was some concern about the gelding injuring himself on the ranch's barbed-wire fencing. But McLemore first introduced him to a small smooth-wire paddock. Old Rosebud romped around until he collided with the fence and was knocked to the ground. He stood up, sniffed the posts and the wire, and had no further issues. After giving the gelding some time to acclimate, the rancher turned Rosebud out in a mile-wide pasture with a stream at one end, where horses liked to cool their legs and escape the insects. The ranch proved to be an ideal environment to let nature perform its restorative magic, but it would be nearly a year before Old Rosebud would again set foot on a racetrack.[1]

Far to the west of the tranquil McLemore spread, tensions at the border were reaching a crisis level. In response to the Wilson administration's decision to recognize Carranza as Mexico's de facto leader, Pancho Villa issued a statement to the Mexican press declaring that he would no longer concern himself with the safety of American nationals in the course of his insurgent activity: "I have much to thank Mr. Wilson for, since he has freed me of the obligation to give guarantees [of safety] to foreigners and, above all, to those who were once free citizens and are now vassals of an evangelizing professor of philosophy."[2]

In January 1916, a band of Villa supporters stopped a train near Santa Isabel, Chihuahua, and executed seventeen American passengers who were on their way to reopen a silver mine that had been shuttered amid revolutionary violence. Theodore Roosevelt and New Mexico senator Albert Fall called for immediate military intervention. William Randolph Hearst joined the chorus, lambasting Wilson's "too proud to fight" philosophy in an editorial:

> Lying where they fell in the Mexican chaparral, beneath the cruel blows and the stabs and shots of their tormentors, another ghastly company of mutilated corpses are waiting for their countrymen to avenge their blood. . . .
>
> Just as it has watchfully waited while other American men and women—yes, and little children, too—have been tortured, outraged and murdered by these Mexican savages. . . .
>
> A nation which is too weak or too cowardly to resent insult and outrage is sure to be insulted and outraged. . . .
>
> Then, if it is UNPREPARED TO FIGHT and unable to fight, it is BRUTALLY AND BLOODILY BEATEN AND PLUNDERED AS WELL. . . .
>
> Why, even a little despicable, bandit nation like Mexico murders our citizens, drags our flag in the dirt and spits at and defies this nation of ours with truculent insolence. AND WITHOUT PUNISHMENT. . . .
>
> On Mexico's bloodsoaked soil the vultures tear the flesh and the coyotes gnaw the bones of our butchered and unburied dead.
>
> But if there is any manhood and courage left in our fathers' sons, these bandit dogs shall not much longer leave American dead to be the obscene feast of the foul birds and beasts of the desert.[3]

American newsreels depicted a borderland in violent disarray, and word of the Santa Isabel attack sparked violent confrontations between Anglos and Tejanos in El Paso, resulting in the arrest of twenty-three Villistas. Villa felt betrayed by American leadership. He had gone out of his way to protect US interests in Mexico and had once called Woodrow Wilson "the most just man in the world." Following an El Paso jail fire that killed more than two dozen when someone trying to light a cigarette accidentally ignited delousing chemicals sprayed on new inmates, Villa became further convinced that Americans were trying to exterminate his supporters. "The United States intends to swallow Mexico," he told his troops. "Let us do what we can to make it stick in their throats." Before dawn on March 9, 1916, four hundred Villistas under the general's command stormed into Columbus, New Mexico, a town of seven hundred that could boast of a bank, four hotels, several saloons, a train station, a Baptist church, and a US Army garrison. The raiders shouted, "Viva Villa, viva Mexico," as they shot out windows, burned buildings, and ransacked stores and homes for two hours. Eighteen Americans and dozens of Villa's men were killed in the first major attack on US soil by a foreign military in more than a century.[4]

Americans were shocked. Senator Fall, who owned substantial acreage in Chihuahua and served as a lawyer for the Terrazas family, called for half a million troops to invade Mexico. Following an emergency cabinet meeting, President Wilson authorized an American military incursion into Mexico, led by Gen. John J. Pershing.

The stated objective of what was officially labeled the Punitive Expedition was to capture Villa. Six days after Villa's raid, some 4,800 US soldiers were in pursuit. With Carranza refusing to allow the Americans use of the Mexican railroad system to supply their troops, 4,000 animals were employed along with any motorized vehicles that could be procured. The caravan included a Hearst camera team that captured exclusive footage for news reels (until rival film companies petitioned the secretary of state for an order compelling Hearst to share the images). Pershing's men engaged and defeated pockets of Villistas, but most dispersed into the desolate Mexican interior. After a 500-mile chase, the broader purpose of the mission—to limit the risk of further attacks—had largely been achieved. But with Villa hiding among a friendly population and unlikely to be captured, the American effort could hardly be called a complete success. Despite Carranza's repeated insistence that the US troops return home, Wilson would keep Pershing's forces in Mexico for nearly a year. Following another Villista raid on Glenn Springs, Texas, in May 1916, Congress dramatically expanded the US National Guard, and by the end of the summer, there would be more than 100,000 guardsmen on the border from California to Texas, while sixteen warships monitored the Mexican coast.[5]

The Punitive Expedition of 1916–1917, led by Gen. John J. Pershing, encountered many obstacles in trying to capture Pancho Villa following his deadly raids on Columbus, New Mexico. (Library of Congress)

The show of force failed to quiet critics like Roosevelt, who lamented what he saw as the feeble condition of the US military. "We, through our representatives at Washington[,] have absolutely refused in the smallest degree to prepare during these twenty-two months of world cataclysm [since the start of the Great War]," Roosevelt told a Detroit audience. "We have endured to deceive ourselves by announcing that in this policy of supine inaction and a failure to perform duty, we are actuated by the loftiest motives. There is not a nation in the world which believes that our course of conduct has been dictated by anything save timidity, unworthy shrinking from effort and responsibility, and cold and selfish love of money-making and soft ease." The demobilization that followed the Spanish-American War and suppression of the resultant Filipino independence movement had indeed left the US military in a paltry state. At the onset of World War I, due in part to Americans' long-standing disinclination toward maintaining large peacetime armies, the American infantry had been smaller than Greece's. In 1916, the US military remained a small fraction of the size of major European powers, with most American servicemen stationed overseas.[6]

Proponents of American horse racing seized on an opportunity to pitch their sport as a partial solution to growing concerns regarding military preparedness. In a letter to the editor first published in the *New York Sun* and reprinted in the *Daily Racing Form*, a pseudonymous writer argued, "The experience of our cavalry in Mexico has brought to the attention of the American people in startling fashion the fact that good horses were never so essential to the success of our [military] as at present. . . . So competent an authority as [chief of staff of the US Army] Major General Hugh L. Scott is on record as favoring the horse of mixed blood, half or three-quarters thoroughbred, for such work as our cavalry is doing in Mexico; and for officers he would have the absolutely clean thoroughbred."[7]

The push to promote Thoroughbreds and horse racing as critical components of American national security would only intensify as the gruesome war in Europe dragged on and US involvement seemed imminent. Since the start of combat there, belligerent nations had procured hundreds of thousands of horses in the United States to be sent to Europe. In total, more than a million North American equines would be exported for military service. As many as eight million horses and mules would perish during the fighting.[8]

Among the strongest voices in the effort to frame horse racing as a vital national interest was Matt Winn's. The Churchill Downs executive plainly understood the potential for lasting benefits to the sport if Thoroughbreds could be seen as valuable to the American military. "With war looming up ahead of us and statistics showing how badly depleted the horse family of America is, it behooves us to work out a preparedness schedule along all lines," Winn told the press. "These gaps have to be filled and it has been shown that the thoroughbred presents the correct solution to the problem. I am anticipating a great advance in racing."[9]

Charles Brossman, who had gained fame as the trainer of the brilliant racemare Imp and later became a respected racing journalist, would strike a similar chord, trumpeting "the essential position that the thoroughbred horse occupies in the defense of the nation." Writing in the *Daily Racing Form*, Brossman contended that "uninformed persons, possibly with good intentions, demagogues, unscrupulous politicians that always have an ulterior motive in any reform they advocate, have about had their day and from now on people will listen only to men that know. They don't want theories; they want facts. Efficiency and capability in every man and horse in the army with the fighting spirit of the thoroughbred is required."[10]

The notion that clever branding of the sport could help to keep anti-racing activists at bay was not a new one. The full name of the entity that conducted the racing at Saratoga—the Saratoga Association for the Improvement of the Breed of Horses—was adopted in 1865 to avail that organization of a midcentury loophole in an 1802 New York antigambling law that allowed racing if it were conducted for "improving the breed of horses." Commercialized horse racing in America had still been in its infancy at the end of the Civil War, but by the height of the Progressive Era, the sport supported thousands of livelihoods. The stakes for its survival were high, and opposition to racing and gambling was stronger and better organized than ever. But if American racing officials could convince a portion of the public that their sport was patriotic and crucial to national defense, perhaps they could stave off efforts to ban it long enough for political winds to shift.[11]

It had been nearly two years since Old Rosebud had started in a race, but he had not been forgotten by the horse-racing community. Churchill Downs honored the sidelined gelding with a race bearing his name on Derby Day in 1916. Building on the publicity generated by Rosebud's record-setting triumph in 1914, the Kentucky Derby's national stature had been further enhanced the following year by a win for prominent sportsman and leading light of New York racing Harry Payne Whitney and his brilliant filly Regret, who became the first of her sex to wear Derby roses. Whitney, heir to a fabulous industrial fortune and husband to artist, heiress, and socialite Gertrude Vanderbilt, had considered scratching the filly after learning of the sinking of the 787-foot luxury liner *Lusitania* by a German submarine off the coast of Ireland the day before the 1915 Derby. Whitney's brother-in-law Alfred Gwynne Vanderbilt had been aboard and was among the nearly 1,200 passengers, including 128 Americans, to lose their lives in the attack. But his death would not be confirmed until later, and Whitney decided that Regret would run.

Following his filly's dazzling wire-to-wire victory, an elated Whitney exclaimed, "I don't care if she ever wins another race, or even runs again, for she has done enough this afternoon by winning America's greatest race." Churchill Downs had pushed the phrase "America's greatest race" in the wake of Rosebud's headline-making Derby win, and the parroting of the label by someone of Whitney's stature further enhanced the Derby's place in American sports culture.[12]

In 1916, with Old Rosebud recuperating on the ranch, a handsome, black-colored colt named George Smith would join the list of Derby champions, just holding off British-bred colt Star Hawk at the wire. Named for the gambler better known as "Pittsburgh Phil," George Smith was ridden by Johnny Loftus and would later serve as a stallion for the Army Remount Service. Winning owner John Sanford, a former congressman who would later serve on the New York state racing commission, accepted postrace congratulations from Kentucky governor Augustus Owsley Stanley, an anti-Prohibition Progressive reformer, at the judges' stand. Sanford's presence at the race confirmed that the Derby had the support of the Eastern racing establishment, and Churchill Downs reported a track record attendance of fifty thousand along with an American record pari-mutuel handle.

"Society's representation was never more brilliant nor more numerous," the *Louisville Courier-Journal* reported. "The big quota drawn from the city's population was never more eager for the occasion, nor more obviously enspirited by the contest it came to see. The smaller proportion from places throughout the land, from the East and from Europe, showed by its presence that the obstacles of distance are minor considerations in the matter of a Kentucky Derby." The newspaper noted that a good portion of the Derby patrons had arrived in automobiles, of which there were two million on American

The year after Old Rosebud's triumph, Regret's win in the 1915 Kentucky Derby continued a run of positive publicity for what some were starting to call "America's greatest race." (Wikimedia Commons)

roads by 1916. The contraptions were still something of a novelty, but by 1920, there would be nearly eight million cars in the United States, a trend that would eventually shift horse racing toward anachronism status in American culture. But by that time the sport would be on much firmer economic and political footing.[13]

Weir continued to receive encouraging reports from Texas and never wavered in his belief that his champion would return to the track. The trainer went to visit his favorite horse at the McLemore ranch in the fall of 1916. Frank G. Menke, sportswriter for the Hearst newspaper syndicate and later publicity director for Churchill Downs, would disseminate an appealing, if presumably exaggerated, story about the visit that would become an oft-repeated part of Old Rosebud's legend. While Weir watched his gelding graze, an automobile came roaring by, frightening Rosebud and his pasture mates. They all took off, with Rosebud leading the charge. Weir was supposedly so thrilled by his horse's condition that he sent the horse for a breeze the very next day. When Old Rosebud ran six furlongs in 1:14 and a mile in 1:44 without being hurried, Weir was convinced that it was time to return Rosebud to the racetrack.[14]

Rosebud was rugged and rested from his eleven months with McLemore when he arrived at Juárez in late November 1916. He was ready to resume light training, including daily gallops alongside a pony. Despite plans to keep him lean in Texas, the staff at the Weir barn reported that he was a hundred pounds heavier than when they last saw him. The Bud flourished in his morning exercise and soon progressed to sterner breezes. But there was some question as to how long racing would continue in the border town. Two hundred miles to the south, Pancho Villa had been threatening Chihuahua City. Swirling rumors suggested that his next target would be Juárez, but track officials assured the racing public that all was well. President Carranza had sent reinforcements to the region, and a squadron of soldiers would be stationed at the racetrack to preserve order and watch for signs of trouble.[15]

Despite the uncertainties, racing proceeded as scheduled. The track even set an attendance record on "El Paso Day," when all enjoyed free admission and pari-mutuel wagering was introduced to an initially skeptical racing public. Tens of thousands of American soldiers were living in the area, including those stationed at nearby Fort Bliss, and many regularly found their way to the racetrack, propping up the meet's early attendance figures. Some were militiamen from the East, ready to protect the border and jump into the hunt for Villa if called. Others had been mustered out of service and simply stuck around El Paso. But by late January 1917, amid growing civil unrest, the challenges of conducting racing in Juárez became too great. Track officials terminated the meet and left town. Though horsemen were understandably frustrated, administrators at the Juárez Jockey Club received mild praise for providing track employees an extra week's pay. Winn would publicly attribute the closure to tensions at the border, a paucity of horses, and "too much Villa," but the final straw leading to the decision to end the meet may have been the riots that had broken out at the Santa Fe Bridge connecting the United States and Mexico.[16]

In response to reports of typhus in Juárez, despite some question as to whether the disease was significantly more prevalent there than it was on the northern shore of the Rio Grande, the mayor of El Paso sent a telegram to the US surgeon general in Washington demanding that a quarantine system for people coming into Texas be established to slow the daily passage of "hundreds [of] dirty, lousy, destitute Mexicans," most of whom crossed the border for work. Public health officials insisted that a quarantine was unnecessary but did set up a disinfecting station. Border crossers were required to remove their clothes and undergo a physical examination for lice. Their possessions were steamed, and objects that could be damaged by water would be exposed to toxic gas instead. After travelers passed the inspection, they were sprayed with a solution of soap and kerosene. Believing that border officials had been salaciously photographing women during their examinations, and with public memory of the previous year's deadly El Paso jail fire still relatively fresh, a Mexican teenaged housecleaner named Carmelita Torres refused to leave a trolley crossing the international bridge when prompted by inspectors. She requested an examination without a bath, which was refused, then asked for a refund of her fare. Fellow passengers, many of them domestic workers, seized control of the streetcar, hurling rocks and bottles at American officials. Soon they were joined by thousands of Juárez residents.[17]

The racetrack, gambling houses, and other places of amusement were closed all day due to the disturbance. Some Americans returning from the shuttered track reported having to "run the gauntlet of rocks and abuse" as they traversed the bridge. Mounted soldiers eventually dispersed the crowd after it became apparent that no one in the baths was being harmed, but a mob reconvened the following day. This time it consisted largely of men protesting the Carranza regime and voicing support for Villa. Rumors that Mexican officials would reciprocate the quarantine turned out to be false. "We will give Americans a bath if they think they need it," a Carranza spokesman told an El Paso newspaper, "but we have not adopted any reprisal measures." The protests lasted three days and produced gridlock in the streets. American businesses and homeowners appealed to the local Chamber of Commerce when they found themselves without laborers, and the unrest eventually subsided.[18]

As officials in Washington monitored trouble on the border, Germany announced its intent to resume unrestricted submarine warfare in the Atlantic that would target American shipping. Theodore Roosevelt, still a leading advocate of American militarism, saw the war as a test of the nation's manhood and was frustrated by the president's reluctance to enter the conflict, privately calling Wilson "yellow all through in the presence of danger." After the president called for arming American merchant vessels but reemphasized his commitment to neutrality, Roosevelt wrote that he was sick of Wilson's "shilly-shallyings" and aggressively campaigned for permission to personally lead a division of American warriors to the front lines in France.[19]

Wilson had won reelection in November with a campaign slogan of "He Kept Us Out of War," narrowly defeating vocal horse-racing opponent Charles Evans Hughes, who had been appointed to the US Supreme Court by William H. Taft and carried Roosevelt's endorsement. Wilson's decision to sever diplomatic relations with Germany in February 1917 pushed the United States to the brink of war, and days later, the last of Pershing's troops quietly returned from Mexico to US soil.

Theodore Roosevelt was a leading voice among critics who believed that the Wilson administration was too passive in its foreign policy and that the US military was ill-prepared for war. (Library of Congress)

Frank Weir and the other American trainers stabled in Juárez were left scrambling for new plans. Old Rosebud was ready to run. Weir wired the Fair Grounds racetrack in New Orleans, where racing had recently returned after a years-long battle with reformers and hostile political cabals, to inquire about the availability of stalls there. Track officials offered to create a marketable stakes race for Rosebud during Mardi Gras, but Weir needed to run his gelding sooner. When horsemen at the Juárez track banded together to organize a short continuation of the abandoned meeting, Colonel Applegate announced that Rosebud would make his return to the races in Mexico.[20]

On February 18, 1917, Old Rosebud made his first trip to the starting post since the 1914 Withers. His reputation had apparently not been hurt much by the thirty-two-month layoff; on the strength of his strong morning works, he was saddled with a 122-pound impost, conceding up to 32 pounds to his rivals in the featured five-and-a-half-furlong sprint handicap on the special Sunday program. For the first time since early in his two-year-old season, Rosebud would have a new rider. Johnny McCabe would later explain that he had gotten "mixed up" and had to get out of Juárez that winter. He went to San Antonio and fell out with Weir "some way or another," then injured his knee in a fall from a horse in Kentucky that spring, which put him out of the saddle for most of the year. Journeyman jockey George Molesworth, a Texas native, took the mount.

A good crowd was on hand despite one of the heaviest sandstorms in memory, and the wind was howling as the five-horse field approached the barrier. Old Rosebud broke well and set an aggressive pace. He outlasted two early challengers, but on the turn for home, an eight-year-old gelding named Zim passed the pacesetter on the inside and rolled to a four-length win. Rosebud held on for second, a respectable result under the circumstances. Most importantly, he pulled up perfectly sound.[21]

The small resort town of Hot Springs, Arkansas, in the Ouachita Mountains, famous since ancient times for its thermal baths, was bubbling with anticipation for the return of horse racing when Old Rosebud and the rest of the Weir stable arrived days after his runner-up performance in Juárez. Hotels and boardinghouses charging unprecedented prices were packed with travelers from St. Louis, Chicago, New York, Cincinnati, and Louisville. Horses shipping from New Orleans, Juárez, and Cuba filled the stables at grand Oaklawn Park. Vacationers and residents readied for top-class racing despite laws still on the books proscribing the sport, or at least the gambling associated with it.

A rival track, Essex Park, had opened in Hot Springs in 1904. It was owned by "Umbrella Bill" McGuigan, a shady character (and onetime member of the Arkansas legislature) who had been a Standardbred driver in the Northeast until he was chased out of the sport for cheating. The early success of Essex, and the cyclonic destruction of the Clinton Park track in nearby Little Rock, had motivated a new group to organize Oaklawn, closer to downtown Hot Springs. They built an elegant grandstand enclosed in glass and heated by steam in time for a meet in 1905. After Essex lost an ensuing war for prime racing dates, and dual tracks proved untenable, McGuigan worked with state senator W. T. Amis to pass a law banning gambling on horse races in the state. A devastating downtown Hot Springs fire in 1913, and a resultant downturn in local tourism, produced a push to resurrect the sport to help attract out-of-town visitors. A 1915 bill to reinstate horse racing was vetoed by Governor George Washington Hays, who would sign a statewide ban on alcohol into law that year. Undeterred, a local group calling itself the Business Men's League conducted an abbreviated race meet at Oaklawn the following year on a nonprofit basis and nominally without gambling. They believed that racing would stoke the local economy, amplify tourism, and foster civic pride. The endeavor was sufficiently successful to compel boosters to revive Essex Park, and the once-adversarial tracks reached an agreement to share the 1917 racing season.[22]

Old Rosebud thrived in Arkansas. Horsemen who had not seen him in years were astounded by the speed he showed in morning workouts. The chance to see how Weir's gelding would fare in his return to racing in the United States drew hardened horsemen and curious neophytes alike amid springlike conditions on the second day of the Oaklawn meet. The Fordyce Handicap was the co-featured race on a track still drying after chilly, wet weather earlier in the week. Rosebud would carry 120 pounds in the six-furlong sprint, 7–14 pounds more than the other five starters. Bettors made him the 4–5 favorite.

The leading contender for an upset was Jeff Livingston's eight-year-old gelding Aldebaran. Arkansas native Charley Peak got the mount on the Bud for the first time since the gelding defeated Roamer at Churchill Downs nearly four years earlier. Peak had been contemplating retirement after riding most of the previous year in Canada, where he had struggled to maintain his weight and continued to find himself in trouble with stewards for on-track misbehavior. But presented with the opportunity to ride Rosebud, he cut fifteen pounds in two weeks.[23]

Peak sent his mount straight to the lead and never looked back. Rosebud lingered a bit in the stretch, and Aldebaran closed to within a length at the wire, but the result was never in doubt. Victorious horse and rider received a standing ovation as they crossed the finish line. "I wouldn't have missed riding Old Rosebud today for anything," Peak told reporters after the race. "The horse came back, and so did the jockey. It was certainly great to be on this horse, and I am proud we won." The mayor of Hot Springs apparently saw little political liability in jumping into the winner's circle photo.[24]

Rosebud's winning effort was more workmanlike than spectacular, and the competition was not what he had once faced. Still, it was a promising reintroduction to American racing. Peak was again in the irons when Rosebud returned four days later for the New Moody Hotel Handicap. The Oaklawn track handicapper added 10 pounds to the gelding's burden, saddling him with 130, two dozen more than six-year-old David Craig, who had run with Rosebud early in the Fordyce and who had won the 1914 International Derby in Montreal.

Old Rosebud again showed good speed, bouncing to an early three-length lead, which he stretched to five by the end of the backstretch with Peak maintaining a snug hold. David Craig made a strong move on the turn, reaching the Bud's hip as they spun into the homestretch, but Old Rosebud shook off the challenge and scampered away to a three-length win under a hand ride.

The performance suggested that he was ready for stiffer competition and a Saturday showdown in the six-furlong Creason Handicap against a world-record-setting sprinter. Named after the daughter of a Juárez public official, Pan Zareta had attained the nickname "Queen of the Turf." The seven-year-old Texas-bred mare would equal or break eleven track records and notch 76 wins in 151 career starts on her way to a spot in American racing's Hall of Fame. The largest crowd of the season showed up at Oaklawn to enjoy balmy weather and what the *Daily Racing Form* called "the best racing offering ever provided patrons of the sport in these parts."[25]

Having won easily with weight assignments of 120 and 130, Bud was dealt a severe 137 pounds for the featured event, two dozen more than Pan Zareta. With Peak again aboard, Rosebud was away slowly from the barrier and had to be hustled into contention through the backstretch. He appeared to be primed to engage the pacesetting Pan Zareta on the turn, but the extra weight proved to be too much. Rosebud faded in the homestretch, barely hanging on for third.

Despite the disappointing result, the Weir trainee continued to impress in the mornings, with Peak handling the exercise duties, as Hot Springs racing moved four miles east to Essex Park. Special trains shuttled patrons from downtown, and the mayor declared a half-holiday to celebrate the reopening of the long-shuttered track.

A capacity crowd of six thousand convened to see if the Bud could carry his speed as far as a mile while lugging 130 pounds, 29–35 more than the rest of the field, in the featured race of the day. Despite the disparity, Old Rosebud was made the 3–5 favorite. He got the best of an untidy start and set sensible early fractions. Not wanting to win by too great a margin, lest the handicapper test him with even more weight next time, Peak slowed his horse when he began to put too much distance between himself and the rest of the field. Their lead had stretched to three lengths after three-quarters, and Peak allowed Rosebud to relax in the stretch. He hoped to coast to the finish line, but a late charge from a Texas-bred named Gordon Russell woke Peak from complacency. Peak shook up his tiring mount, and Rosebud labored through the last seventy yards, just holding off the adversary by a head at the wire. The tight finish gave the crowd a thrill but did not instill confidence that Rosebud wanted any more weight or distance.[26]

Late the next morning, the once-spacious grandstand at Essex Park was a heap of smoldering ruins. Investigators determined that the fire originated with "some rubbish which had been carelessly left in a corner of the second floor." One witness, apparently the first to notice the flames, said that after he saw smoke billowing from the grandstand, he climbed the steps to discover two or three fiery sacks of straw. Unable to locate any water with which to douse them, the man grabbed the bag that was burning the brightest and threw it out a nearby window, but by that time the fire was beyond control.[27]

Trainers, riders, and stable hands dashed away from their morning chores to fight the flames, but brisk winds complicated the effort. Fire damage to large wooden structures could hardly be called rare in those days, but any suspicions regarding the cause of the mysterious blaze were understandable, particularly given the volatile nature of local politics and the tenuous status of horse racing in Hot Springs. A full explanation of the origins of the fire never emerged, but no person or animal was harmed, and racing would resume, back at Oaklawn, two days later. By the end of the year, interests connected to Oaklawn Park would purchase the remains of the Essex property, ensuring that there would be no competition between the entities going forward.[28]

Steady stoking from hawkish newspapers, business interests, and prominent saber-rattlers had prodded American public sentiment toward war as Germany resumed its submarine attacks on US shipping in early 1917. Decision-makers in Berlin knew that the strategy was likely to provoke the United States, but they were willing to bet that an undersupplied Britain and France could be defeated before the Americans would be able to make much of a military impact. Hoping to draw the United States fully into the fray as soon as possible, British officials publicized a telegram from German foreign secretary Arthur Zimmerman, intercepted by His Majesty's intelligence officials, that had instructed the German Embassy in Mexico to propose a German-Mexican alliance in the event that the United States entered the war. Under the proposition, Mexico could reclaim territory in Texas, New Mexico, and Arizona lost to the United States in 1848. As details of the German scheme came to light, the American public's appetite for military intervention in Europe reached a tipping point. On April 2, Woodrow Wilson asked Congress to declare war against Germany for its "cruel and unmanly actions," citing the need to make the world "safe for democracy." More than four million volunteers and conscripts would serve, making it the largest American army ever assembled to that time, and General Pershing would head the American Expeditionary Force on the Western Front in France.[29]

 A week after the war declaration, Wilson created the Committee on Public Information to streamline the government's messaging regarding the war and to cultivate enthusiasm for the undertaking. Cabinet members and military officials would serve on the committee, but its executive director, former journalist George Creel, would be the driving force behind what quickly became the largest propaganda machine the world had ever seen. Creel would call the committee "a plain publicity proposition, a vast enterprise in salesmanship, [and] the world's greatest adventure in advertising." The most visible aspect of the Creel Committee's work was the "four-minute men," seventy-five thousand volunteers who gave more than seven million brief patriotic speeches at theaters, churches, and civic organizations across the country in support of the American war effort. The committee also produced millions of posters promoting war bonds and the military draft, distributed pamphlets to schoolchildren, and controlled the information and images pertaining to the war that would be disseminated to the news media.[30]

Creel got his professional start at the *Kansas City World*, writing book reviews and a gossip column. Tired of tawdry assignments, he decamped for New York, where he found work writing jokes for William Randolph Hearst's *New York Journal*. He became homesick and accepted an offer to start a weekly muckraking magazine in his native Missouri, which he turned into a success before eventually losing interest. Seeking new adventures, he traveled to Mexico in 1909 with an acquaintance who was trying to build a railroad there. Creel was shocked by the poverty he witnessed in Chihuahua, which was governed by his cousin, Enrique Clay Creel. In a meeting with the governor, who owned 1.7 million acres of Mexican land and was a powerful member of the Terrazas-Creel clan, George expressed his concerns about the sustainability of a society that contained such opulent wealth and widespread deprivation. His opinions were ignored, but his prediction of imminent revolution would prove to be accurate.[31]

Returning to the United States, Creel agreed to write a daily column for the *Denver Post*, owned by a group whose other commercial endeavors included a circus. When Creel's politics proved to be too leftist for the paper, he again headed East to write for Hearst's *Cosmopolitan* magazine and reluctantly agreed to ghostwrite an autobiography of heavyweight boxing champion Jess Willard to be published by Hearst, in which Creel was required to adhere to a storyline that emphasized the fighter's clean living as the key to his pugilistic success. In 1916, he was hired by Wilson's reelection campaign to write newspaper pieces defending the president's pacifism and restraint in Europe and Mexico.[32]

The American entry into the war allowed Wilson, with the help of what soon became popularly known as the Creel Committee, to pursue his moral vision for a reshaped world. Domestically, war would provide cover for all sorts of reform efforts. As one journalist noted, wartime emergency allowed the Wilson administration to "seize railways, requisition factories, take over mines, fix prices, put an embargo on all exports, commandeer all ships, standardize all loaves of bread, punish all careless use of fuel, draft men for an army, and send that army to a war in France," all with relatively little public opposition. Across the country, patriotic enthusiasm produced all sorts of legislation and bluster. Iowa outlawed speaking German in public or on the telephone. Boston banned Beethoven. Senator "Cotton Tom" Heflin of Alabama went even further, declaring, "We must execute the [Germans] within our gates. The firing squad is the only solution for these perverts and renegades." Exigencies of war would even produce the first national daylight saving time. Its proponents postulated that "increased daylight will tend to lessen tuberculosis, will decidedly reduce eyestrain, will increase personal efficiency and materially lessen industrial accidents," in addition to the more easily quantifiable savings from the conservation of fuel and electricity.[33]

In such an environment, a bill banning the production of distilled spirits made from anything that could be used for food sailed through Congress and was signed by President Wilson that summer. Labeled the Food and Fuel Control Act, the prohibition was implemented in the name of aiding the war effort, but it was also merely accelerating an existing trend. The Anti-Saloon League's call to "abolish, root and branch, the un-American, pro-German, crime-producing, food-wasting, youth corrupting, home-wrecking, treasonable liquor traffic" made sense to many Americans. US entry into the Great War had created an opportunity for alcohol opponents to push their efforts to ban booze as a patriotic imperative, and red-light districts across the country were being shuttered in the name of protecting the health of young servicemen. Astute horse-racing officials knew that their sport was an even more vulnerable target than sex and booze. While those opposed to gambling were less fervent and less organized than anti-alcohol crusaders, there were also far fewer ardent horse-racing fans than there were regular patrons of saloons in America.[34]

Racing's leaders saw that their sport and livelihood could easily be done away with along similar lines. They wasted little time crafting an aggressive campaign that would ramp up the promotion of Thoroughbred racing as serving a higher purpose beyond mere recreation or commerce. Jockey Club chair August Belmont, who had been among the oldest American volunteers for military service in the Great War, issued a statement declaring that American racing associations had a duty to continue the sport despite calls for its wartime curtailment. Noting that the belligerent nations of Europe had continued their horse racing during the war, and that the American Thoroughbred breeding markets were just starting to recover from years of disorder, he insisted that "it would be a great mistake to stop racing and tear down now what so many men have been at so great pains to build up. I do not think there should be a single day of racing declared off. Even though great crowds may not be able to attend, it will be well to carry it on for the good of the breeding horses, so many of which are certain to be in big demand." In a letter to Gen. Leonard Wood, who had commanded Theodore Roosevelt's Rough Riders regiment in the Spanish-American War before serving as military governor of Cuba and US Army chief of staff, Belmont further contended, "We as a people have no more right to put our young men on an inferior horse than we have to send them forth with an inferior rifle." The sixty-four-year-old Belmont had long been a proponent of utilizing racehorses in military breeding programs, but his views carried more urgency in wartime and, especially after he received his commission as a major in the Army Air Service, would bear more weight as well.[35]

Federal restrictions on wartime travel and consumption would soon impact nearly every facet of American life, including horse racing. In the meantime, racing executives did their best to maintain positive momentum for the sport while also taking care to wrap their product in patriotism at any opportunity. Hoping to build on the record attendance produced by their first meeting, Oaklawn officials arranged a rematch between Pan Zareta and Old Rosebud. A dependable seven-year-old named Robert Bradley rounded out the three-horse field. This time, they would run at nearly equal weights, with Old Rosebud and Robert Bradley assigned only 105 pounds and Pan Zareta 2 pounds less.

Hours after Congress passed its war declaration against Germany, a lively crowd filled Oaklawn Park, energized by pleasant early-spring weather. Old Rosebud was an even-money favorite in the seven-furlong dash. The start was slow, but Rosebud crept to the lead in the opening quarter with lightweight George Molesworth aboard, Charley Peak being far too heavy for the assignment. Molesworth set a solid pace, and Rosebud was never seriously tested. He brushed away a mild challenge from Pan Zareta on the backstretch and extended his lead to three lengths turning for home. Molesworth let the gelding coast to the finish, shaving a full second off the course-record time, a performance that would garner praise in newspapers across the United States and Canada.

To his supporters, Old Rosebud was making a case for consideration as the best racehorse in America. Even impartial observers had to concede that, provided he could remain healthy, the Bud would be a major player in the big handicap races that summer. Capitalizing on the hype surrounding

August Belmont II advocated for continuing to conduct horse racing during World War I and was a prominent promoter of the sport as an essential component of American military preparedness. (Library of Congress)

the comeback, Matt Winn announced a special race, to be held at Churchill Downs on Derby Day, that he hoped would attract Roamer and Rosebud. Like Old Rosebud, Roamer was a record-setting former champion looking to regain some of his past brilliance. A win against Andrew Miller's gelding would be a good starting place for Weir to achieve the goals he had quietly set for his resurgent runner, which included beating Kentucky's best older horses in the Clark Handicap at Churchill Downs, the Kentucky Handicap at Douglas Park, and the Inaugural at Latonia. The Applegates were happy to take Winn's bait, and they insured their gelding for ten thousand dollars before putting him on a train to Louisville. The sum was a far cry from the thirty-five thousand they had once turned down for their star but still quite a bit of money for a six-year-old gelding just returning from years away from the racetrack.[36]

Old Rosebud's resounding wins against Roamer when the pair were two-year-olds had caused Roamer's breeders to sell their once-promising racer. But while Rosebud was on the sidelines, Roamer had blossomed into the top Thoroughbred in America, with twelve wins, a second, and two third-place finishes in sixteen starts as a three-year-old in 1914. The following year, he set a track record for ten furlongs in the Saratoga Handicap on his way to recognition as the top older male of 1915. He had regressed a bit at five, winning only once in thirteen starts, but was still competitive with the top handicap horses in America, notching six runner-up finishes in top-level stakes races. By the spring of 1917, Roamer appeared to be set for a return to great form as a six-year-old.

The Derby was the marquee event, but the Rosebud-Roamer showdown received nearly as much attention from the press leading up to Kentucky racing's biggest day. Old Rosebud appeared happy and healthy in his morning gallops but was not being asked to do too much. Heightened interest in the Derby from Easterners, partially traceable to publicity garnered by headline-grabbing performances from Old Rosebud and Regret in recent years, led Downs officials to expect another record crowd despite the recent war declaration. They had again upped the Derby purse, to fifteen thousand dollars, and made improvements to accommodate increased patronage, including installing three thousand benches about the lawns that surrounded the saddling paddock.[37]

Festivities on a chilly, breezy Derby Day at the Downs began with a flag-raising ceremony that elicited a "mighty cheer" from the crowd. The

Kentucky Militia band performed, and Governor Stanley gave a rambling, patriotic address emphasizing Kentucky horses' importance to the American war effort in Europe:

> It is eminently fitting that on this classic occasion and in the presence of this vast assemblage we should inaugurate this auspicious opening of a great meeting by hoisting to the winds the beautiful and unconquered emblem of the world's liberty.
>
> As that banner is unfurled today, as it is raised aloft, it presents a new significance to us and the world. To us it is an inspiration to deeds of valor; to courage and fortitude; to sacrifice and support, and if needs be, to death. . . . In Kentucky we are prepared to follow that flag to the end of time. We are marshaled sons of marshaled sires . . . and when we shall go in defense of our flag, we go mounted upon the greatest creature God ever made except women—the thoroughbred horse, the Kentucky thoroughbred horse. Our loved and trusted animal in times of peace becomes in times of war our cavalry horse, our artillery horse, and our charger.
>
> The farmers of the land are doing a big share in this war, but no man in the furrow nor no man in the trench is doing more to prepare us for the victory which is to follow than is the breeder of the horses that are to vie for supremacy upon this track today.[38]

Old Rosebud received boisterous applause as a quartet of contestants made its way to the starting line for the mile-and-a-sixteenth contest. It was the first time a Louisville crowd had seen him in three years, and bettors made him the post-time favorite, at odds of 1–2. Off his own long layoff, Roamer was the longest price in the field. Away from the barrier quickly, Rosebud and jockey Danny Connelly—a rising star in Kentucky who was already struggling to maintain weight, a struggle that would ultimately cost him his life—set fast fractions through six furlongs. They were tracked by Roamer and jockey Andy Schuttinger, wearing Andrew Miller's cardinal and white colors. Entering the stretch, Rosebud clung to a short lead, but Roamer's pressure proved to be too much; Rosebud tired in the final furlong as Roamer rumbled ahead for an easy win.

Roamer's owner, pleasantly surprised by his gelding's performance off a long rest, just missed a Derby Day double when British-bred Omar Khayyam,

With Old Rosebud sidelined by injury, Roamer blossomed into the top American racehorse of 1914. (Library of Congress)

owned by a pair of New Yorkers, caught Miller's gelding Ticket in the stretch to win the forty-third running of the Kentucky Derby. Omar's win, the first for a foreign-born horse in America's greatest race, was early evidence that the eastward flow of American racehorses to Europe had started to reverse, due largely to wartime deprivations on the continent. And with top national stables now making the Derby an annual target, recent momentum for the race was showing little sign of abating. Churchill Downs officials claimed another record crowd, with significant numbers of spectators having traveled from outside the region to witness the spectacle.[39]

Old Rosebud exited his race in fine form. Old accusations that he was merely a sprinter reemerged, but Weir and the Applegates were undeterred. They announced that their gelding would be entered in the Clark Handicap the following Saturday. Named for the track founder and dating to Churchill Downs first year in operation, the Clark was the second most prestigious race on the Downs schedule. It had initially been limited to three-year-olds but was opened to older horses and switched to handicap conditions in 1902. Originally run at two miles, it had been gradually reduced to a mile and a sixteenth.

Had Rosebud's people used the Derby Day race as a chance to better position their horse for the richer Clark prize? Rosebud would receive a manageable weight assignment of 117 (11 pounds less than Roamer). Only two other competitors made the starting line. Neither would figure prominently in the running. Roamer had been working well all week, while Rosebud continued his regimen of easy gallops. Despite the weight concession, Roamer was the odds-on favorite at post time.

Perfect temperatures, marred only by high wind, greeted the large Saturday crowd for the rematch. Taking advantage of Roamer's stumble at the start, Danny Connelly sent Rosebud to an early lead and allowed his horse to settle under a gentle hold. He set a more deliberate pace than he had a week earlier, followed closely by 1913 Kentucky Derby–winning jockey Roscoe Goose, aboard Roamer, through the backstretch and around the turn. Goose tried to move at the quarter pole, but before he reached Rosebud's saddle, Connelly let his horse spurt ahead. Despite Goose's repeated efforts to rouse Roamer through the stretch, he could gain no ground. Rosebud coasted to an open-length victory with Connelly sitting perfectly still.

The crowd was ecstatic as the local hero returned to the winner's circle. Rosebud's comeback was complete. But his handlers had still loftier ambitions.

5

King of the Turf

With Rosebud and Roamer each having tallied a win in the rekindled rivalry, the Kentucky Handicap at Douglas Park, which had quickly become one of the premier races in America for older horses, loomed as a likely venue for a tiebreaker. Rosebud had come out of the Clark in good shape, and Weir wanted to give his horse a couple of local preps to ease him up to the Kentucky Handicap's ten furlongs, a distance he had not tried since the Kentucky Derby.

Track officials at Douglas raised the bar on patriotic flair for the start of their late-spring 1917 meet. As the horses stepped onto the track for the first race, a large band struck up "The Star-Spangled Banner," which President Wilson had recently endorsed as the official song for the armed forces, though it would not formally be designated the national anthem until the 1930s. A gigantic Old Glory ascended the 128-foot flagpole in the infield to wild applause, and a cannon round punctuating the festivities caused the excited crowd to squeal with glee.[1]

The air had been heavy with humidity beneath threatening clouds all afternoon. Rain finally came as the horses reached the barrier for the fifth race, the eight-and-a-half-furlong Pendennis Club Special. It looked to be a competitive, boutique field of four challengers for Old Rosebud that included Jeff Livingston's stakes-winning British-bred colt Colonel Vennie, Rosebud's Kentucky Derby runner-up Hodge, and Pif Jr., who would set multiple track records in a long, decorated career. Danny Connelly kept Old Rosebud tightly held and put him just outside a Canadian-owned long-shot pacesetter for the first half mile. Entering the far turn, Connelly turned his horse loose, and Rosebud left his adversary in the dust. He extended his lead to five lengths in the stretch before Connelly allowed him to glide to the finish, in a scene that evoked past glory.

Four days later, Rosebud stretched out to nine furlongs to take the Cherokee Handicap over improving four-year-old King Gorin and Hodge. The popular winner received another hearty ovation as he and Connelly returned to the scales. The time, 1:51⅕, was a fifth of a second off the track record. Just a couple of weeks earlier, it had appeared that Roamer would be the horse to beat in the ten-thousand-dollar Kentucky Handicap, but Rosebud's three-race win streak forced bettors to take another look.

Thanks to a generous weight assignment and his local popularity, Old Rosebud would be the 9–5 betting favorite by post time. Savvy players looked elsewhere for value. Roamer had been pointed to the race all spring and was training up a storm. He would carry six pounds less than he had in the previous year's Kentucky Handicap, when he finished a close second. Sharing highweight designation with Roamer was another standout six-year-old gelding, Boots. Bred in Kentucky by James Ben Ali Haggin, Boots raced competitively in England at two and three before being repatriated to America, where he continued to thrive on dirt for owner Kingsley Macomber, breaking track records in the United States and Canada. Johnny Loftus had come down from New York to ride the six-year-old. The previous year's winner, Ed Crump, and Rosebud's familiar foe Hodge were among the other contenders, along with future champion Cudgel and mud-loving King Gorin.

Douglas Park officials were determined to do all they could to produce a fast track for their signature race, despite two days of rain. The maintenance crew worked through the night, setting fire to portions of the racing surface to burn off standing water, and used sponges and buckets to sop up lingering puddles. The return of scattered showers in the morning mitigated the efforts, but the skies cleared in time for the arrival of the largest crowd in the track's history.[2]

Though the surface was officially labeled "good," it was wet in some places, soft in others. Fans filled the stands, clubhouse, and grounds to witness one of the deepest fields ever to race in Kentucky. After a slow start, Rosebud seized the lead on the rail for jockey Connelly, flanked by a 50–1 long shot named Opportunity. The front-running pair pushed through a quick half mile, with Roamer and jockey Andy Schuttinger looming. Roamer moved up on the backstretch to join the fray and poked a head in front entering the far turn. The trio raced three abreast, but the gummy going had cooked the pacesetters. Groans from Rosebud's backers resounded through the grandstand as Roamer passed his spent rivals and rolled into the final straight. The Miller gelding persevered gamely through the stretch but was overtaken by deep closers King Gorin and Cudgel in the final strides to finish third.

Despite his ninth-place finish, Rosebud largely received a pass from the press. Most turf writers were generous in their assessment of his race, noting the track conditions, relatively heavy impost, and stiff early challenge from a horse with little chance to win. Perhaps the mile-and-a-quarter distance was a bit too far. Frank Weir was disappointed but not discouraged. He suspected that shortening Rosebud up a bit would be just what his horse needed to return to his winning ways. By the end of the week, the Weir string was on a train to northern Kentucky for the start of the summer meet at Latonia.

Cincinnati-area manufacturers were humming around the clock to supply the Allied armies. At the start of the Great War, the American economy had been in a recession. But demand for food and armaments had been a boon to US agriculture and industry. American entry into the conflict had only accelerated the growth. US exports had risen from $2.3 billion in 1913 to $4.3 billion in 1916 and would reach $6.3 billion in 1917. On Wall Street, stock prices had doubled in less than three years. In packed Cincinnati hotels, guests spoke of little but horse racing and war.[3]

Frank Weir and company would not have to wait long to see Old Rosebud avenge his loss. The featured race on opening day was the Inaugural Handicap at a mile and a sixteenth. Off his surprise Kentucky Handicap score, King Gorin received a substantial bump in weight assignment, to 119, still 5 pounds less than Old Rosebud, who would be making his first trip to the Latonia starting line in four years. Hodge was ready to take another crack at the Applegates' gelding and was the second favorite at odds marginally more generous than Rosebud's 2–1.

Long before the first race, the parking lots were filled with automobiles, many of them new, fancy models. The bridge spanning the Ohio River between Cincinnati and Kentucky was crowded with cars ferrying racegoers to the track. The wartime pageantry at Churchill Downs and Douglas Park had established a standard that Latonia officials managed to exceed. As the horses made their way to the post for the day's first race beneath cloudless skies, two American-flag projectile parachutes were launched high into the air along with a large balloon shaped like a horse and jockey, as part of an elaborate prerace extravaganza in the infield. An enormous Stars and Stripes was dramatically unfurled atop a 130-foot flagpole, with the British and French flags beneath. Accompanied by patriotic music, the scene elicited vigorous cheers from the capacity opening-day crowd.[4]

Hodge broke sharply from the rail in the featured race. He set a moderate pace around the first turn and into the backstretch with King Gorin tracking closely. Danny Connelly saved ground aboard Old Rosebud, a length and a half behind the pacesetters. King Gorin moved up to challenge on the turn, and the tiring Hodge swung wide entering the homestretch, leaving a hole on the rail. Connelly sent Rosebud through the gap and hustled him on to a two-length win. The cranked-up Latonia crowd loudly welcomed the victorious gelding and his hometown-hero jockey back to the winner's circle. It was Rosebud's eighth win in twelve starts on the year.

Weir decided that his horse was ready for steeper competition and a start in the Brooklyn Handicap on opening day of the summer meeting at Aqueduct. The trainer had hoped that Charley Peak, who had ridden the Bud to three of his four wins in Arkansas, would take the mount. But The Jockey Club refused to grant Peak a license. No reason for the decision was provided, but the jockey's long rap sheet for riding infractions (despite a reputation as personally well-mannered) was well known. Connelly would instead be back in the saddle. Unconvinced by his recent run of success, some New York sportswriters still questioned whether the resurgent Old Rosebud could handle the best horses from the East Coast.[5]

The Brooklyn Handicap had been run at Gravesend, near Coney Island, from 1887 until the shuttering of New York racing following the 1910 season. That track never reopened, and the Brooklyn race was resurrected at Aqueduct in 1914. In twenty-eight previous runnings, the race had never attracted as talented a field as Old Rosebud would face in the 1917 edition. Some were calling it the greatest in the history of American racing. It would be the first on-track meeting of three Kentucky Derby winners. The all-star cast that included three future Hall of Famers would produce a race that would somehow exceed the heavy journalistic hype it had received all week. Five of the starters, and four of the leading contenders, were geldings. The *Daily Racing Form* called the glut of top-level, castrated competitors an "unfortunate circumstance" for American racing, lamenting that those elite runners would be unable to produce generations of successors. But in the meantime, fans would enjoy a compelling summer of competition among an elite group of familiar horses at a time when the sport still needed every bit of positive publicity it could get, particularly in New York.[6]

Roamer, who had set a new track record in his most recent outing when he beat a strong bunch in the Excelsior Handicap at Jamaica, was the highest-weighted contestant, carrying 128 pounds. He had established a new American record for the Brooklyn's nine-furlong distance the year before and was well regarded by the punters at 4–1. Off his recent win in the Suburban Handicap, the well-traveled Boots would be the post-time favorite at odds of 3–1. Bettors made Harry Payne Whitney's two-horse entry the second choice. His nine-year-old gelding Borrow had notched several stakes wins in England before returning to the United States on the outbreak of the Great War. Recent runner-up finishes in the Suburban and the Excelsior indicated a late-career renaissance. His Kentucky Derby–winning entry mate Regret was one of the greatest American female runners of all time. She had lost only once in eight career starts, and six of her wins had come against males. The Whitney pair was priced at 7–2 in clandestine betting. Reigning Kentucky Derby champion Omar Khayyam, recently purchased by Canadian cookie manufacturer Wilfrid Viau for $26,500, would accumulate wins in the Brooklyn Derby, Travers Stakes, Saratoga Cup, and Lawrence Realization among a slew of stakes scores that year. As a three-year-old facing older horses, the colt named for a twelfth-century Persian polymath would carry only 110 pounds. Stromboli, August Belmont's brawny six-year-old gelding—a past winner of the Metropolitan, Jerome, and Suburban Handicaps—was largely ignored at 20–1. Rosebud would tote 120 pounds and was 8–1. A quartet of other stakes-quality horses rounded out the field.

The stellar lineup drew a huge crowd for the opening card at Aqueduct on a late-June Monday afternoon, producing a scene reminiscent of pre-shutdown days. As in his earlier appearances in New York, Rosebud had plenty of supporters and detractors. A group of his hometown fans took a train from Louisville to witness the spectacle. The weather was pleasant, but a strong breeze kept a cloud of dust billowing from the homestretch toward the grandstand and clubhouse. Fans arrived in waves through much of the afternoon as the Long Island Railroad had trouble handling local passenger volume.

"This horse is fit," Weir told jockey Connelly before the race. "The only way they can beat you is to [break the American record for nine furlongs].

Just ride him as you always do, and they'll drink to your health and Old Rosebud out in Cincinnati tonight."[7]

The eleven-horse field proved to be a challenge for starter Mars Cassidy, who took five minutes to get the fractious bunch in line. Once the barrier was sprung, all were away in good order except for Omar Khayyam, who was on his heels and would lag near the back of the pack for the rest of the race. Breaking from the rail, emerging star of the saddle Frankie Robinson rushed Regret straight to the lead. Ormesdale and Chiclet, the two longest shots in the race, pressed her through a half mile in forty-seven flat. Roamer and Old Rosebud were forwardly placed, three lengths behind the pacesetters. As Ormesdale faded on the turn, Roamer plowed ahead to reach Regret's hip, and the front-running mare's stablemate Borrow moved up on the rail.

Regret chugged steadily onward and was separating herself from Roamer turning into the homestretch, with Old Rosebud gearing up for a challenge on the outside. After a mile in 1:36⅖, which would have equaled the track record for the distance, Regret was tiring. Connelly sent Rosebud into a drive. Roamer had nothing left and began to fall back, but half a dozen horses still had a chance in the final sixteenth. As the field reached the grandstand, the din of the crowd jumped an octave.

Down on the rail, top-notch rider Willie Knapp had been steadily chewing up ground aboard Borrow. Knapp knew that Whitney and trainer Jimmy Rowe wanted to see their beloved mare win, but he sensed Old Rosebud threatening on the outside. Clinging to a diminishing lead, Robinson popped Regret with the whip and glanced over his shoulder, relieved to see Whitney's Eton-blue silks. His wearied mount drifted to the outside, opening a lane for her surging stablemate. Fifty yards from the finish, Borrow stuck a head in front. Rosebud had cost himself ground swerving through the stretch, and Borrow slid under the wire a neck in front of the real star of the race, Regret, with an exhausted Old Rosebud a close third. The time, 1:49⅖, was a new American record, surpassing the mark set by Roamer three years earlier.

As the Whitney pair returned to be greeted by the winning owner making an appearance at the Queens track, the crowd renewed its raucous ovation, drowning out the trackside band that had started a postrace tune. "It seemed as if the entire grandstand had got up and cheered itself hoarse," a New York reporter noted, "while the women folk split their gloves in clapping." The scene provided proof, if anyone needed it, that New York sports fans could still be captivated by big-time horse racing.[8]

The field for the 1917 Brooklyn Handicap, including Old Rosebud (6), Regret (4), and Borrow (leading), was one of the deepest in American horse-racing history. (Keeneland Library Cook Collection)

Knapp sounded slightly apologetic in his postrace comments. "I wouldn't have beaten [Regret] if I had been sure she would win," the jockey told the press. "Old Rosebud was coming fast at the end, and rather than take any chances of defeat, I moved up and went past the mare."[9]

Connelly fielded questions from a reporter before catching a train to Latonia, perhaps trying to preemptively absolve himself of blame for what some would say was a premature move in the stretch. "At the sixteenth pole I felt sure of winning," the rider said:

> Rosebud was going strong under me, and I was in the lead. Yes, I was a good neck in front of Regret who was tiring fast from cutting out that terrific pace. To keep him ahead I cut him twice with the whip. Then what does the honest old feller do but hang—something he had never done under me before. He was beaten but they had to smash the world's record to do it. It was a great race and no disgrace

for a cripple like Rosebud to lose. If he stands up, he'll show you Easterners some great performances.[10]

If Old Rosebud did hold the lead at some point in the stretch, it was only very briefly. And though Weir never directly criticized Connelly in the press, it would be the last time the jockey would ride the great gelding.

Rosebud returned to winning ways five days later, cutting back to a mile in the Queens County Handicap. After a soaking rain on Friday, the racing surface was slow, but clear skies and a chance to see the most talked-about horse in America drew another capacity crowd to Aqueduct. A steady breeze created a homestretch headwind and helped the swarming patrons tolerate the late-June heat. Off his strong showing in the Brooklyn, Rosebud was the top choice at 5–2 and seemed to have the support of those who had no pecuniary interest in the race. The field included Brooklyn Handicap starters Roamer, Chiclet, and Ormesdale, as well as 1915 Belmont Stakes winner The Finn and seven-year-old gelding Leochares, who had won a handful of stakes in a long career that would include 62 victories in 175 starts. Neither Borrow nor any other horses from the H. P. Whitney stable would run; Whitney's uncle Oliver Hazard Payne, who had made a fortune in Standard Oil, American Tobacco Company, and US Steel, had died that week. With no Whitney runners in the race, Weir tapped Frankie Robinson to ride Old Rosebud.

Robinson kept his horse stuck to Ormesdale for a half mile before the pacesetter gave way and faded to the back of the pack. Roamer plodded steadily along but never posed a real threat to Rosebud, finishing a length and a half behind the winner.

If the Queens County win earned him a spot on the list of top American handicap horses, his score in the seven-furlong $3,500 Carter Handicap as the 130-pound topweight four days later made a strong case for him to be placed at the head of the division. Colonel Applegate arrived from Latonia in time to be among the Fourth of July crowd of fifteen thousand that embraced Rosebud as a sentimental choice. Gamblers made him the 11–5 chalk in a strong nine-horse field.

With Frankie Robinson obligated to ride H. P. Whitney's Bromo (running in the colors of Whitney's friend Lewis Thompson, son of the former treasurer of Standard Oil, out of continuing respect to Whitney's deceased uncle), Andy Schuttinger was aboard Old Rosebud. As he had earlier in the week, Rosebud pranced to the post ready to race. Unlike his previous

Beginning with the Queens County Handicap, Old Rosebud would win seven of eight starts to finish a championship 1917 racing season. (Keeneland Library Cook Collection)

two starts, Rosebud got the early jump on the eager Ormesdale and ran Richard T. Wilson's colt into submission after a half mile. After repelling a series of mild challenges on the turn, he held a two-length lead headed into the homestretch. Bromo mounted a late rally, but Old Rosebud dug in gamely under a vigorous hand ride from Schuttinger. The "cannonade of applause" emanating from the stands intensified as The Finn came flying from the back of the field in the final yards. But Rosebud prevailed by a safe half length. The grandstand "jumped clear out of plumb," according to one witness, when Rosebud crossed the finish line to the delight of a frenzied crowd.[11]

Old Rosebud's breeder, John Madden, flashed a broad grin as he watched one of the best horses he had ever raised, winner of twenty-four races in thirty-two starts, gallop back toward the grandstand to be unsaddled. "He was bred in old Kentucky," Madden proudly told a reporter for the *New York Tribune*, "where horses are of the true type. He is bred in the purple, and it is no wonder he wins. I know of no more wonderful horse."[12]

Rosebud was making a strong case for recognition as the best sprinter in America. But Weir and the Applegates were determined to show that their horse could carry weight and win at any distance. He would not race at less than a mile the rest of the year. Weir firmly believed Old Rosebud would have already been acknowledged as the best American racehorse in history had it not been for his breakdown and subsequent extended layoff. He wanted to reclaim as much reputation for his beloved charge as he could. "Old Rosebud is the kind of a horse that one sees once in a lifetime," Weir said. "He is certainly the fastest horse I ever trained or ever saw."[13]

The Bud was bouncy the next morning and seemed primed for a try four days later in the eight-and-a-half-furlong Red Cross Handicap on a special card at Aqueduct to benefit war-relief organizations. The first US soldiers had reached Europe in June. General Pershing immediately requested a million more troops, but it would be another year before most of those would arrive. Conducting horse races on behalf of charitable causes gave fans a chance to be generous. And at a time when the lingering reformist spirit of the era was combining with wartime exigency to open the gate for broad commercial and social restrictions, benevolent racing events also burnished the image of a sport whose footing in American society remained precarious. Earlier in the spring, Churchill Downs leadership had planted potatoes in their track's infield. After harvest, Matt Winn and other Churchill Downs executives would parade five truckloads of potatoes from Churchill Downs to the Jefferson County courthouse steps, accompanied by a military brass band. The sale of three thousand bushels of spuds, facilitated by a Shakespearean actor serving as celebrity auctioneer, provided well-publicized cash for a Christmas fund to benefit soldiers stationed nearby at Camp Zachary Taylor, and contributions to Red Cross charities from the American racing industry were expected to exceed $750,000 the following year, with Kentucky tracks promising 10 percent of gross receipts and a similar portion of all purse money won by horse owners.[14]

The Red Cross race at Aqueduct had the makings of another blockbuster with Regret, Roamer, Borrow, and The Finn named as possible contestants. But after a rash of scratches, due in part to the sloppy racetrack, only three runners toed the starting line. Old Rosebud would again be saddled with 130 pounds by handicapper Walter Vosburgh. With a 10-pound advantage, H. P. Whitney's Bromo, still running in the Thompson colors, would try to turn the tables on the Bud. Joseph E. Widener's French-bred colt Chiclet, who had run competitively to finish fourth at long odds in the Brooklyn Handicap, would carry only 110. Despite the disparity, Rosebud was the odds-on favorite.

Five thousand fans braved rainy conditions, and many of the sport's leading figures filled the clubhouse to support the patriotic cause and to see whether Old Rosebud could further validate his claim to consideration as America's top racehorse. Chiclet was away from the barrier first, with Bromo and jockey Johnny Loftus glued to him on the rail. The pair raced neck and neck for the first quarter, while Willie Knapp, Rosebud's fourth rider in as many starts, found better going on the outside, well positioned just off the pace. After a half mile in forty-eight seconds on the slow, wet track, Chiclet was fading. Bromo eased into the lead headed into the far turn with Rosebud at his flank. Rounding into the homestretch, Knapp smooched to his horse, and Rosebud darted ahead. Opening a bit of daylight, it looked like he would draw away. When Rosebud started to linger, tiring under the encumbrance, Loftus roused Bromo for one last push on the inside. But Knapp held off the challenge, without employing the whip, to prevail by a long neck.

With the Red Cross win, his third in the two weeks since his third-place effort in the Brooklyn, Old Rosebud was positioning himself as an early leader in the chase for year-end divisional championship honors. He would have another chance to enhance his résumé five days later in the Frontier Handicap, the most valuable prize in Canada, on opening day at Windsor.

Light rain fell off and on through the afternoon, but it was not enough to prevent record attendance for what was being billed as the greatest event in the history of Canadian racing. Ferry boats were loaded with racegoers well before noon. Twelve thousand spectators filled the Windsor Jockey Club grounds, just across the river from Detroit, whose automobile plants had shifted production to military trucks and airplanes for the war that was entrenched in a horrific stalemate, with most American forces still making their way toward Europe. Though the track would be rated "good" by post time, Roamer was a late defection, his handlers scared off by the intermittent showers. The co-top-weights, Old Rosebud and Boots, were the star attractions in a loaded eight-horse field that also included Rosebud's old antagonists Hodge and Bromo, as well as the good three-year-old filly Fruit Cake, recently the beaten favorite in the Preakness. Since his disappointing sixth-place finish in the Brooklyn, Boots had equaled the American record for nine furlongs in the Brookdale

Handicap at Aqueduct. He appeared ready for a game effort and was made the 5–2 chalk, with Rosebud the second choice at 3–1.[15]

Hodge and Old Rosebud were the primary causes of an eight-minute delay at the starting line. After everyone was finally brought under control, jockey George Molesworth put Rosebud just off a moderate early pace set by long shots Waterbass and Fruit Cake. Nearing the far turn, Molesworth turned his horse loose, and they slid into the lead. After finding early traffic trouble on Boots, Johnny Loftus chased the Bud the rest of the way on the outside. Boots made a bid in the homestretch, but Old Rosebud had plenty left. A thrilled crowd shook the grandstand with appreciative applause as he passed the wire a length and a half in front to score a fourth straight win and bank a ten-thousand-dollar payday. Molesworth, who would go on to a career as a racing official when his riding days were finished, was awestruck by his horse. "He was like a machine," the jockey said. "He ran like a machine."[16]

The American press was ready to anoint Old Rosebud a phenomenon. The *New Orleans Times-Picayune* called him "the most wonderful come-back in American turf history." Dubbing him the "Miracle Horse," Hearst columnist Frank G. Menke wrote, "What Old Rosebud has performed since [his return] has been history, has added glory to his name and won for him the love of the great mass of Eastern horse enthusiasts." Walter Vosburgh had seen enough to rate him the top racehorse in America. When he issued weight assignments a week later for the Saratoga Handicap, set for opening day at the upstate track, Rosebud received the highest impost of 132 pounds.[17]

Old Rosebud would make one more start in Canada before heading back across the border. The Kenilworth Handicap was the featured race on opening day at Kenilworth Park, another racetrack in Windsor that served the population of greater Detroit, where gambling remained illegal. The Kenilworth meeting would conclude an abbreviated Canadian racing season, as officials there had decided that the nation's resources, time, and attention could be better focused on achieving Allied military victory in Europe.

Rosebud carried 132 pounds, including jockey George Molesworth, giving up to 30 pounds to his five challengers. No other horse toted more than 108. Still, Rosebud was made the overwhelming 3–20 favorite for the race at a mile and seventy yards. He would win just as easily as expected. A record crowd of nine thousand Tuesday-afternoon fans tried to stay cool beneath the steel roof of the grandstand. Rosebud fought his rider's efforts to keep him restrained before settling down through the backstretch as he tracked

George Molesworth rode Old Rosebud in Mexico, the United States, and Canada in 1917, winning four of six starts. He drew heavy criticism for his ill-advised tactics in the Saratoga Handicap. (Keeneland Library Cook Collection)

pacesetter Kinney, winner of the 1915 Breeders' Futurity. Rounding into the homestretch, Molesworth urged Rosebud to the front, and he kicked on to a two-length win, lopping nearly two seconds off the track record without being asked for full exertion. As Kenilworth had been in operation for less than a year, that accomplishment was less remarkable than the headlines made it appear. Still, the win put Old Rosebud atop the North American earnings list for the year.

The 1917 Saratoga Handicap was shaping up to be a doozy. Borrow and Roamer, the winners of the 1914 and 1915 editions, joined top-weighted Old Rosebud on the list of entries for the ten-furlong contest. Other expected starters included the top two-year-old colt of 1916, Richard T. Wilson's Campfire; 1916 Kentucky Derby winner George Smith; 1917 Kentucky Derby runner-up Ticket; and Spur, winner of the 1916 Travers and Withers. Hotels, boardinghouses, and owners of private residences at Saratoga boosted their rates in anticipation of a return to pre-shutdown vitality, with the nation galvanized for war but protected from threat of physical harm by thousands of miles of ocean.

Though Roamer had been winless since his record-breaking score in the Excelsior back in June, he had been competitive in each of his nine races on the year and was thriving in Saratoga. His recent eye-catching eight-furlong work, combined with the ten pounds he would be receiving from Old Rosebud, drew sharp punters' money toward Miller's gelding. Still, Weir was confident. "Rosebud made [Roamer's breeders] think Roamer was only a plater when they met as two-year-olds," the trainer reminded a reporter. "He has done everything I have ever asked him, and if the track is good on Wednesday the public will see a great race."[18]

Less than an hour before the start of the afternoon racing, a ferocious storm walloped the racetrack and surrounding town. Telegraph poles and trees were ripped from the ground, and awesome lightning lit up the sky. Hail pelted rooftops, and thunder rattled windows. The accompanying deluge turned the Saratoga racing surface to a muddy bog, which seemed to favor Old Rosebud rather than Roamer, and bettors would make Rosebud the 9–5 favorite. Though Roamer had managed to win in the slop when he was able to take an early lead, his reputation as mud-averse caused his odds to drift to 5–1.

The squall marginally deflated attendance, but the grounds were still lively and the stands largely full for the featured Saratoga Handicap. Heeding orders to sit off the pace as he had done in Canada, Molesworth took a firm hold of Rosebud after a good start, allowing Roamer an uncontested lead. Roamer's stablemate Ticket moved up to join the pacesetter through a half in : 50⅗. Molesworth kept his horse under a tight pull into the backstretch, content to lie nearly three lengths behind the leaders as Rosebud bristled at the restraint. Finally allowed to run entering the far turn, Old Rosebud gave his backers some hope for a few jumps that he might catch Roamer. But he had expended too much energy fighting his rider and flattened out in the stretch. Thanks to the deliberate early pace, Roamer had enough in reserve to outlast a fast-closing Spur for a half-length victory. Seeing that Rosebud was hopelessly beaten, Molesworth saved his horse for another day and let him coast to the finish, just a couple of lengths ahead of the trailers.

The press pinned the blame for Old Rosebud's defeat squarely on his rider. "If Molesworth had purposely put on 'the brakes' he couldn't have done it to better advantage," carped the *New York Evening World*. Weir was disappointed with the result but acknowledged that he had told Molesworth to stay off the lead and save his horse for a stretch run. He had not thought it necessary to issue a caveat to account for the possibility that the pacesetter might be merely strolling on the lead. "The pace was slower than Molesworth thought, and he obeyed orders too strictly," Weir said after the race. "I expect Old Rosebud to run a better race the next time." The Applegate gelding returned to the barn with a mouth full of mud and some minor flesh wounds incurred at the start. The rider had done Rosebud no favors, but there were other excuses.[19]

Weir gave Old Rosebud and Molesworth a chance at redemption a week later in the one-mile Delaware Handicap at Saratoga, where Rosebud was saddled with 133 pounds. Despite his recent win, Roamer would carry 6 fewer and was the 3–2 favorite. Other starters included multiple-stakes-winning three-year-old Cudgel, who had run well on the Kentucky circuit that year, and New York grocery store magnate and racetrack owner James Butler's capable five-year-old stakes-placed mare Capra, carrying only 104 pounds.

After a good break, Molesworth again took Rosebud back, securing a ground-saving spot on the rail and letting Capra and long shot British-bred colt Hollister set a quick pace. But Molesworth was careful not to pull on his horse this time, and Rosebud stalked the leaders a length ahead of Roamer. Odds-makers had assumed that Miller's gelding would be closer to the lead, but jockey Jimmy Butwell was content to hang near the back of the tightly bunched pack. By the end of the backstretch, Hollister had folded. Molesworth clucked to Rosebud and began to reel in the front-running Capra. Turning for home, Rosebud had reached the mare's flank. Despite carrying twenty-nine more pounds, Rosebud wore down Capra in the final furlong and was a head in front at the wire. Roamer made a late charge to finish third, a half length behind the winner.

Apologists for the Miller gelding said that Roamer needed more distance and that his jockey's saddle had slipped during the stretch run. But most credited Rosebud for beating Roamer on the square while conceding weight. The handicap divisional championship was starting to seem all but decided in Old Rosebud's favor.[20]

With Rosebud having won seven of his past nine starts, it was becoming difficult to find fault with the horse. One critic noted that Rosebud was not drawing away in his wins, doing just enough to win. Perhaps it was a sign of the horse's maturity. Or perhaps, as one Brooklyn writer posited,

Molesworth had cagily given the appearance of a tough struggle at the finish to fool the handicapper into dropping Rosebud's weight assignment for his next race, "mask[ing] the wonderful gelding's capabilities with a degree of skill which Isaac Murphy or any of the other master horsemen of bygone days could not have surpassed." Regardless, it would be Molesworth's last ride on Rosebud.[21]

Observant railbirds began to notice that Old Rosebud was looking a bit light in the flesh, which some took as a sign that he might be tiring from what had already been a long campaign. But Weir insisted that it was his intention to keep as much weight off his horse as possible, to limit the strain on his previously injured leg and reduce the chance of recurrence of tendon problems. All conceded that Weir had done a masterful rehabilitation job and were inclined to give him the benefit of the doubt when he said that he could keep his star pupil on the track long enough to secure a championship. The trainer eyed the mile-and-three-quarters Saratoga Cup on closing day, where Rosebud might demonstrate his stamina and prove once and for all that he could carry his brilliant speed any distance. All the top older horses still on the grounds were pointed to the marathon Saratoga finale. Weir was inclined to race, rather than train, his horse up to the Cup. He just needed to figure out a schedule.[22]

Kentucky Derby winner Omar Khayyam had emerged as a leader of the three-year-old division with wins in the Brooklyn Derby and Kenner Stakes, prompting trackside debate over which horse would be better at a mile, Omar or Rosebud. Calls for a match race ensued, and Weir paid them lip service. "I would be delighted to enter in a sweepstakes with Omar Khayyam for $5,000 a corner," the trainer said. "I've got to meet [him] in the [Saratoga] Cup anyway, and the race would be a good preparation for the longer distance." As tantalizing as the matchup sounded, there would prove to be no room amid the busy Saratoga stakes schedule for such a showdown.[23]

Weir decided that a run in the Merchants and Citizens Handicap at a mile and a half would set up Rosebud nicely for a shot at the Cup five days later. The trainer did not need to do much with his horse to keep him fit. The day before the race, he arranged a public afternoon breeze, between races, with Charley Peak aboard. The embattled rider had finally received a license from The Jockey Club and would replace Molesworth when he could make the weight, which wouldn't be a problem if Rosebud continued to receive such substantial assignments from the handicapper.

Weir brought his horse to the paddock to give fans a chance to see him getting saddled. As Peak waited for a leg up, Weir tightened the girth. Without warning, Rosebud collapsed. Bystanders scrambled for buckets of cold water to revive the motionless horse. Someone called for ice. R. W. McCulley, a track veterinarian standing nearby, hurried over. He quickly ascertained that Rosebud was not dead, as some onlookers feared, but merely unconscious. The doc made the curious diagnosis of "acute indigestion, which caused reflex action of the heart." When a block of ice arrived, he applied it to the patient's neck and administered an unidentified restorative medicine orally. Soon Rosebud was revived and, ten minutes later, was on his feet. After a couple of laps around the saddling area, a groom led him back to his stall for some rest, apparently fully recovered.[24]

Witnesses said Rosebud had fallen as if he had been shot or hit on the head with a club, but there was no sign of foul play. Amateur diagnosticians noted that the air had been quite humid and that the gelding tended to eat his food quickly; the vet's explanation of the fainting spell thus somehow made sense to them. One Weir employee later posited an alternative theory. Though he offered no specific evidence, handyman Willie Kuchen determined that Rosebud had been stung by a bee and had flopped to the ground trying to crush the insect. "Wise hoss, that Bud," Kuchen said. "Just as smart as they make 'em. Got almost human intelligence."[25]

Though he had initially indicated that his horse would still make the Saratoga Cup, Weir kept Old Rosebud on the sidelines for the conclusion of upstate racing. And the trainer's superstitiousness made him disinclined to tempt fate with a return at Belmont, the site of his star's 1914 breakdown. But Rosebud would be back in action at Aqueduct for the mid-September Bayview Handicap at a mile and a sixteenth. He received no sympathy from the handicapper for the mysterious medical incident; Rosebud would carry 133 pounds, 10 more than Borrow, whose record-setting win in the Brooklyn Handicap three months earlier was still among the best performances of the year, and 31 more than Runes, a two-time winner of the Toronto Cup at Woodbine. Other starters included James Butler's mare Capra, recent winner of the Kings County Handicap, and Kentucky Oaks victress Sunbonnet. Despite the heavy impost and lingering questions about his health, Rosebud would be the 5–4 favorite.

The grandstand and clubhouse were full, and thousands spilled onto the Aqueduct lawns for the Monday start to the September meet. A good portion of the sizable crowd expressed their appreciation for the Applegate gelding as the field headed for the starting line. Breaking from the middle of the seven-horse lineup, Charley Peak sent Old Rosebud to the lead, putting a length between his horse and Capra in the first dozen strides. Sunbonnet overcame a slow start to secure third position. The trio maintained their spots through the backstretch, with Capra and Sunbonnet ridden aggressively to keep up with Rosebud. Peak gave his mount a breather around the turn, providing Capra the chance to gain ground, and Butler's mare had nearly pulled alongside the pacesetter at the top of the stretch. But when Peak let loose at the eighth pole, Rosebud surged forward. Peak popped a glance over his shoulder midway through the straight and saw no surprises. He let his horse glide the last hundred yards to the finish, crossing the wire two easy lengths in front. When the time, 1:44⅗, was posted in the infield, a new round of cheers and hoots lifted from the stands. He had equaled the track record set two years earlier by a mare carrying thirty-three fewer pounds.

Though it was not the most formidable field that he had faced that year, the win was sufficiently impressive to remove all but the slimmest of doubt that Rosebud was the most accomplished older horse in America. The six-year-old gelding was running as well as he ever had. When he returned to the judges' stand, a mob of well-wishers swarmed Peak and his record-matching mount. Weir expressed as much relief as elation. "I had an idea that he would never race [again] when he took sick at Saratoga," the trainer told a gaggle of reporters.[26]

Trying to capitalize on Old Rosebud's popularity, Aqueduct management petitioned Weir to run his star one more time at the Queens track. They dangled a two-thousand-dollar purse for a special race they hoped could entice the owners of Rosebud, Roamer, and Regret for a nine-furlong late-season clash, but Weir did not take the carrot. He was headed to Kentucky to run Colonel Applegate's precocious two-year-old colt Jack Hare Jr. in the Breeders' Futurity and would be taking Charley Peak with him. The trainer left open the possibility that Rosebud might make the Aqueduct Handicap the following Saturday, but Vosburgh's 135-pound weight assignment killed that idea. Ham Applegate told reporters in Kentucky that Rosebud would return to Louisville and would race in front of the hometown fans that fall. His local supporters were planning a reception to welcome the conquering hero back to the Bluegrass, but Ham had evidently not cleared that vision with his trainer. After fifteen wins in twenty-one starts on the year, Rosebud had done enough. He had competed on ten different tracks and in three countries. He was finished for the year.[27]

Perhaps Ham had his mind on the whiskey business. That fall, he and his father unloaded a large stock of booze and would sell the Old Rosebud Distillery in Bardstown, Kentucky. The Illinois buyers planned to crank up production once wartime regulations were lifted, but the push toward a permanent ban on alcohol was already well underway. In December, a proposal for an amendment to the US Constitution prohibiting the manufacture, sale, and transportation of intoxicating beverages would be approved by Congress and submitted to the states for ratification.[28]

For the first time in years, Frank Weir would not winter in Juárez. Citing tightened border security, wartime restrictions on rail travel, and heightened tensions between the United States and Mexico, Matt Winn announced the cancellation of the 1917–1918 meet. Though he declined to rule out a return in the future, there would be no more racing in Juárez under the American-led syndicate's supervision. But the track had served its purpose, providing a lifeline for the US racing industry in some of its darkest hours. Weir instead took his string to the defunct Gravesend track in Brooklyn. During his hibernation, Rosebud attracted a parade of well-wishers making pilgrimages to the stable for a chance to see the most famous comebacker in the history of American horse racing.[29]

Though the winter temperatures were far colder in New York than they would have been in Mexico, Weir and his staff could bask in the warmth of the year-end accolades bestowed on Old Rosebud by journalists in various publications' reviews of the racing season. He was the consensus pick as top handicap horse in America, among a historically deep group of older horses. The *New York Sun* crowned him "king of the turf," and newspapers across the country hailed the "Miracle Horse." Horse of the Year would not be a recognized title until the 1930s, but Old Rosebud was the most accomplished and most popular American racehorse of 1917.[30]

As Weir and the Rosebud team looked forward to continued prosperity in the spring, American racing officials were guardedly optimistic about the future of their sport and industry. The wave of anti-racing legislation seemed to have crested, and with Europe still embroiled in catastrophic war and no longer an option for top American owners seeking alternative racing venues, a sustainable future for horse racing seemed within reach. The wartime regulatory machine still chugged along, and American horse racing was not completely out of harm's way, but Old Rosebud's comeback had captured the public imagination at a crucial moment for the sport.

With the Juárez racetrack shuttered, Weir intended to start Old Rosebud's 1918 racing season in Hot Springs, Arkansas. But a severe winter had disrupted his training schedule, and wartime limitations on train travel complicated interstate shipping of racehorses. Rosebud would remain at Gravesend until the start of spring racing in Maryland. He could have been retired as one of the greatest Thoroughbreds in the history of American horse racing, with twenty-nine wins, three seconds, and three third-place finishes in thirty-eight career starts. But he gave little indication that he was quite ready for the pasture.

Rosebud had wintered well and was looking sharp in his first workouts of 1918. He was on schedule for a return to the races at the start of the season. But when he missed a few days of training toward the end of March, rumors swept through the Gravesend barnyard that Old Rosebud had broken down again. Weir gave a statement to reporters, insisting that all was fine. "The horse is going as sound as ever in his works," the trainer said, "and from present indications, he should race as well as last year."[31]

When Old Rosebud did not make the trip to Maryland, Weir maintained that his gelding was still just getting over a little cough. He received the highest weight assignment from Walter Vosburgh for the Metropolitan Handicap, set for Memorial Day, an acknowledgment of Rosebud's lofty achievements in 1917. But murmurs about an injured leg continued. Maryland race meets at Havre de Grace and Pimlico came and went, highlighted by a score for the Weir-trained, Applegate-owned Jack Hare Jr. in the Preakness Stakes (run in two divisions that year). Old Rosebud was still nowhere to be seen.

The Maryland horse-racing community was breathing a heavy collective sigh of relief. It had just won a major battle in the state legislature over the future of horse racing in the state, defeating an anti-racing bill that had been considered alongside other contentious issues of the day, including alcohol prohibition and women's suffrage. Racing's stakeholders enlisted a coterie of US military officers to attest in committee hearings to the genetic utility of Thoroughbreds in breeding dependable military mounts. Colonel Winn, who managed Laurel Park, situated between Baltimore and Washington, in addition to his duties at Churchill Downs, was overjoyed at horse racing's triumph in Annapolis. "It foreshadows a coming country-wide appreciation of the real mission of racing," Winn said. "Now that the developments of the great war have made the maintenance of a great permanent military force in this country indispensable . . . the racing associations of the Old Line State, working in harmony with Maryland's sportsmen and breeders, will do their utmost toward encouraging the production of military horses of the right sort in numbers that will be of real military value to the nation."[32]

While horse racing's proponents cited military necessity as a reason to continue the sport, its foes contended that it was an inappropriate and inefficient use of national resources to conduct race meetings in wartime. August Belmont addressed calls to shutter racetracks for the duration of the war, saying, "If the government asked us to discontinue racing for the period of the war we should do so unhesitatingly. But the government has not asked us to do anything of the sort. No person in government service, who has given the subject of horse production serious consideration, looks on racing now as a mere sport. In well informed quarters, racing is regarded as a military necessity, because it is upon the continuance of well managed racing that thoroughbred production depends."[33]

To fend off anti-racing activists' efforts to cancel the Kentucky Derby that spring, Winn solicited the help of Admiral Cary T. Grayson, personal physician to Woodrow Wilson and a noted racing enthusiast, in securing assurances that the president supported the Derby being run as scheduled. The *Courier-Journal* reminded Churchill Downs patrons to donate their binoculars, claiming that forty-eight thousand pairs had already been contributed to the war effort by racing fans. There would also be booths at the track where patriotic racegoers could buy Liberty bonds and get information from the Red Cross and Knights of Columbus about how to assist in war-relief charities.[34]

A late-morning rain shower, restricted rail travel, and long lines as a result of the time required for clerks to make change for the war tax collected at the gates were blamed for the marginally depressed attendance figures at the 1918 Derby. A crop of rye had been planted in the infield, and the free-admission policy was suspended, further suppressing crowd size. The gravities of wartime made for a more subdued atmosphere than usual at the Downs, but the presence of khaki-clad officers and soldiers gave the scene an "added glamour of romance," according to a local newspaper. And, under the circumstances, merely conducting the Derby was no small achievement. In a

Matt Winn managed racetracks in Kentucky, Mexico, New York, and Maryland in the 1910s. He helped blunt legislative efforts to regulate horse racing through his painting of the sport as patriotic and in service to the US military. (Herald-Post Collection, University of Louisville Photographic Archives)

surprising result, a lanky gelding named Exterminator, making his three-year-old debut, took the Derby roses that afternoon over a solid field of eight that included bellicose-sounding names like Viva America, War Cloud, and American Eagle. Exterminator's owner, New York patent-medicine manufacturer Willis Sharpe Kilmer, who had made a fortune selling his uncle's Swamp Root concoction, was overjoyed.[35]

"You must excuse me from talking, as I am too happy to know what I am saying," Kilmer told a reporter. "Gee, but it is great to win a Derby." Exterminator, affectionately nicknamed "Old Bones" by his admirers, would become a fan favorite, winning more than a quarter-million dollars in his long career, though he had been purchased by Kilmer as a workmate for his 1917 champion two-year-old, Sun Briar. Exterminator's win would become part of Derby lore thanks in part to his humble beginnings and to Matt Winn later taking credit for convincing Kilmer to start him in the Derby after an injury had forced Sun Briar from the race.[36]

In June, Frank Weir announced that Old Rosebud's return to training was imminent. "He has been sick but has not taken a lame step and is getting along well now and will soon be in action again," the trainer told reporters. Skeptics became noisier. The *Ottawa Citizen* noted "a growing belief that the cough is in his leg, and that his turf career is over."[37]

There were plenty of powerful people who would have been happy if there were no racing for Rosebud to return to. Louisville mayor George Weissinger Smith, an anti-vice, anticorruption Republican, joined the chorus of critics questioning the propriety of racing horses in a time of war. And he further indicated that it would be fine with him if the sport were permanently outlawed. In a letter to Johnson N. Camden, chair of the Kentucky State Racing Commission, Smith wrote, "This is not the time to test the will of the people with a sport whose existence depends on betting and leaves the trail of crime and despair wherever it thrives."[38]

The inclination to end horse racing in Kentucky was not limited to the GOP. Months earlier, Thomas B. Cromwell, turf writer and later publisher of *Blood-Horse* magazine, had reported that a faction of Democrats was crafting a bill that would close all racetracks in the state. In a piece published in the *Cincinnati Enquirer*, Cromwell warned that an attempt to end racing "at a time when the allied armies of the United States, France, England and Italy are in greater need of horses than ever in their histories" was "dangerous business for politicians." But given the torrent of reform legislation being passed in the name of wartime emergency, such an assertion sounded more hopeful than declarative.[39]

By late spring 1918, 650,000 US troops had landed in France, along with thousands of horses that would supplement the hundreds of thousands of American animals that had already been shipped to Europe during the Great War. American forces would be instrumental in stemming a final German offensive and mounting an Allied counterattack that would compel Germany to end the fighting by November. But that outcome was not yet assured.

In August, months after Exterminator had become the second gelding in five years to win the Kentucky Derby, Colonel Winn announced that castrated horses would henceforth be barred from the race. The ban reemphasized the notion that American horse racing was being conducted to improve the equine breed, rather than for pleasure or profit, and that the sport was a vital part of the American war machine. Winn justified the new policy by stressing that if racing associations did not take a proactive step, government would intervene.

"The new position of leadership in which American participation in the great war has thrust the United States imposes upon us the obligation of maintaining a great military establishment," Winn explained. "The Government must have horses by the hundreds of thousands, and horses of the right sort." It went without saying that the "right sort" were horses with Thoroughbred genetic influence. The government supposedly needed thousands of Thoroughbred stallions; the virility of the US military—the very security of the nation, Americans were told—depended on disincentivizing the gelding of racehorses.

"This is more than a mere duty; it is a solemn obligation," Winn declared. "Racing in the United States is no longer a mere sport. It is no longer a medium of gambling. It must henceforth be regarded as an essential factor in our great scheme of national defense. By voluntarily meeting its obligations and responsibilities, [racing] will ensure its own permanency and win for itself a popularity greater than it has ever had in the past." Winn's announcement came on the heels of a similar proclamation from the Westchester Racing Association, presided over by Maj. August Belmont; geldings would also be excluded from Belmont Park's highest-profile races for three-year-olds, including the Withers and Belmont Stakes, as well as the Suburban Handicap for older horses. Administrators of other American racing organizations would join the push to ban geldings from major American races, and Winn acknowledged that the prohibition could be extended much further. "It is within the bounds of possibility that the unsexed horse may ultimately be excluded from all races not of the selling-plate variety," he warned.[40]

The need for horses to aid the war effort in Europe was real. Some wild estimates suggested the US military would need three or four million horses in the next few years, especially if the war in Europe was to persist much longer. But racing officials did not bother trying to explain exactly how the elimination of geldings from certain races would significantly address the warhorse shortage. It was enough to ingratiate the sport to the American public and to governmental authorities with the power to regulate or eliminate it.

The move to curtail castration was well received within racing circles, and many predicted that the list of gelding-free races would continue to grow. Prominent Pennsylvania breeder and Jockey Club member Edward B. Cassatt, a West Point graduate, Spanish-American War veteran, and son of a railroad baron, was among the vocal supporters of the move to ban geldings, which, he said, "are not horses at all." In a letter printed in the trade publications, Cassatt wrote, "The sole excuse for the existence of racing is the improvement of the general breed of horses. Racing is not maintained to provide enjoyment for the people; nor yet to enable me or any other breeder to sell thoroughbred yearlings at the highest possible price; nor to enable racing associations to draw the largest possible crowd. . . . Racing is for the purpose of selecting the very best reproducers possible . . . and this object is defeated by permitting geldings to compete [for the sport's top prizes]." Jockey Club steward Frank Hitchcock concurred, noting the importance of public perception in considering regulatory changes. "I take it that we are all sincere in the protestation that we are racing for the purpose of improving the horse," he told the *Daily Racing Form*. "As long then as we allow geldings to meet our entire horses and mares in the important stakes of the turf, we leave the way open to criticism."[41]

The initial wave of gelding bans would primarily target top races for three-year-olds, but broadening the scope of the prohibition was still very much on the table. Racing's leaders appeared to be willing to preemptively exclude some of the sport's biggest stars from its higher-profile events if such a policy would enhance the public's opinion of their sport and keep hostile legislators at bay. The Jockey Club would amend its rules, excluding geldings from all major stakes races in New York early the following year. Whether

The need for military horses was real; as many as a million equines were sent from North America to European battlefields during World War I. Thoroughbred industry leaders capitalized on that demand by pushing horse racing as a partial solution to the problem. (National Archives)

Old Rosebud would be able to avail himself of an exception for geldings that had been castrated before passage of the amendment remained to be seen. First, he would once again have to make it back to the racetrack.[42]

An influenza pandemic forced racing associations to alter their schedules amid restrictions on public gatherings into the autumn of 1918, and Old Rosebud's return continued to be delayed. By October, it was clear that he would not make it to the races before the end of the year. Weir announced plans to ship his stable to Cuba for the winter, but that nine-horse string would not include Old Rosebud. Before his December departure for Havana, where he would be among the leading trainers that winter, Weir acknowledged that his equine star had been turned out, though he declined to say where. Later reports would reveal the secret location to have been Rancocas Farm in New Jersey, which would soon be acquired by Harry Sinclair, who had extracted a colossal fortune from the oil fields of the United States and Mexico and would be a central figure in the Teapot Dome political scandal of the 1920s. Weir was happy to divulge that Rosebud had again been pin fired and that his legs were in good shape. He was luxuriating in a large paddock with a band of fillies, which he regularly engaged in impromptu races, spotting them a lead before tossing his head and charging to the front, according to reports from his attendant.[43]

The armistice of November 11 halted fighting on the Western Front in Europe and ushered in months of negotiations that would finally end the Great War. Transition to peacetime in the United States would coincide with some of the worst domestic discord of the twentieth century, including race riots, a Red Scare, terrorist bombings, a brief economic recession, and violent repression of widespread labor unrest. Amid the tumult, Churchill Downs would quietly announce that geldings would not in fact be banned from the Kentucky Derby. But in Maryland, where anti-racing legislation had been narrowly defeated only months earlier, geldings would not be allowed back at the Preakness until 1935. And in New York, where memories of racing's shutdown were still fresh, castrated horses would continue to be excluded from some of the state's biggest races for decades, with the Belmont Stakes remaining gelding-free until 1957.

Eschewing presidential norms, Woodrow Wilson sailed to Europe to personally participate in the conferences that would produce the Treaty of Versailles. His traveling entourage included his physician Cary Grayson and

Committee on Public Information chair George Creel. While in France, Wilson found time to attend the horse races at Longchamp with Grayson. The US president was welcomed as a conquering hero on the continent. Enormous crowds cheered him in the streets of Paris, London, and Rome, expressing gratitude for the American intervention that helped secure Allied victory. The adulation hardened Wilson's resolve to reshape the world order under the stewardship of a new League of Nations, but Republicans had taken control of Congress in US elections that fall and were skeptical of portions of the treaty that Wilson was championing. They were tired of his sanctimonious activism and were particularly disinclined to support the collective security provision of the proposed league.

Despite warnings from Grayson regarding his fragile health, Wilson had contemplated seeking a third presidential term in 1920 and would take his case for ratification of the peace accord directly to the American people in a wildly ambitious cross-country whistle-stop speaking tour. But he collapsed after a speech in Pueblo, Colorado, and cut his trip short. After returning to Washington, he suffered a debilitating stroke, resulting in partial paralysis. Wilson would be a near-invalid for the remainder of his presidency, carefully guarded and handled by his wife, his personal secretary, and Admiral Grayson. Across the nation, the Progressive impulse that had energized American politics for decades was fading as quickly as the president's health.

6

Last Campaigns

Sent to Gravesend under the care of Weir's assistant to begin preparation for a return to the races in the spring of 1919, Rosebud drew plenty of visitors. He was his typically spirited self and enjoyed the attention, particularly when it involved a lump of sugar. Though many quietly doubted whether the old-timer would ever race again, the mere possibility intrigued local sportswriters. "If he were to come back as he did the first time, Old Rosebud would be rightly entitled to be called the wonder horse of all times," declared a Brooklyn reporter.[1]

Weir needed the Bud to run well. Some of the horses he had taken to Cuba were sold there, and others remained on the island when Weir returned to New York in early March. More troubling, Colonel Applegate was scaling back his involvement in horse racing and had announced his intention to dissolve most of his stable. Weeks earlier, the acquisition of the major Kentucky racetracks by a syndicate of leading local breeders was finalized. It was perhaps the most significant transaction of its kind to that time. Calling itself the Kentucky Jockey Club (KJC), the new group purchased Latonia, the Kentucky Association track in Lexington, Churchill Downs, and Douglas Park; this marked the end of Applegate's long run as a major player in racetrack administration, though Ham would remain an executive at Churchill Downs, and the Colonel would later acquire a substantial interest in the KJC. Matt Winn would oversee the consolidated entity as general manager.[2]

Though Colonel Applegate would retain a few horses, including Jack Hare Jr., moving his Preakness winner to Kay Spence's care later that summer, his separation from Weir, for reasons never reported, dealt the trainer a serious blow. Ham Applegate would also temporarily abandon racehorse ownership. Perhaps the new regime at Churchill Downs frowned on employees owning racehorses. Maybe there were disagreements regarding the trainer's handling of Old Rosebud or a rift pertaining to money. Whatever the cause, Weir assumed Ham's share in the horse, and Old Rosebud would run in the trainer's name for the rest of his career. Weir would aggressively campaign the now-eight-year-old, running his aging star thirty times in seven months, facing—and occasionally beating—some of the fastest horses in America.

When Old Rosebud made his 1919 debut on April 25 at Havre de Grace in Maryland, he looked ready to run, if a bit light. The most noticeable difference was Weir's red and white silks being worn by jockey Joe Dreyer. Rosebud was the 3–2 second choice in a five-and-a-half-furlong allowance. A two-horse entry owned by Commander J. K. L. Ross—a Canadian industrialist, heir to a railroad fortune, and a world-record-setting fisherman—would be the even-money favorites. Ross had earned his naval title by donating two of his yachts to the Royal Canadian Navy during the Great War and skippering one of them on patrol missions in the North Atlantic. His colt Sir Barton would soon become the most famous in his sizable racing stable, but the commander had several outstanding runners that included Milkmaid, one of the top American three-year-old fillies of the year, who would finish second in the Kentucky Oaks weeks later, and the multiple-stakes-winning colt Boniface. Rosebud would be the popular darling in his latest return to the races, following a nineteen-month layoff, but the Ross entry would provide a stern test.[3]

A good crowd enduring a biting springtime wind whipping from the Susquehanna River affectionately cheered the returning hero as the field made its way to the starting post. Rosebud's rider was on the tail end of a middling career, having recovered from a nasty fall in New York a few years earlier that left him with a compound fracture in his leg, which many assumed would put him permanently out of the saddle. But he had performed well for Weir in Cuba over the winter, earning himself a contract to ride in the United States. Rosebud jumped to an early lead, with Milkmaid stalking a length behind. Jockey Earl Sande, one of the top young riders in America, urged the filly to challenge on the turn but failed to overtake the front-runner, who skipped home with his ears pricked. Dreyer snuck a couple of glances over his shoulder through the stretch but otherwise sat perfectly still. Returning to the scales, Rosebud bobbed his head, apparently pleased to be racing again. Fans and journalists were astounded. Several papers reported that Weir's gelding had never looked better as they hyped another extraordinary comeback. The sports editor for the *Brooklyn Times* declared, "There have been few more remarkable thoroughbreds in the history of the American turf than Old Rosebud."[4]

Calls for a resumption of the rivalry between Rosebud and his old adversary Roamer began to circulate. While Rosebud was on the shelf in 1918, Roamer had put together another splendid season as a seven-year-old. Running against the clock at Saratoga, he went a mile in 1:34⅘, breaking an American record that had stood for twenty-seven years. But Andrew Miller's gelding had been sick with an equine influenza that ravaged the Gravesend stables that winter and would be late making his 1919 debut. Another showdown between the ageless geldings would have to wait until the summer.

A week after his successful return at Havre de Grace, Rosebud won a six-furlong allowance on opening day at Pimlico in a thick fog that obscured the view of most of the race from the grandstand. On a track rated sloppy, he beat track-record-holding gelding Flags, one of the top sprinters in America. Five days later, Rosebud was a 3–10 favorite as he stretched out to a mile. He faced another salty allowance field that included a pair of top three-year-olds: Dunboyne, winner of the Futurity Stakes at Belmont; and Sweep On, who took the Grand Union Hotel Stakes at Saratoga and would later equal the North American record for six and a half furlongs. Rosebud again broke quickly under Dreyer and set a moderate pace while opening a four-length lead on the backstretch, which he maintained through the final turn. But he was probably not totally fit for the distance. Dreyer allowed his horse to dawdle in the stretch, and they were nipped at the wire by a late-surging Sweep On.

The Weir trainee suffered another narrow defeat four days later in the six-furlong Equity Handicap on a heavy Pimlico track. But the Bud ran gamely, and some of his defenders blamed Dreyer for the loss. Named for his confectioner owner's "penny-a-pound profit" candy-selling slogan, four-year-old colt Papp had won the Flash, United States Hotel, Sanford Memorial, and Futurity Stakes in 1917 for trainer Max Hirsch. Despite being saddled with a whopping 132 pounds to Papp's 111, Rosebud was the even-money favorite on the cold, wet Saturday. Dreyer bided his time in third position through the backstretch and into the far turn. Rounding into the final straight, he urged his horse forward, and Rosebud responded. They rolled into second place, a length behind Papp, before flattening out with a sixteenth to go. With Dreyer giving an effort in the closing yards that the *Daily Racing Form* called "amateurish," Papp persevered to complete the mild upset.[5]

With two wins and two runner-up finishes against stiff competition in his latest comeback, Rosebud was again capturing the attention of the American sports world. "Another miracle is being unfolded before the eyes of the racing public," Frank G. Menke reported. "In all turf history, perhaps no achievement is more remarkable. Once in a while in sporting history a man or a horse proves an exception to the rule that 'they never come back' by returning for a brief spell. But never before, until Old Rosebud showed the way, has man or horse come back twice after being retired as a 'hopeless cripple.'"[6]

The end of the bloodshed in Europe produced a palpable spike in American enthusiasm for sports and other trivialities, including horse racing. As treaty negotiations continued in Paris, the 1919 Kentucky Derby again drew record crowds, reported to be near sixty thousand, despite dreary weather. The *Louisville Courier-Journal* society page celebrated the return of "all the romance, the rich flavor of tradition and the far-famed glamour" of prewar Derbies. "Everybody was present, and everybody seemed to have plenty of money or at least looked like a million dollars. . . . And from every section of the country the clans gathered to become Kentuckians temporarily." The winning horse, Sir Barton, bred by John E. Madden and owned by Commander Ross, would add scores in the Preakness and Belmont to become the first to capture what would later be recognized as the American Triple Crown.[7]

Before he presented the trophy to the winning connections, Governor Stanley gave a long-winded soliloquy on the centrality of horses to military heroics since the dawn of time. "It is peculiarly fitting that the lovers of this kingly sport should make this commonwealth their mecca," Stanley declared. "Courage, grit [and] a fine and aspiring spirit that does not brook defeat are the common heritage of the Kentuckian and his horse." After discussing Alexander the Great, Robert E. Lee, and their beloved warhorses, the governor meandered toward a conclusion, proclaiming,

> Civilization but yesterday was saved by the courage of the hero and the endurance of his horse. An army without its cavalry is as lacking in inspiration as if its banners were furled and its music were silenced. The charger's ancestor is here. These swift and exquisite creatures, miracles of endurance and grace and strength, in the hour

of peril are as essential to the nation's security and its honor as [its naval] fleet or fortress of frowning guns. I felicitate you upon a prize nobly won. Second only to the warrior's laurels is the coveted crown of the winner of the Kentucky Derby.[8]

A long poem titled "The Phoenix Horse," appearing in the Sunday *Pittsburgh Gazette Times* the day after Sir Barton's Derby score, rhapsodized Old Rosebud in complex rhyming verse. Like the gubernatorial windbaggery at the Derby, the poem's opening stanza reflects not only the poet's pronounced admiration for the renascent gelding but perhaps also aspects of a nation in transition from the restrictions of wartime to a new postwar era:

> The ashes again are aflame, Old Rosebud, the dust
>   with new fire is aglow.
> The heart that was silenced is beating
>   The eyes that were glazed are agleam.
> The faithful are calling your name, Old Rosebud, like
>   echoes of ages ago,
> And lo! like a god for new greeting,
>   You leap from the depths of a dream![9]

Old Rosebud was again the highweight on May 15 for the five-thousand-dollar Paumonok Handicap, the featured race on the opening card at the short Jamaica meet in Queens that would begin the New York racing season. He would carry a crushing 134 pounds against a stout field of fourteen that included the speedy Flags; Sam Hildreth's multiple-stakes-winning four-year-old colt Lucullite, who had been among the top juveniles of 1917 before an injury forced him to miss his three-year-old year; the previous year's Paumonok victor, Old Koenig; and the outstanding two-year-old filly of 1918, Elfin Queen. A crowd of twenty thousand filled the grounds despite a chilly breeze and scattered showers. The parking lot was overflowing early, and extra trains ran all afternoon. Advocates for racing took this promising start to the season as evidence of brighter days ahead for the sport as wartime restraints evaporated. "If racing improves the breed of horses proportionately to public interest displayed," quipped a *New York Tribune* scribe, "then America sure is destined to send some veritable fliers to the post in the immediate future."[10]

Popular sentiment was with Old Rosebud, though Lucullite was made the slight favorite by the bettors, thanks to a fifteen-pound weight advantage. Joe Dreyer again got the call to ride the Weir gelding. After a cluttered start, he found himself shuffled back, seven lengths from the front in the early going. Moving up on the turn, Dreyer took the Bud wide into the homestretch, where he began to pick off tiring front-runners. But Flags had clung to the rail and had an earlier start on the late running. Old Rosebud was gobbling ground on the outside but fell a length and a half short at the wire.

Though he had lost three straight, Rosebud was spotting weight to some of the best sprinters in America and competing at the highest levels. Weir found a softer spot for him in a five-and-a-half-furlong allowance on the Metropolitan Handicap undercard, where Old Rosebud ran to his heavily favored status in a four-horse field and romped to a six-length victory. With Johnny Loftus, widely regarded as the top jockey in America, replacing Dreyer for his next race, Rosebud was again an odds-on favorite five days later. He faced an overmatched group of ten in a six-furlong allowance race. Perhaps uncomfortable with the new rider, Rosebud acted badly at the starting line, delaying the commencement for seven minutes. He and Loftus rebuffed an early challenger on the turn and, after dallying at the sixteenth pole, refocused to grind out another win. It was a second consecutive score but not a particularly impressive one. The sheen of Rosebud's latest comeback had started to dim.

"Old Rosebud is still a good horse, but he is not what he was two years ago," a *Brooklyn Times* reporter wrote. "He is as willing as ever and there is an edge to his speed, but he begins to labor after he has gone about six furlongs." Weir seemed to have made a similar assessment. He shipped Rosebud and the rest of his dwindling six-horse stable to Kentucky, where he could expect softer competition.[11]

Old Rosebud began his early-summer Kentucky residency in the featured one-mile Milldale Purse at Latonia as part of a seven-horse field that included 1916 Latonia Derby winner Dodge. A heavy 3–10 favorite, Rosebud again displayed some once-uncharacteristic misbehavior at the post, delaying the start for five minutes. But he went straight to the lead at the spring of the barrier for local teenaged jockey Tommy Murray and led at every call. He was easing up when he crossed the wire a diminishing length and a half in front. The crowd voiced its admiration as the Kentucky-bred hero returned to the winner's circle at the northern Kentucky track for the first time in nearly two years. A week later, he was the 1–2 chalk in the Grand Hotel Purse at six furlongs on a steamy afternoon before an overstuffed grandstand. Rosebud extended his win streak to four on a lightning-quick racetrack but was all out to escape with a narrow triumph over an ordinary lot of sprinters, albeit in near-track-record time. Weir's gelding had lost a step from his peak form but not his competitive bent.

After a sharp five-furlong work the following week, Weir entered him in the $2,500 Gibson Hotel Handicap. Old Rosebud was saddled with a 133-pound impost, spotting a decent six-horse group between 19 and 32 pounds for the six-furlong sprint. He was a lukewarm favorite but broke slowly on the muddy track and was never in the race, finishing next to last, some sixteen lengths behind the winner, Beaverkill, a five-year-old who had won the Clark Handicap the previous year.

Rosebud put in a better effort the following week, stretching out to a mile and a sixteenth in the Eden Park Handicap. He received a bit of relief from the handicapper but still toted 128 pounds, 20 more than 1918 Kentucky Oaks winner Viva America and 22 more than the reigning Oaks champion, Jeff Livingston's Lillian Shaw. Rosebud broke well for veteran Texas jockey Jack Howard, who was rumored to have participated in a failed betting coup in Havana the previous winter. Howard let the Bud set the pace, pressured by Viva America. But they went too fast and had no answer when the longest shot on the board, an Irish-bred gelding named Barney Shannon, showing what the *Daily Racing Form* called "sudden and unhealthily improved form," swooped past the front-runners for a two-length win.[12]

Four days later, in the one-mile Burnett Woods Handicap, before a record crowd on the closing day of what was called the most successful spring racing season in Kentucky racing history, Rosebud again made the lead with Tommy Murray back aboard, conceding as much as twenty-six pounds to the rest of the four-horse field. Murray settled his mount on the rail and carved out sensible fractions most of the way around the oval before being engaged in a gripping stretch duel by slight betting favorite Sennings Park, recently fifth in the Kentucky Derby. The youngster prevailed by a neck at the wire, with the third-place finisher ten lengths back, and the time of 1:36$\frac{4}{5}$ equaled the track record. The *Courier-Journal* called it, somewhat dubiously, "the best race that [Rosebud] ever ran during his long and honorable racing career." A dozen races into what would be a long 1919 season, Rosebud was still competing at a high level. But he was difficult to classify—too good to be dismissed as a has-been but too inconsistent to garner much faith.[13]

That summer, Pancho Villa reassembled a rebel force in a last-ditch effort to liberate Chihuahua from Carrancista control. In mid-June, several thousand Villistas attacked Ciudad Juárez. They seized the racetrack and made it a field base, using the sturdy grandstand and adobe perimeter walls for protection from artillery fire as close-range fighting raged through the city streets. When shots crossing into El Paso wounded several civilians, three thousand American troops stormed across the border. After shelling the racetrack, they surrounded the rebel stronghold, forcing the Villistas to retreat under heavy fire. The Americans briefly pursued the fleeing insurgents as they scattered into the mountains southwest of the city. The US troops returned home, again having failed to capture Villa. But he would no longer pose a serious threat, and it would be the last major US incursion into Mexico.

Unable to run for reelection to the Mexican presidency the following year under the terms of the new constitution enacted under his regime, Venustiano Carranza would back a civilian diplomat as his replacement. The popular general Álvaro Obregón, Carranza's former minister of war who had helped to subdue Villa and was widely assumed to be the successor to the presidency, was not happy. Obregón determined that Carranza would not leave office peacefully and led an army to Mexico City to remove him. Carranza fled the capital and would later be assassinated by Obregón partisans. Before Obregón assumed power, Villa reached a truce with an interim government. Agreeing to retire from revolutionary activity, Villa received amnesty for past crimes and a twenty-five-thousand-acre ranch in Chihuahua. Three years later, he would be gunned down in an ambush, with at least tacit approval from Obregón, while on an automobile excursion. The confessed leader of the band of assassins would serve one month of a twenty-year sentence.[14]

Having concluded the Latonia meet on a relative high note, Weir moved his stable to New York for the rest of the summer. The trainer decided to try another high-level middle-distance race, entering Rosebud in the one-mile Mt. Vernon Handicap at Empire City in Yonkers. There he would face two of the top racehorses in America, Lucullite and Sun Briar. After finishing behind Old Rosebud in the Paumonok to start the season, Sam Hildreth's Lucullite had set a track record at Jamaica in the Clarendon Handicap at five and a half furlongs. He was quick as lightning, though there was some question as to how far he wanted to run. Sun Briar, owned by patent-medicine manufacturer Willis Sharpe Kilmer, had been the top American two-year-old colt in 1917. He took the Travers and Delaware Handicap at Saratoga as a three-year-old, but he had since spent the winter servicing mares at his owner's Binghamton, New York, farm. In his return to the racetrack a week earlier, Sun Briar was beaten by less than a length by Roamer at Aqueduct while spotting the future Hall of Famer sixteen pounds. That promising performance earned him favored status in the Mt. Vernon.[15]

Jockey Laverne Fator sent Lucullite to an early lead on a track listed as good but reported to be drying and heavy. Sun Briar and jockey Johnny Loftus followed the pacemaker into the clubhouse turn, tracked by Old Rosebud, who had broken a step slowly. Rosebud's rider, Harry Lunsford, a talented young lightweight, found a spot on the rail in the backstretch and eased his mount past Sun Briar as Loftus kept a tight hold on his horse into the far turn. When Loftus finally asked Sun Briar to quicken in the homestretch, he lacked the fuel to catch Rosebud, who hung on for second, four lengths behind the free-running Lucullite.

Despite being well beaten, Rosebud received the loudest cheers from the crowd as the horses returned to the front of the grandstand. Some saw a half-full glass and emphasized that he had soundly defeated one of the best horses in America; the *Brooklyn Times* called Rosebud's performance proof "that he is still some racehorse." But others stressed that he had been trounced by the winner. Then there was the fact that Rosebud was starting to display some serious roguishness at the starting line, often requiring an assistant starter to take a stout hold of his bridle. He had been prone to fractiousness in the past, but this was a new level of misbehavior that bordered on belligerence. Was Rosebud positioning himself for a late-summer surge and a bid for another championship, or was he showing his age and telling his owner that he was ready to be retired?[16]

In assigning weights for the Yonkers Handicap at Empire City the following week, Walter Vosburgh seemed to believe that Rosebud was still among the best horses in America. Weir's gelding received a 127-pound impost, 7 more than Roamer. Empire City track owner James Butler's 1917 Jerome Handicap winner Bally, who had beaten Lucullite earlier that month, and 1916 Travers Stakes champion Spur, who had won the Yonkers the previous two years, would carry 109 and 113. Latonia Derby winner Be Frank rounded out a star-studded field.

A record crowd of more than twenty thousand filled the Empire City grounds for the last Saturday of downstate racing before the sport's caravan moved north to Saratoga. An overflow area was opened to reduce crowd congestion, and spectators lined the rail from near the top of the stretch to the first turn. Cloudy skies and a steady breeze made the summer temperatures tolerable. Bettors made the Butler entry the 2–1 favorite, though most spectators were hoping for a dramatic revival of the old rivalry between Roamer and Old Rosebud. For six furlongs, they got just that. With Johnny Loftus in the irons, Rosebud got away from the barrier quickly and set the early pace on the rail under a light hold. Andy Schuttinger applied pressure aboard Roamer, two lengths in front of a lurking Bally. By the end of the backstretch, the pacesetter was tiring. Rosebud began to shorten stride and conceded the lead entering the far turn. Roamer opened daylight on the rest of the field and appeared to be headed for an easy win. But, finding himself alone early in the stretch, he stalled, allowing Bally to breeze by. When it was clear that his horse was beaten, Loftus allowed Rosebud to canter to the finish line, nearly twenty lengths behind the winner. Some thought he was limping as he walked back to the scales.

Rosebud and Roamer seemed to be going in opposite directions. But days later, Miller's gelding came up sore in his right hind leg after a training session at Saratoga. He was sent to a New Jersey farm for recuperation at the conclusion of the meet. His owner held some hope that he might return to the track the following year for a chance to push his career earnings past $100,000, but the great gelding slipped in his paddock that winter, broke his leg, and had to be humanely destroyed. Coincidentally, Miller had died of a heart attack only hours earlier. If Roamer's sudden death served as a reminder to Weir of the capricious nature of a racehorse's life and health, he never said so publicly. But he would continue to campaign his beloved Old Rosebud as if he was aware that it could all end at any time.

Weir was happy with his horse's condition on arrival at Saratoga in early August. After three weeks of downtime, Old Rosebud returned to the track for some easy gallops in preparation for a try in the Uncas Handicap on the last Friday of the meet. For the first time since his ill-fated Withers run more than five years earlier, he would be reunited there with Johnny McCabe, the rider who had guided him to a championship two-year-old season and Kentucky Derby glory. Since then, McCabe had endured a series of injuries and had recently been discharged from the army after a tour of duty in France, where the fighting had ended before his unit reached the front lines. Weir was confident that the gelding was rounding back into form.

"The old horse earned a well-deserved rest," the trainer told the press, assuring reporters that there was nothing wrong with Old Rosebud. "He raced steadily during the spring over all sorts of tracks and was in need of the let up." The Paumonok-winning Flags received the top weight of 130 pounds and favored status from the bettors. Rosebud would carry 125. After exhibiting some irritability at the start, Rosebud, pressed by Flags, carried an early lead into the homestretch but was passed by two closers to finish third.[17]

Three days later, twenty-five thousand people showed up to Belmont Park for racing's return to New York City. The first contest on the Monday card was a competitive six-furlong allowance. Old Rosebud again misbehaved at the starting line and was away slowly. Lucullite stalked Greentree Stable's French-bred pacesetter Peter Piper around the turn and zipped past him in the stretch to win by five, setting a track record on an unusually quick surface. While never in contention for the win, Rosebud was less than a length from third-place money. His poor start was enough of an excuse for Weir to wheel him back against a tough bunch in the Autumn Highweight Handicap three days later. Joseph Widener's imported gelding Naturalist lugged 140 pounds and caught Commander Ross's Kentucky Derby runner-up Billy Kelly at the wire to take the winner's share of the two-thousand-dollar purse. Rosebud was left at the starting line after knocking one horse sideways and refusing to break. The *New York Times* cited a pattern of misbehavior and declared, "Old Rosebud has become so unmanageable that he mars every race he starts in."[18]

A change of venue yielded similar results in the opening race of Aqueduct's September meeting. Rosebud broke last of twelve in the six-and-a-half-furlong Luke Blackburn Handicap and found traffic through the stretch to finish seventh, behind a good group of horses led by Gazelle Handicap champ Fairy Wand. Two days later, he showed some improvement in a fourth-place effort in the Averne Handicap, finishing less than two lengths behind the winner, Sam Hildreth's multiple-stakes-winner Lord Brighton. But, as the *Brooklyn Times* noted, Old Rosebud was "far from the horse he was two years ago."[19]

Yet, under the right conditions, he was still capable of stealing a win. Those conditions presented themselves the following week in the seven-furlong Salvator Handicap on a muddy Aqueduct racetrack. Made the 6–5 favorite in an underwhelming field that included a two-year-old filly that had recently won the Schuylerville at Saratoga, Rosebud again gave starter Mars Cassidy trouble, albeit a milder form of what was becoming his trademark shenanigans. He surged to the front after another slow start and was never threatened as he splashed along the rail, notching his first win since May. When Johnny McCabe returned him to the winner's circle, the crowd gave Rosebud a warm reception, an indication of both lingering affection for past accomplishments and the fact that he had received heavy play from the betting public.

In his long career, Rosebud had never raced so deeply into a season. Only once had he run as late as September. He had made twenty starts in 1919, more than most top twenty-first-century Thoroughbreds make in a lifetime. He received two and a half weeks of downtime, then ran third to Flags as the 126-pound highweight in the six-furlong Consolation Handicap on the closing Saturday of the Jamaica fall meet in front of the largest crowd of the season. Facing a decent field of eight, Rosebud again got away poorly after acting up at the start. McCabe did well to put him into the race by the far turn, but he was never within shouting distance of the winner.

A wet track at Empire City two days later was cause for hope of a better effort in the Lecompte Purse, but the results were similar. Rosebud was away from the barrier quickly for a change and ran with the pacesetters early. But he was spent after a half mile and finished fourth. Weir hoped to build on the fast start and brought his gelding back in the featured two-thousand-dollar Knightsbridge Handicap after a single day's rest, his third race in five days. But Rosebud sulked at the starting post for journeyman rider Charles Fairbrother, causing a delay of more than five minutes before starter Mars Cassidy had enough and released the barrier. Weir's gelding spotted the rest of the field nearly a sixteenth of a mile before he got rolling. It was too much to overcome, and he finished ahead of only his stablemate Toto, ridden that day by Johnny McCabe.

A sharp half-mile blowout the following week demonstrated that Old Rosebud had not entirely lost his inclination to run. The next day, he won the six-furlong Sir Archy with McCabe back aboard, holding off a late-charging Flags after breaking from the outside and securing a stalking trip behind a long-shot pacesetter for the first half mile. It was an unexpectedly inspired performance. Even McCabe received some rare, if mild, praise in the press, one writer calling his ride "creditable."[20]

With Rosebud showing signs of soreness, an increasing propensity for misbehavior at the starting line, and variable levels of interest in competing, the end of the New York racing season would have been an opportune time to send him to the farm for the winter. Instead, he got a couple of weeks' rest as the Weir stable moved to Maryland for the last of the year's East Coast racing. Following a pair of easy works, Rosebud finished third in the six-furlong Linstead Handicap at Pimlico after leading the four-horse field into the homestretch in heavy going. Three days later, stretching out to seven furlongs at Bowie, he won the Hampton Roads Purse against a competitive field as the odds-on favorite. Pleased with the return to the winner's circle, McCabe said Rosebud traveled so smoothly that he felt like he was "sitting in a parlor chair." He was back in the irons the following Saturday for the Oriole Handicap, where Rosebud pressed the favored Flags early but could not stay with him late, just hanging on for second after tiring badly through the stretch.[21]

McCabe had ridden Old Rosebud in eleven of his last twelve starts, but he had not been getting many other mounts since returning from France. Two days after what would be his last ride of the year on Rosebud, he was unseated from another of Weir's horses on the first turn of a race at Bowie. He suffered a broken leg and would be out of action for months. Still, Weir persisted with Old Rosebud, enlisting handy local jockey Dave Stirling to ride for the remainder of the meet.[22]

Rosebud was running competitively, and his antics at the starting line seemed to have subsided. Perhaps most importantly, Weir had bills to pay. Under threatening skies and a new jockey in the Meadowbrook Handicap at a mile and seventy yards, Old Rosebud chased pacesetting Ophelia, one of the top three-year-old fillies in America. But when Stirling was unable to find another gear in the stretch, he let Rosebud gallop on to a third-place finish. It was a decent effort for which the stable took home $150. And he did finish ahead of odds-on favorite Leochares, another aging gelding past his prime, one that had once drawn comparisons to Weir's old charge Roseben. But Old Rosebud was clearly no longer capable of offering anywhere near his former best.

With the racing season nearing its conclusion, Weir squeezed two more starts out of his favorite horse. A record holiday crowd was on hand two days later as Rosebud toed the starting line for the Thanksgiving Handicap at eight and a half furlongs. Forwardly placed through a sluggish first quarter, Stirling let Rosebud settle on the backstretch before mounting a good late charge to finish third behind a pair of stakes winners to score another two hundred dollars for Weir.

Two days later, making his fourth start in a week, Rosebud finished his year with a runner-up effort in the eight-furlong Southern Maryland

Handicap, the closing-day feature at Bowie, before a good crowd on a cold, drizzly Saturday. He set a fast pace for Stirling and led a seven-horse field deep into the stretch but could not hold off six-year-old gelding Slippery Elm, losing by a widening neck.

Rosebud headed to winter quarters tired but sound. He had made thirty starts in 1919, with nine wins and twenty-one top-three finishes. His $12,182 in purse money was third best among American runners at least six years of age. Though it was less than half of what he had earned in 1917, by nearly any metric it was a successful year—except that he had once been mentioned in the same breath with the greatest American Thoroughbreds in history.

While Old Rosebud rested that winter, fans across the country could catch him in a blockbuster movie. *Checkers*, a high-budget melodrama with an all-star cast, based on a successful stage play and produced by William Fox (founder of the Fox Film Corporation, which would, through mergers, later become 20th Century-Fox), depicted a reformed racetrack tout who falls in love with society dame Pert Barlow. Checkers, working as a groom, enters Pert's horse Remorse, "played" by Old Rosebud, in the Big Race in New York. A cad named Kendall, who plans to run his own horse in the race and is a rival for Pert's affection, endeavors to prevent Remorse from getting to the track. Thrills ensue, including a jump from a moving automobile, a plunge into a river as a burning train approaches a broken drawbridge, a car chase to save the trapped Remorse, and a daring escape aboard a seaplane. In the climactic scene, filmed in front of a lively crowd at Belmont Park, Pert secretly rides Remorse to victory after Kendall's henchmen wickedly blind his regular jockey. *Checkers* opened in New York City and played to packed houses and rave reviews across the country.[23]

After watching Old Rosebud on the big screen, some pundits were surprised to see him return to the racetrack for the 1920 season. But reports from Havre de Grace in anticipation of the start of East Coast racing indicated that Rosebud looked healthy and was training as well as ever. In his first race as a nine-year-old, the five-thousand-dollar Harford Handicap, he showed a bit of speed with Johnny McCabe back in the saddle but faded in the stretch, finishing ahead of only one horse and nearly a dozen lengths behind the winner, 1918 champion two-year-old Billy Kelly. The results were similar in his next start, where he ran fifth in a Havre de Grace allowance, conceding weight to a solid field that included several stakes winners. Rosebud showed some improvement a week later, perhaps owing to the muddy conditions, in the Fort McHenry, where he set the early pace but could not hold off Commander Ross's 1918 Champagne Stakes–winning colt, War Pennant, at the finish. As the *Baltimore Sun* noted, Rosebud's "heart was there, but his legs were not."[24]

Weir pressed on and entered Old Rosebud in the Paumonok at Jamaica on May 15. The stands and clubhouse were full for the opening-day fixture. Rosebud broke well in the sloppy going and forced the pace set by Dunboyne, the 1918 Futurity winner making his return after a long layoff. McCabe and Rosebud doggedly chased the accelerating front-runner into the stretch but were passed by Billy Kelly and a middling handicapper named Ticklish in the final sixteenth to finish fourth.

The following week, Rosebud lost the Californian Handicap in a head bob, on another sloppy track at Jamaica, after a late surge in the homestretch. Encouraged by the effort, Weir brought him back in the featured Babylon Handicap at six furlongs on the Belmont straight course a week later. After some balking at the starting line, McCabe had Old Rosebud away in good order and cleverly moved him to the outside rail, a half length behind the favored Peter Piper, who set the pace in the middle of the track under jockey Clarence Kummer. Peter Piper had gone a bit too quickly early and was losing steam as the pair entered the homestretch. McCabe roused his horse to the lead at the sixteenth pole and floated on to win by a comfortable length and a half.

Spectators and scribes were duly impressed. "Just when it had been generally agreed that Old Rosebud, for years an idol on the American turf, had seen his best days and had joined the pathetic class of has-beens, the old gelding showed a large and applauding crowd that the reports of his hopeless condition were at least premature," the *New York Times* proclaimed. Brooklyn turf writer W. C. Vreeland went a step further in his praise. "No horse that has ever trod the American turf—and I make this statement without reserve—has ever accomplished the great things that he has after becoming a cripple," the columnist wrote. "Hats off to a fine old racehorse!"[25]

Was this the beginning of yet another late-career renaissance or merely a nice win under favorable circumstances? Weir hoped the former and ran Rosebud back four days later in the Toboggan Handicap over the same Belmont course. He again behaved meanly at the starting line and swerved out several times through the stretch. Though he did beat the favored Dunboyne, who found traffic early in the race, Rosebud finished a nonthreatening fifth. If Weir had been looking for signs that his horse's interest in racing was waning, they were there.

Instead, he gave Rosebud a couple of weeks off before shortening him to five and a half furlongs in the Richmond Handicap back at Jamaica, where, after a slow start, he finished sixth of ten, nine lengths behind the winner, Peter Piper. It would be Rosebud's last start of the year. His health and various prognoses had once made headlines in the sports sections of American newspapers, but the premature end of his 1920 season came without fanfare or public announcement. With Rosebud resting up for a possible return the following year, Weir carried on with a bare-bones stable through the summer and fall.

As one superhorse was fading, another was capturing the imaginations of American sports fans and leaving commentators searching for historical comparisons. Man o' War was a powerful chestnut colt bought at auction in Saratoga by textile mogul Samuel Riddle from his breeder, August Belmont, who was busy with his military service at the time. Man o' War won nine of ten starts as a two-year-old in 1919, his lone defeat coming to Harry Payne Whitney's aptly named colt Upset in the Sanford Memorial Stakes at Saratoga, for which jockey Johnny Loftus was widely criticized. Man o' War began his three-year-old campaign with a win in the Preakness and an American record-setting performance in the Withers. Facing only one horse in the Belmont Stakes, he set a world record for a mile and three-eighths. That September, he would win the Lawrence Realization by what chartmakers determined to be one hundred lengths.

While conceding that Man o' War was a singular specimen, the *Daily Racing Form* chose Old Rosebud as the nearest point of reference:

> It is probable that Old Rosebud, in his early three-year-old form, before he went wrong, nearly approached Man o' War for speed, up to as far as one mile and a quarter. The son of Uncle had practically the same motion while in action as the Riddle colt. He did not appear to be going fast, but his frictionless gait took him over the ground with the precision of a machine.... Like Old Rosebud, [Man o' War] is a quick breaker and runs so smoothly that there does not seem to be any horse now in training which can keep pace with him.

No one was mistaking the nine-year-old version of Old Rosebud for Man o' War, but comparisons to Big Red served as a refresher, for any readers who needed reminding, as to what a phenomenal racehorse Rosebud had been in his prime.[26]

In November, Ohio senator Warren G. Harding won the presidential election in a landslide on the promise of a "return to normalcy" for the nation after years of war and Progressive reform. Even William Randolph Hearst, who had never publicly supported a Republican, gave his endorsement to Harding, having become generally disillusioned with Progressivism—but more specifically frustrated by Woodrow Wilson's unwillingness to entertain war with Mexico, his decision to enter what Hearst still believed to have been a pointless war in Europe, and his advocacy of a League of Nations. Theodore Roosevelt had toyed with another run for the presidency but died in his sleep in January 1919 at age sixty, months after his youngest son was killed in an aerial fight over France. Harding's win spearheaded broad conservative Republican electoral success that year, ushering in a more freewheeling,

Man o' War's brilliance in 1919–1920 drew comparisons to Old Rosebud in his prime. (Keeneland Library Cook Collection)

deregulated atmosphere in Washington and signaling a decisive end to Progressive idealism on the federal level.[27]

American racing would continue to grow amid a golden age of commercialized sports in the Roaring Twenties. With new tracks supported by legalized pari-mutuel wagering soon to sprout in places like Chicago, Miami, and Cincinnati, the future looked promising for the first time in decades. But Frank Weir would not share in the good times. That fall, Weir's wife, Ida, suffered a fatal heart attack, and his own health was not great. According to one report, he had grown too "corpulent" to ride his bicycle, a longtime favorite pastime. He was struggling to keep horses in his barn, and Old Rosebud would turn ten years old on January 1, Thoroughbreds' universal "birthday." A century later, the New York Racing Association would issue a regulation making horses ten years of age or older ineligible to race in the state, but no such rule existed in 1921. By mid-March, Rosebud was galloping well at Gravesend and would soon be on his way to Maryland for the start of spring racing.[28]

The day after a six-furlong leg stretcher at Havre de Grace, clocked in 1:19, Weir entered his former champion in a thousand-dollar claiming race. Weir was subjecting Rosebud to the possibility of being purchased but was willing to suppose that a ten-year-old gelding with a long history of soundness issues might not garner much interest, even if his name was Old Rosebud. Johnny McCabe was unavailable to ride, having broken his nose earlier that month after being tossed from a horse and kicked in the face during a morning gallop. He would continue to eke out a living as a jockey until 1931, when, struggling to get mounts, he found work as an assistant trainer. He would exercise horses well into his sixties until a broken stirrup at Belmont Park caused another spill and forced him out of the saddle for good. With young Linus "Pony" McAtee, a future Hall of Fame rider, aboard, Rosebud was sent off as a 6–5 favorite for his first race of 1921. He chased a hot pace set by Uncle's Lassie (a daughter of Rosebud's sire who would, incidentally, become the dam of 1929 Kentucky Derby winner Clyde Van Dusen) and tired in the stretch, finishing sixth. He was limping when he returned to be unsaddled.

There were excuses for the poor result. He was probably a bit short of full fitness for his seasonal debut, and he had sustained a muscle strain during the race, but some members of the racing press had seen enough. The *Baltimore Evening Sun* lamented, "Though he looks the part, age and infirmity have robbed [Old Rosebud] of most of his speed, and it is doubtful if he has any great liking for the track." A correspondent for the *Philadelphia Inquirer* wrote, "Old Rosebud has earned a rest and his owner, Frank Weir, should take pity and retire the Derby winner to a life of ease." The injury turned out not to be too serious, but Rosebud would again be out of action until late summer. Weir was soon down to one horse in his barn after Frank Farrell, Weir's lone remaining client, moved his stock.[29]

Rosebud rounded back into shape that summer in New York and was at the starting line in September for a six-and-a-half-furlong claiming race at Belmont. There he would face Cum Sah, who had finished second in the 1918 Withers and third in the Belmont Stakes but had since suffered from leg ailments and was only a shell of his former self. Weir did not expect a great performance from Rosebud, telling friends in the paddock, "The old fellow is going to do his best, but I don't think that best is good enough to win. He might be second, but I don't believe he can beat Cum Sah." Bettors shared the trainer's lack of faith, and Rosebud's odds drifted to 6–1. With another future Hall of Famer, Laverne Fator, riding, Rosebud stalked the early pace set by long shot Old Sinner and Cum Sah before seizing the lead at the eighth pole and charging on to a three-length win. The crowd of eight thousand greeted the old warrior with booming applause as he returned to the winner's circle. He earned seven hundred dollars for his owner but again appeared to be sore when pulling up. He was finished for the year.[30]

Weir managed to assemble a string to take to Cuba for the winter, and Rosebud was left in the care of an assistant at Gravesend with an eye to yet another return to the races in the spring. By the time the trainer arrived back in New York in early May, Rosebud was working at Aqueduct, pointing to a start at Jamaica. He appeared to be in good shape for an eleven-year-old.

Rosebud was made the 8–5 favorite against a mediocre octet of eight-hundred-dollar claimers in a five-and-a-half-furlong sprint carrying a one-thousand-dollar purse on the first Saturday in May 1922. Jockey Earl Sande, who would win the first of his three Kentucky Derbies the following year aboard Harry Sinclair's colt Zev, had Rosebud forwardly placed. Sande moved his mount to the front in the stretch and started to pull away before Rosebud seemed to run out of gas. He gave his best after being collared by a five-year-old British-bred mare named Liberty Girl deep in the stretch, but she lumbered past him to win by a widening half length. Rosebud again moved stiffly as he returned to the grandstand to be unsaddled. A reporter for the *Buffalo Courier* predicted this would be his final race and that he would "be turned out in the clover fields to spend the rest of his days in comfort." Though specialized retirement farms for Thoroughbreds were still decades away, there would have been plenty of good homes available to a horse like Old Rosebud. Still, it was a two-hundred-dollar payday for Weir, who had become dependent on the horse for his livelihood.[31]

In Louisville, the undefeated Morvich won the 1922 Kentucky Derby the following week, becoming the first California-bred to accomplish the feat and the first two-year-old champion to wear Derby roses since Old Rosebud. The winner's share of the purse, some fifty-three thousand dollars, was nearly six times Old Rosebud's Derby haul only eight years earlier. Governors, cabinet members, congressmen, and movie stars were among the record-smashing seventy-five thousand in attendance on a flawless spring afternoon. Journalists and photographers from across the country gave the scene rave reviews. The Kentucky Derby had cemented its place as not only the most important horse race in America but an event that transcended even its lofty significance within the sport.

"It's the greatest day of my life," Wall Street stockbroker Benjamin Block said as Governor Edwin P. Morrow presented him with the winner's trophy. "I feel too much to talk about it. My horse has won other races, but there is only one Kentucky Derby. Morvich could bring to me, or to himself, no greater honor."[32]

Colonel Matt Winn was just as delighted. "It was the greatest Derby Day we have ever enjoyed," he told the press. "It was the biggest crowd ever in Churchill Downs, and what a cosmopolitan crowd it was! Notables from all over America were present and, besides, every section of the nation was represented by the men of modest means whose love for the thoroughbred caused them to make the pilgrimage. The popularity of racing with the American people was illustrated well by the assemblage at the Downs." Winn would continue to oversee his beloved Kentucky Derby through a long period of growth until his death in 1949, when he would be replaced by former sportswriter and broadcaster Bill Corum, who had been credited with attaching the moniker "Run for the Roses" to the race.[33]

An eight-furlong spin around the Aqueduct oval in a leisurely 1:52, along with a three-quarter-mile gallop in 1:26 the following day, was enough to convince Weir that Rosebud was ready for another race. The sky was cloudy, and the wind was cold on May 17 for the opening contest, a thousand-dollar six-furlong allowance race on a Wednesday card at Jamaica. Rosebud started a step slowly for Sande but hustled toward the front of an eleven-horse scrum. He dogged the front-runner, a nine-year-old gelding named Ting-a-Ling, down the backstretch through slow early fractions and labored to keep pace around the turn. He continued to fade after going wide into the homestretch and finished a well-beaten seventh, nine lengths behind the winner, a five-year-old named Victor S. It would be Old Rosebud's final race.[34]

Out for a gallop the following Sunday, he took a bad step and hobbled back to the barn. Veterinarians did all they could, but they determined that the situation was hopeless. Most press reports did not specify the nature of his injury, though some mentioned that he had torn ligaments in his lower leg. Johnny McCabe would later recall that he had shattered a small bone. The capacities of veterinary diagnostics and surgery were limited compared to what they would later become, and there was nothing the docs could do. After two days, Weir made the awful decision, in consultation with Dr. McCulley, to allow the horse to be put down. Ham Applegate sent a telegram to Weir a day later, which read, "The Kentucky Jockey Club would like to have the bones of OLD ROSEBUD so they could be buried in the center field of CHURCHILL DOWNS with all the honors due to a Prince of the Turf. Let me hear from you." Weir responded, "MESSAGE TOO LATE WOULD HAVE GIVEN HUNDRED DOLLARS FOR THAT MESSAGE TUESDAY." Rosebud had been carted off under local animal disposal regulations. Newspapers across the country announced his death and rhapsodized one of the most accomplished and beloved racehorses in the history of the American turf.[35]

That fall, the *Daily Racing Form* reported that the only horses Frank Weir owned were a couple of three-year-olds that were turned out in Cuba. But Weir retained his love for the sport and was often spotted at the racetrack, admiring the Thoroughbreds and conversing with old colleagues. A columnist caught up with Weir and asked him for recollections of his former charge and companion. The veteran trainer became emotional. "Oh Lord. Old Rosebud, so far as disposition and accomplishments go, was a perfect horse," Weir said.

> He had no faults and no meanness. Some horses are born stubborn like some men. Some are mean or savage or nervous or cranky, so

that you can't count on them. But Old Rosebud—there was a good horse. You ask me what a fellow learns from an animal like that. He learns kindness, willingness, determination, fidelity. That horse had brains. He could think and reason . . . he knew when he won a race and was as chirky and proud as anything. He'd toss his head and give the glad eye. When he lost, he was downcast and a wee bit irritable. But when he did lose, it was no fault of his. He always did his best. . . . I loved that horse.[36]

Epilogue

Three months after Old Rosebud's death, Weir's thirty-two-year-old daughter would pass away following a short illness. His other child, a son, had died at age eleven in 1899. By April, Weir had sold his horses in Cuba. That summer, he went to Chicago to live with his sister. On August 11, he was found in his automobile, dead of an apparent heart attack at age sixty-three. He had pulled to the side of Jackson Boulevard and was still clutching the steering wheel.[1]

The following year, on October 20, 1923, Belmont Park would host the biggest extravaganza American horse racing had ever seen—one of the most spectacular events of the 1920s golden age of American sports. In a showdown organized by August Belmont and billed as the Race of the Century, Kentucky Derby winner Zev (the fourth of five Derby victors bred by John E. Madden) would square off against the top three-year-old colt from England, Epsom Derby winner Papyrus, for an astounding $100,000 purse, the largest in the history of America's oldest sport. The *Daily Racing Form* called the race and the unprecedented hype that surrounded it "the beginning of a new era" for horse racing in the United States. On the eve of the big race, the racing publication reported that New York City was "on the verge of hysterics" and predicted the largest crowd ever to witness a horse race in North America. The race itself was anticlimactic as Zev, ridden by Earl Sande, trounced the English colt in the Belmont mud. But weeks of publicity in American newspapers appealed to national pride and confirmed that horse racing had returned to the American cultural mainstream.[2]

On October 20, 1923, Kentucky Derby winner Zev beat Epsom Derby champ Papyrus by five lengths in what was billed as the "race of the century." The heavily hyped event was one of the grandest American sports spectacles of the 1920s and served as an announcement that the sport had survived its Progressive Era troubles. (Keeneland Library Cook Collection)

ↄ

Winner of forty races in eighty lifetime starts and one of the greatest equine athletes in the long history of Thoroughbred racing, Old Rosebud would be inducted into American Thoroughbred racing's Hall of Fame in Saratoga Springs, New York, in 1968. Neither Colonel Applegate nor his son Ham lived to see it. Ham had died in 1960, thirty-two years after his father, leaving an estate valued at $1.5 million to a sister and nephew. Johnny McCabe proudly accepted the honor on the great gelding's behalf. For the rest of his life, McCabe would swear that Old Rosebud was the best racehorse ever to run in America. "Old Rosebud was as good as any of them," the jockey insisted, "Man o' War, Count Fleet, Citation, Secretariat . . ."[3]

Though McCabe was surely biased in his assessment, Ben Jones, longtime trainer for Calumet Farm, who was credited with saddling six Kentucky Derby winners between 1938 and 1952, claimed Old Rosebud as his all-time favorite Thoroughbred. When asked about a talented runner in his barn toward the end of his illustrious career, Jones remarked, "He's a right nice horse, but he sure isn't any Old Rosebud."[4]

Before the advent of quasi-official championship designations, Old Rosebud was the first twentieth-century racehorse to be broadly recognized as an American champion two-year-old male, champion handicap horse, and horse of the year. Since then, nine horses have accomplished the feat, each a titan of the sport: Equipoise, Whirlaway, Citation, Native Dancer, Tom Fool, Buckpasser, Affirmed, Seattle Slew, and Spectacular Bid. Most Thoroughbreds that have attained an exalted place in racing lore either retired near the peak of their abilities or achieved immortality through an early death that left admirers to imagine what might have been. Old Rosebud's overlong career cost him a prominent place among Thoroughbred racing's most beloved equine figures. His untimely end deprived him of a retirement in which he might have been visited and celebrated, memories of his accomplishments allowed to seep into the sport's canon of lore alongside a new generation of heroes as horse racing roared into the 1920s.[5]

It would be an exaggeration of one horse's significance to suggest that Old Rosebud was directly responsible for changing the public perception of American horse racing or for the shifting political, cultural, and economic tides that would facilitate a decades-long period of growth and prosperity for the sport after years of attacks from those who wanted to see it eliminated. But Old Rosebud was the most famous racehorse in America at a pivotal moment for horse racing, and the legend of the "miracle horse" cast the sport in a positive light during turbulent times. While military preparedness is no longer a useful justification for horse racing in the face of calls for its abolition, stories about Thoroughbreds and the countless thousands of people who care for them are as capable of affecting public opinion and policymakers today as they were more than a century ago.

Acknowledgments

This book's origins lie in a meeting with the late Arthur Applegate at Tack House Pub in Lexington, Kentucky, which was facilitated by my cousin-in-law Bret. Arthur thought that his great-grandfather William Edward Applegate would make a good book subject. I was vaguely aware of the historical Applegate, thanks largely to Samuel Thomas's *Churchill Downs: A Documentary History of America's Most Legendary Race Track*, and I agreed with Arthur's assessment that his ancestor was someone whose contributions to American horse racing and, more specifically, to Churchill Downs had been underrecognized. I promised to do some digging. After determining that I could not unearth enough material to justify a longer study of Applegate, I shifted my focus to Old Rosebud. I regret that Mr. Applegate did not see this book's completion, but I understand that he was pleased I was working on it. English Drews had produced a wonderful overview of W. E. Applegate and Old Rosebud for Arthur and his family, and an early draft that was shared with me provided a most helpful place from which to start my research.

Patrick O'Dowd was the acquisitions editor at the University Press of Kentucky attached to this project for years as it slowly progressed. I will miss our conversations about UPK's Horses in History series that he played such a crucial role in advancing, but I know he will continue to succeed in his new professional endeavors. Margaret Kelly inherited the project and capably saw Old Rosebud to the finish line.

When I told him that I was working on a book about Old Rosebud, my brother-in-law Jordan asked whether that was the horse that had served as the inspiration for the name of the sled in *Citizen Kane*. There have been several books, movies, and lawsuits that have tried to clarify who was responsible for which elements of the *Citizen Kane* screenplay, and it's not clear that there was a connection between the Derby-winning horse and the famous cinematic sled. But the question emphasized the fact that, at least at some point in the twentieth century, Old Rosebud reached a fairly prominent place in American culture. And it convinced me that I wasn't too far off base in the decision to inject William Randolph Hearst (supposedly the inspiration for Charles Foster Kane) into this story—primarily to tie some divergent themes, issues, and events together.

Thank you to Kelly Coffman and everyone at Keeneland Library, Amy Purcell at University of Louisville Libraries, and Jessica Whitehead at the Kentucky Derby Museum for their help in accessing photos and research material. Thank you to everyone at the University Press of Kentucky who helped to make this a better book. And thank you to Maegan, Boone, Lyle, and Dell for being yourselves.

Notes

Introduction

1. William H. P. Robertson, *The History of Thoroughbred Racing* (Hoboken, NJ: Prentice-Hall, 1964), 261; David M. Kennedy, *Over Here: The First World War and American Society* (New York: Oxford University Press, 2004), 97.

2. Stephen A. Reiss, "The Cyclical History of Racing: The USA's Oldest and (Sometimes) Most Popular Spectator Sport," *International Journal of the History of Sport* 31, no. 1 (March 2014): 1–2, 30–33.

3. See, for example, T. J. Jackson Lears, *Something for Nothing: Luck in America* (New York: Viking, 2003); Ann Fabian, *Card Sharps, Dream Books, and Bucket Shops: Gambling in 19th-Century America* (Ithaca, NY: Cornell University Press, 1990); Kenneth Cohen, *They Will Have Their Game: Sporting Culture and the Making of the Early American Republic* (Ithaca, NY: Cornell University Press, 2017).

4. John Dos Passos, *U.S.A.: The Big Money* (New York: Library of America, 1996), 1199.

1. Origins

1. "How Old Rosebud Came Back," *Buffalo Times*, July 16, 1917.

2. Matt J. Winn and Frank G. Menke, *Down the Stretch* (New York: Smith and Durrell, 1945), 83–84; Edward Larocque Tinker, "Campaigning with Villa," *Southwest Review* 30, no. 2 (Winter 1945): 148.

3. Robert Ryal Miller, *Mexico: A History* (Norman: University of Oklahoma Press, 1985), 268–72; Eileen Welsome, *The General and the Jaguar: Pershing's Hunt for Pancho Villa* (Lincoln: University of Nebraska Press, 2006), 16; P. Edward Haley, *Revolution and Intervention: The Diplomacy of Taft and Wilson with Mexico, 1910–1917* (Cambridge, MA: MIT Press, 1970), 11–12; Karl M. Schmitt, *Mexico and the United*

States, 1821–1973: Conflict and Coexistence (New York: John Wiley and Sons, 1974), 104.

4. Jose M. Ponce de Leon, "Francisco Villa, Outlaw and Rebel Chief," *Current History* 19, no. 1 (October 1923): 124–27; Haldeen Braddy, "Pancho Villa, Folk Hero of the Mexican Border," *Western Folklore* 7, no. 4 (October 1948): 349–55; David Dorado Romo, *Ringside Seat to a Revolution: An Underground Cultural History of El Paso and Juárez, 1893–1923* (El Paso, TX: Cinco Puntos Press, 2017), 81–83, 96.

5. "Juarez Racing Now Well Established," *Daily Racing Form*, March 9, 1913; Stephen A. Reiss, "The Cyclical History of Racing: The USA's Oldest and (Sometimes) Most Popular Spectator Sport," *International Journal of the History of Sport* 31, no. 1 (March 2014): 1–2, 37–38; William H. P. Robertson, *The History of Thoroughbred Racing* (Hoboken, NJ: Prentice-Hall, 1964), 261.

6. Allowances were (and remain) midlevel races in which all horses carry a set amount of weight unless a horse has yet to meet certain performance criteria, as established in the conditions of the race, in which case that horse will receive a reduction in weight assignment—an *allowance*. Allowances were a step up from selling races (a precursor to the modern claiming race), in which the horses could be purchased following the race, and a step down from stakes races, for which owners had to pay a nomination, entry, and/or starting fee, which would be added to the race's prize money. And unlike handicap races, in which a racetrack official assigned weights to each horse with the goal of producing a close finish and more robust betting, weights to be carried in allowance races are determined by the application of the rules, or "conditions," of the race as promulgated by track officials.

7. "Trouble Brewing at Gloucester," *Philadelphia Inquirer*, November 13, 1892.

8. "The Evils of Monmouth," *New York Tribune*, July 30, 1893; "Frank Weir Dies in Chicago," *Brooklyn Daily Eagle*, August 14, 1923; "Great Record of the Veteran Trainer Weir," *Lexington Leader*, January 24, 1908; "Made Old-Time Killing," *Washington Post*, December 27, 1914; "Doings in the Legislature," *New Brunswick Daily Times*, April 25, 1894; "Gloucester's Track: Its Inception, Completion and Promising Future," *Philadelphia Times*, June 13, 1891; John Whiteclay Chambers, *The Tyranny of Change: America in the Progressive Era, 1890–1920* (New Brunswick, NJ: Rutgers University Press, 2006), 148.

9. David Nasaw, *The Chief: The Life of William Randolph Hearst* (Boston: Mariner, 2001), 127; W. A. Swanberg, *Citizen Hearst: A Biography of William Randolph Hearst* (New York: Galahad, 1996), 108; W. Joseph Campbell, *Getting It Wrong: Debunking the Greatest Myths in American Journalism* (Oakland: University of California Press, 2017), 9–25.

10. Stephen A. Reiss, *The Sport of Kings and the Kings of Crime: Horse Racing, Politics, and Organized Crime in New York, 1865–1913* (Syracuse, NY: Syracuse University Press, 2011), 167; "Percy-Gray Law Upheld," *New York Times*, March 3, 1897; "Racing Cases Argued," *New York Times*, December 19, 1895.

11. "The Racetrack," *New York Tribune*, February 20, 1900; "Victory of Cameron Was a Costly One," *Brooklyn Daily Eagle*, May 2, 1903; "Cracks in Charge of Frank Weir," *Daily Racing Form*, November 17, 1908.

12. Roseben won 52 of his 111 lifetime races, carrying 147 pounds to victory on four occasions. After retirement, he became US senator James Wadworth's daughter's pleasure horse. His track record at Belmont would finally be broken by Bold Ruler in the 1957 Vosburgh Handicap.

13. "Gossip of the Racetrack," *New York Sun*, April 20, 1907; "Weir's Extremely Successful Career," *Daily Racing Form*, January 28, 1908; "Anti-gambling Is a Party Issue—Hughes," *New York Times*, March 8, 1908; "Situation Discussed by the Men Who Will Suffer from the Action at Albany," *Cincinnati Enquirer*, June 12, 1908. The president resented the publishing king's "enormous popularity among the ignorant and unthinking people" and feared that, if elected, Hearst would "reap the reward of the sinister preaching of unrest which he and his agents have had so large a share in conducting." Nasaw, *The Chief*, 207–8.

14. "Gillett Dodges the Racetrack Gambling Issue," *Los Angeles Express*, August 8, 1908.

15. *Cincinnati Enquirer*, February 12, 1895.

16. J. Stoddard Johnston, *Memorial History of Louisville from Its First Settlement to the Year 1896* (Chicago: American Biographical Pub. Co., 1896), 537; Daniel Okrent, *Last Call: The Rise and Fall of Prohibition* (New York: Scribner, 2010), 3.

17. "Will Sell His String," *Louisville Courier-Journal*, April 20, 1894; "Notables Seen in the Betting Shed," *Cincinnati Enquirer*, July 19, 1896; "Applegate & Sons," *Louisville Courier-Journal*, January 1, 1891.

18. "Notables Seen in the Betting Shed," *Cincinnati Enquirer*, July 19, 1896; Johnston, *Memorial History of Louisville*, 537; "The Book-Makers: The Peculiar Methods They Employ to Induce Their Patrons to Bet," *St. Louis Post-Dispatch*, June 17, 1886; "New Louisville Jockey Club," *Louisville Courier-Journal*, January 15, 1895; "No Change at Churchill Downs," *Louisville Courier-Journal*, March 8, 1895; "Applegate Wins Suit over Perkins," *Cincinnati Enquirer*, March 16, 1905.

19. "General Sporting Gossip," *Memphis Commercial Appeal*, September 15, 1898; "The Belle of New York," *New York Times*, September 29, 1897; "Will Applegate's Way," *Chicago Inter Ocean*, December 26, 1897; "Applegate as 'Angel,'" *Cincinnati Enquirer*, September 5, 1897; *Cincinnati Enquirer*, March 6, 1898.

20. *Indianapolis News*, February 7, 1903; "From Program Boy to Prince of Racetrack Plungers," *Cincinnati Enquirer*, April 3, 1927; *Fort Wayne News*, July 18, 1896; "Rawhide People Bid Farewell," *Reno Gazette-Journal*, April 11, 1908; "A Forgotten Prince of Plungers," *Dayton Daily News*, March 4, 1928; Kent Hollingsworth, "Coups of Gambler Riley Grannan Are Recalled," *Lexington Leader*, March 7, 1957. By one estimation, Grannan had won and lost more than twelve million dollars in his brief career.

21. "Puzzled Are the Horseplayers," *Cincinnati Enquirer*, April 30, 1902; "Old Rosebud Real Pickup for Owner," *Anaconda Standard*, June 15, 1913.

22. "Stake Events Well Filled," *Louisville Courier-Journal*, December 1, 1912; "Notes of the Turf," *Daily Racing Form*, February 18, 1913; "Gossip from Juarez Track," *Daily Racing Form*, March 23, 1913; "Juarez Racing Closes," *Salt Lake Tribune*,

March 23, 1913; "Turfmen Ready for Last Bugle," *Louisville Courier-Journal*, March 23, 1913; "Old Rosebud Almost a Gift," *Salt Lake Tribune*, June 15, 1913; "Old Rosebud Has Made Great Record," *Cincinnati Enquirer*, August 15, 1913; "Coming Here at End of Meeting," *Louisville Courier-Journal*, August 15, 1913; "Mudders in Evidence," *Cincinnati Enquirer*, February 17, 1913; "Old Rosebud Is Still Unbeaten," *Louisville Courier-Journal*, March 6, 1913; "Old Rosebud Should Prove Star," *Chattanooga News*, March 28, 1913; "A Crack Two-Year-Old," *Toronto Star Weekly*, March 29, 1913; "Some Hoss," *Cincinnati Enquirer*, August 5, 1913; "Facts about Winner," *Louisville Courier-Journal*, May 10, 1914. Various contemporary accounts placed Old Rosebud's value for the purposes of the sale between $450 and $900, but the gelding was usually described as something of a deal sweetener, so there may not have been a specific dollar figure assigned to each horse. The rounder number of $500 eventually attached itself to Old Rosebud's legend and became the conventionally accepted figure, which could reflect an assumption that there were six horses purchased. Reports varied as to the number of yearlings in the deal—as many as six and as few as four. Weir would take five yearling fillies to Juárez in the fall, but at least two, including Ida Lavinia and Della Mack, are listed elsewhere as having been acquired separately at auction. Johnny McCabe claimed to have been at Hamburg when Weir made the purchases. McCabe recalled that Weir bought four yearlings from Madden, with one filly later being returned to Madden, which could explain some of the confusion. Turf writer Hy Scheider identified the returned yearling as Nellie Irene (*Lexington Herald*, February 21, 1929), but she raced at least once in Frank Weir's colors, at Latonia in 1913, finishing last of twelve. The best of the fillies was Edith W. (named for Weir's only daughter), who would win the Golden Rod Stakes as a two-year-old at Churchill Downs. Aunt Mamie (who shared a name with Ham's sister) would run second in the Juvenile Stakes at the same track. Another of the purchases, Hattie Mc, was unremarkable.

23. "Turfmen Praise Little Gelding," *Louisville Courier-Journal*, July 7, 1913; Jay See See, "She Was Bred in Tennessee," *Nashville Banner*, May 21, 1914. In acquiring Ida Pickwick, Madden was fulfilling his personal vow to have the three greatest mares in America residing on his Hamburg Place farm. He had already acquired the fast and tough Ohio-bred racemare Imp, winner of 62 races in 171 career starts, including the 1899 Suburban Handicap, and the world champion Standardbred Nancy Hanks (named for Abraham Lincoln's mother).

24. W. C. Vreeland, "From a Foot Runner to the Leading Breeder of North America," *Brooklyn Daily Eagle*, March 15, 1925; W. H. Gocher, "Trotting and Pacing World Mourns Passing of Madden," *Hartford Courant*, November 10, 1929; W. C. Vreeland, "John E. Madden, the Strenuous, Most Notable Character of the Turf," *Brooklyn Daily Eagle*, December 8, 1929; "John E. Madden: The Wizard of the Turf," *Louisville Courier-Journal*, March 4, 1917; "Old Rosebud Not in the Latonia Derby," *Anaconda Standard*, May 24, 1914. Most sources say Old Rosebud was born March 13. Madden recalled the date to be March 21.

25. "Negro Jockeys Shut Out," *New York Times*, July 29, 1900; Hugh Keogh, "Passing of the Colored Jockeys," *Louisville Courier-Journal*, January 14, 1902; "Few Negro Jockeys Left," *Washington Post*, January 11, 1907.

26. "Hildreth Regrets Having Sold Uncle," *Daily Racing Form*, March 26, 1910; "Great Speed Shown by Uncle," *Daily Racing Form*, May 15, 1908; "Madden Sells Uncle to Hildreth," *Daily Racing Form*, August 7, 1907; "Great Racing Record Made by S. C. Hildreth," *Indianapolis Journal*, April 3, 1904; "Madden Admires Hildreth's Methods," *Daily Racing Form*, July 14, 1907; "Old Rosebud's Sire Fastest Horse Ever," *Anaconda Standard*, May 31, 1914. Hildreth had beaten Madden senseless a few years earlier at Morris Park in the culmination of a personal dispute. But their mutual love of fast horses allowed them to patch up their differences, and they would later partner in several profitable equine transactions.

2. Freak

1. Ed Comerford, "Baldwin Man Led 1914 Derby Field," *Newsday*, April 27, 1976; Johnny McCabe, interview by Jim Bolus, tape recording, Elmont, New York, 1975, Kentucky Derby Museum (call number 1985.155.0031).

2. "Little Nephew Takes Feature," *Louisville Courier-Journal*, May 2, 1913; *Thoroughbred Record*, April 14, 1917; Kent Hollingsworth, *The Great Ones* (Lexington, KY: Blood-Horse, 1970), 221.

3. Adolph Mathis, "Nags Race Well for Old-Time Race Rider," *Collyer's Eye*, January 6, 1923, cited in Dorothy Ours, *Man o' War: A Legend Like Lightning* (New York: St. Martin's Press, 2007), 37.

4. "Little Nephew Wins Feature in Drive with Old Rosebud," *Louisville Courier-Journal*, May 20, 1913; *Louisville Courier-Journal*, May 21, 1913; "Old Rosebud Is Beaten," *Daily Racing Form*, May 20, 1913.

5. Ed Cole, "A. L. Aste Encounters Bad Luck," *Daily Racing Form*, August 8, 1917; "Tobacco-Chewing Thoroughbred Wins 4 Races," *Collyer's Eye*, September 9, 1922.

6. "Race Tracks to Pool Interests," *Chicago Tribune*, February 26, 1907; "Louisville Race Tracks Merged," *Cincinnati Enquirer*, February 26, 1907; "Louisville Tracks Are in a Pool," *Daily Racing Form*, February 27, 1907; "Victor Establishes New Track Record for Distance," *Louisville Courier-Journal*, May 27, 1913; *Daily Racing Form*, May 28, 1913. Ham Applegate would serve as secretary of the consolidated entity.

7. *Daily Racing Form*, May 29, 1913; "Chat of the Course," *Louisville Courier-Journal*, June 6, 1913.

8. "Old Rosebud Easily Defeats Rivals for Juvenile Honors," *Louisville Courier-Journal*, June 1, 1913; "Chat of the Course," *Louisville Courier-Journal*, June 1, 1913. The Breeders' Futurity was run in the spring at that time.

9. "Old Roamer Is King of Horses," *Washington Herald*, October 15, 1918.

10. "Brilliant Sport Marks Close of Local Racing Season," *Louisville Courier-Journal*, June 8, 1913.

11. "Louisville Racing Ends," *Daily Racing Form*, June 8, 1913; "Notes of the Turf," *Daily Racing Form*, July 20, 1913. Prodigal son Willie Applegate inserted himself in the situation from New York and told a newsman at Belmont Park, "I am looking after proposals to purchase Old Rosebud. I can sell him for $25,000 to three different parties, but he has been priced at $30,000 and will not be sold for one cent less." "Owner of Punch Bowl Hopes Old Rosebud Will Come East," *Cincinnati Enquirer*, June 16, 1913.

12. "Star Racers Arrive Here," *Louisville Courier-Journal*, September 6, 1913.

13. "Turfmen Praise Little Gelding," *Louisville Courier-Journal*, July 7, 1913.

14. "Turfmen Praise Little Gelding"; T. H. Schneidau, "Two-Year-Old King," *El Paso Times*, July 10, 1913.

15. "Spa Quivers at Joy of Racing," *New York Sun*, August 3, 1913; "Month of Racing On at Saratoga Today," *New York Sun*, August 2, 1913; "Racing Returns in Glory to Saratoga," *New York Tribune*, August 3, 1913; Ed Cole, "Saratoga Gay with Inpouring Racing Crowd," *New York Evening Telegram*, August 1, 1913.

16. "Old Rosebud to Race Again," *Brooklyn Daily Eagle*, December 15, 1918; "Notes of the Turf," *Daily Racing Form*, August 1, 1913; *Daily Racing Form*, August 2, 1913.

17. "Old Rosebud to Race Again," *Brooklyn Daily Eagle*, December 15, 1918; "Some Hoss," *Cincinnati Enquirer*, August 5, 1913.

18. "Wonderful Speed by Old Rosebud," *New York Sun*, August 2, 1913. As late as April 28, 1920, the *Washington Herald* observed that Old Rosebud was "not herself this season."

19. "Woman's Beauty, Grace, and Art Bewilder at the Capital," *Washington Post*, March 4, 1913; "To Ride in Pageant," *Washington Evening Star*, January 10, 1913; Eliza McGraw, *Astride: Horses, Women, and the Partnership That Changed America* (Lexington: University Press of Kentucky, 2025). The women's suffrage movement would enter the realm of horse racing that summer in England when suffragist Emily Wilding Davison was fatally struck by King George V's horse Anmer while trying to attach a suffrage scarf to the colt's bridle as the field rounded into the homestretch in the Epsom Derby. Vanessa Thorpe, "Truth behind the Death of Suffragette Emily Davison Is Finally Revealed," *Guardian*, May 25, 2013; Michael Tanner, *The Suffragette Derby* (London: Robson Press, 2013).

20. "Racing Returns in Glory to Saratoga," *New York Tribune*, August 3, 1913; "Racing Season Inaugurated at Famous Saratoga Course," *Louisville Courier-Journal*, August 3, 1913.

21. "Some Hoss," *Cincinnati Enquirer*, August 5, 1913.

22. "Cock o' the Walk Wins the Saratoga," *New York Times*, August 3, 1913; "Racing Returns in Glory to Saratoga," *New York Tribune*, August 3, 1913; "Spa Quivers at Joy of Racing," *New York Sun*, August 3, 1913.

23. "Glorious Times in the Old Town," *Cincinnati Enquirer*, August 3, 1913.

24. *Brooklyn Times*, August 4, 1913; "Flying Fairy Lands Feature at Saratoga," *Lexington Herald*, August 5, 1913; "Spa Quivers at Joy of Racing," *New York Sun*, August 3, 1913; "Old Rosebud Makes a Hit," *Daily Racing Form*, August 5, 1913; "Racing Returns in Glory to Saratoga," *New York Tribune*, August 3, 1913.

25. "Spa Quivers at Joy of Racing," *New York Sun*, August 3, 1913; "Old Rosebud," *Buffalo Morning Express*, August 6, 1913; "Racing Warmly Welcomed," *Daily Racing Form*, August 3, 1913. Healy trained for Captain E. B. Cassatt and was no relation to Tom Healey.

26. *Louisville Courier-Journal*, August 4, 1913.

27. "Rowe Tosses Bomb among Westerners," *New York Sun*, August 13, 1913. The record Pennant matched had been set by James R. Keene's brilliant filly Maskette in 1908 while carrying ten more pounds.

28. Ed Cole, "Best Little Horse in Annals of Turf," *Anaconda Standard*, August 17, 1913; "Great Gelding Breezes Home," *Louisville Courier-Journal*, August 14, 1913; *Brooklyn Citizen*, August 14, 1913.

29. Cole, "Best Little Horse in Annals of Turf." Like others searching for a point of reference to describe Rosebud's talent, Cole looked to the past. He chose to compare him to legendary fillies rather than colts. He noted that, like August Belmont's homebred champion Beldame, Old Rosebud could "kill his opponents early, take a breathing spell and then come home." And, like the resilient racemare Imp, he possessed remarkable speed from the barrier but also had the athleticism to stop after a few strides in the event of a false start.

30. "Gallops at Saratoga Track," *Lexington Leader*, August 17, 1913; "Pennant Meets Old Rosebud Wednesday," *Brooklyn Times-Union*, August 18, 1913; "Saratoga Stables Go to Maryland," *Washington Times*, September 1, 1913; "Trainer Weir Denies Report That Old Rosebud Has Broken Down," *Cincinnati Enquirer*, September 17, 1913. The Adirondack was open to all two-year-olds at that time and was restricted to fillies beginning in 1930.

31. "Old Rosebud Sent to Stable Here," *Lexington Leader*, October 26, 1913.

32. "Old Rosebud to Race Again," *Brooklyn Daily Eagle*, December 15, 1918; "Noble Old Rosebud a Wonderful Horse," *Anaconda Standard*, January 12, 1919; "Old Rosebud—Frank Weir: Some Intimate Details concerning One of America's Most Popular Racehorses," *Daily Racing Form*, June 9, 1922.

33. "The Champion Two-Year-Old of This Year," *Daily Racing Form*, November 15, 1913.

34. Peter V. N. Henderson, "Woodrow Wilson, Victoriano Huerta, and the Recognition Issue in Mexico," *The Americas* 41, no. 2 (1984): 151–76. The coup was reportedly abetted by the outgoing American ambassador to Mexico, Henry Lane Wilson.

35. "Juarez Racing to Go On," *Daily Racing Form*, November 16, 1913; "Transferred to Juarez," *Daily Racing Form*, November 19, 1913; "Villa Takes Juarez," *New York Times*, November 16, 1913; "Terrazas Must Pay $250,000 or Die," *New York Times*, March 6, 1914.

36. Matt J. Winn and Frank G. Menke, *Down the Stretch* (New York: Smith and Durrell, 1945), 91, 100; "Rebels Cheered at the Juarez Track," *Cincinnati Enquirer*, November 28, 1913; "Meet Auspiciously Opens," *Louisville Courier-Journal*, November 28, 1913.

37. "Impressed by Derby Material," *Daily Racing Form*, March 16, 1914; Jack Sallee, "Kentucky Derby Has Fine Field," *Tampa Tribune*, December 21, 1913; "Rosy Outlook for the Derby," *Louisville Courier-Journal*, April 5, 1914; "Kentucky Derby to Become the Classic of American Turf," *Cincinnati Enquirer*, April 5, 1914; "Have Ambitious Plans," *Daily Racing Form*, April 5, 1914.

38. Theodore Roosevelt, *The Works of Theodore Roosevelt*, vol. 1 (New York: P. F. Collier, 1897), 259.

39. LeRoy Parker, "The Trial of the Anarchist Murderer Czolgosz," *Yale Law Journal* 11, no. 2 (December 1901): 93; "The President Speaks: Through Elihu Root He Denounces William R. Hearst," *Buffalo Evening News*, November 2, 1906; Theodore Roosevelt, *The Strenuous Life: Essays and Addresses* (New York: Century, 1902), 279–97; Kim Brink-Johnsen, "Playing the Man: Masculinity, Performance, and United States Foreign Policy, 1901–1920" (PhD diss., University of New Hampshire–Durham, 2004), 3.

40. H. W. Brands, "Woodrow Wilson and the Irony of Fate," *Diplomatic History* 28, no. 4 (September 2004): 503.

41. "Little Jingoism Here," *Baltimore Sun*, April 21, 1914.

3. Roses

1. "Derby Day," *Louisville Commercial*, April 25, 1875, quoted in Samuel W. Thomas, *Churchill Downs: A Documentary History of America's Most Legendary Race Track* (Louisville: Kentucky Derby Museum, 1995), 46.

2. "A New Deal," *Louisville Courier-Journal*, August 7, 1894; "A Cake Walk," *Louisville Commercial*, May 16, 1894; Marjorie Rieser, "Horse Racing in Central Kentucky and Jefferson County with Special Reference to Churchill Downs" (master's thesis, University of Louisville, 1944), 61; "Tuesday's Big Races," *Chicago Tribune*, May 14, 1894.

3. Thomas, *Churchill Downs*, 110.

4. "Will Not Allow Betting," *Lexington Herald*, May 4, 1908; "Sheriff Will Stop Betting at Track," *Louisville Courier-Journal*, October 12, 1907; "Racing Will Continue," *Lexington Herald*, May 7, 1908; Rieser, "Horse Racing in Central Kentucky and Jefferson County," 81–99; *Grinstead v. Kirby*, 110 S.W. 247 (Ky. 1908).

5. "Jeff Livingston, Turf Patron, Dies," *New York Times*, February 10, 1931; "Jeff Livingston Would Pay $30,000 for Old Rosebud," *Cincinnati Enquirer*, April 5, 1914; Harvey T. Woodruff, "Chicagoan Bids for Old Rosebud," *Chicago Tribune*, April 5, 1914; "Livingston Offers $30,000 for Old Rosebud," *Louisville Courier-Journal*, April 5, 1914. Livingston was also a descendent of Robert Livingston—American founding father, negotiator of the Louisiana Purchase, and facilitator of the first commercially viable steamboat.

6. "Price for Derby Favorite Set at $40,000 by Owners," *Chicago Tribune*, April 6, 1914.

7. "Jeff Livingston after a Horse to Win the Kentucky Derby," *Cincinnati Enquirer*, April 7, 1914; "Decline Offer for Favorite," *Louisville Courier-Journal*,

April 8, 1914; "Jeff Livingston to Buy More Horses in England," *New York Tribune*, April 16, 1914; "$35,000 Refused for Old Rosebud," *Thoroughbred Record*, April 11, 1914.

8. "Chinn Sees Old Rosebud," *Cincinnati Enquirer*, April 8, 1914; Andrew G. Leonard, "Uncle Heads Extensive Stud at Beaumont Farm," *Lexington Herald*, April 15, 1917. Lexington breeder Hal Price Headley had acquired Rosebud's sire, Uncle, one of the most exciting young stallions in America, for "only" thirty-eight thousand dollars at auction a few months earlier, a number that underscores the high value being placed on Old Rosebud.

9. "Clever Trials Mark Training," *Louisville Courier-Journal*, April 16, 1914; "Belloc Must Be Reckoned With," *Cincinnati Enquirer*, April 27, 1914.

10. "Old Rosebud Ships Well," *Louisville Courier-Journal*, April 22, 1914; "Lexington Horses Speeding Up," *Daily Racing Form*, April 23, 1914.

11. Weir did not think the Blue Grass Stakes was a viable option. A win there would have earned Rosebud a heftier weight assignment in the Derby, while any wins in allowance races would go unpenalized.

12. *Cincinnati Enquirer*, May 1, 1914; *Cincinnati Enquirer*, May 5, 1914; *Daily Racing Form*, May 5, 1914.

13. "Old Rosebud Now 4 to 1," *Nashville Tennessean*, April 14, 1914; "Hodge in Sensational Workout," *Daily Racing Form*, April 23, 1914; "Sensational Derby Trial," *Daily Racing Form*, May 2, 1914; "New Mark for Derby Trials," *Louisville Courier-Journal*, May 2, 1914.

14. Johnny McCabe, interview by Jim Bolus, tape recording, Elmont, New York, 1975, Kentucky Derby Museum (call number 1985.155.0031).

15. "Grover Hughes Wins," *Louisville Courier-Journal*, May 6, 1914; "Old Rosebud Worked," *Cincinnati Enquirer*, May 6, 1914; "Talent Jolted Many Times," *Lexington Leader*, May 6, 1914; "Old Rosebud in Grand Form in Final Trial," *Louisville Courier-Journal*, May 8, 1914.

16. "Slow Track for Derby," *Daily Racing Form*, May 9, 1914; "Largest Crowd in Derby Annals," *Louisville Courier-Journal*, May 10, 1914.

17. James R. Conant, "Tom Young Came to Landscape Downs in 1911, Stayed 44 Years," *Louisville Courier-Journal*, May 8, 1955; "Old Rosebud Makes a New Track Record," *Daily Racing Form*, May 10, 1914; "Largest Crowd in Derby Annals," *Louisville Courier-Journal*, May 10, 1914; "Running of the Fortieth Kentucky Derby," *Thoroughbred Record*, May 16, 1914; "Great Crowd Sees Contest," *Louisville Courier-Journal*, May 12, 1912; "Relluf's Chances Are None Too Rosy in Kentucky Derby," *Lexington Herald*, May 1, 1910; "Donau Gamely Stood Drive," *Cincinnati Enquirer*, May 11, 1910.

18. "John Gund Has an Excellent Chance," *Cincinnati Enquirer*, May 6, 1914.

19. "Largest Crowd in Derby Annals," *Louisville Courier-Journal*, May 10, 1914; "Running of the Fortieth Kentucky Derby," *Thoroughbred Record*, May 16, 1914; Francis Nelson, "Old Rosebud for Dorval," *Thoroughbred Record*, May 16, 1914.

20. McCabe, interview by Jim Bolus, 1975.

21. "View of Classic Race from Quarter-Mile Pole," *Louisville Courier-Journal*, May 10, 1914 (quote). Churchill Downs lists a William Taylor as Hodge's rider, but he was consistently referred to as Walter in trade publications. "Ralph and Hodge Continue to Train Well," *Daily Racing Form*, April 28, 1914.

22. "Son of Uncle Gallops Home," *Louisville Courier-Journal*, May 10, 1914.

23. McCabe, interview by Jim Bolus, 1975.

24. "Famous Star of Yesteryear Passes On," *Collyer's Eye*, May 27, 1922; "McCabe's Great Ride,'" *Louisville Courier-Journal*, May 10, 1914; "Old Rosebud Wins Kentucky Derby," *Birmingham News*, May 10, 1914; "Breezing Was Old Rosebud," *Cincinnati Enquirer*, May 10, 1914.

25. "Chat of the Course," *Louisville Courier-Journal*, May 10, 1914.

26. George Biggers, "Ham Applegate Breaks Record," date and publication unknown, Applegate family scrapbook; "Breezing," *Cincinnati Enquirer*, May 10, 1914.

27. "Derby Winner Called a Freak," *Nashville Banner*, May 11, 1914; "Senators See Kentucky Derby," *Washington Post*, May 18, 1914; Francis Nelson in *Toronto Globe*, "The Speed of Old Rosebud," *Daily Racing Form*, May 14, 1914; Patrick McGilligan, *Young Orson: The Years of Luck and Genius on the Path to Citizen Kane* (New York: Harper, 2015), 697; Thomas Stackpole, "Who Really Wrote 'Citizen Kane,'" *Smithsonian*, May 2016. Mankiewicz's son would insist that the inspiration for the sled's name was a Rosebud-brand bicycle that was stolen from his father when he was a boy. Frank Mankiewicz with Joel Swerdlow, *So As I Was Saying: My Somewhat Eventful Life* (New York: Thomas Dunne, 2016), 33–34. Others say it was a reference to Hearst's mistress's genatalia. Quinn Hough, "Mank: What Really Inspired Citizen Kane's Rosebud (Was It Marion Davies?)," *Screen Rant*, December 7, 2020.

28. "Son of Uncle Gallops Home," *Louisville Courier-Journal*, May 10, 1914; "All Sports," *Cincinnati Enquirer*, June 28, 1914.

29. *Louisville Courier-Journal*, May 13, 1914; "Gossip and Comment from Kentucky," *Daily Racing Form*, May 19, 1914.

30. "Old Rosebud to Leave for East Sunday Night," *Louisville Courier-Journal*, May 21, 1914; *Thoroughbred Record*, May 23, 1914; "Old Rosebud Works Out," *Cincinnati Enquirer*, May 23, 1914.

31. "Gossip and Comment from Kentucky," *Daily Racing Form*, May 22, 1914.

32. "Old Rosebud Met with Accident and Has Been Killed," *Corsicana (Tex.) Daily Sun*, June 3, 1922; "Turfmen of Kentucky Mourn the Passing of Famous 'Old Rosebud,'" *Springfield (Mo.) Leader and Press*, June 3, 1922; "'Jinxed' by a Photo," *New Orleans Times-Picayune*, June 4, 1922; *Louisville Courier-Journal*, May 25, 1914.

33. "Big Crowd at Belmont," *Baltimore Sun*, May 31, 1914; "Old Rosebud Beaten for the Withers," *New York Times*, May 31, 1914; "Society Folk Make Merry at Belmont Park," *New York Tribune*, May 31, 1914; Herbert Daley, "Old Rosebud, Idol of West, Runs Bad Last," *New York Tribune*, May 31, 1914.

34. "Walden's Two Kentucky Derby Horses," *Daily Racing Form*, May 4, 1915; "Old Rosebud Put Out of Training," *Thoroughbred Record*, June 6, 1914.

35. "Old Rosebud Went Lame," *Cincinnati Enquirer*, June 1, 1914; "Old Rosebud Loses," *Washington Evening Star*, May 31, 1914. Applegate concluded his statement by giving credit to McCabe for not making a bad situation worse.

36. "Kentucky Derby Winner Runs Disappointingly in Withers," *Louisville Courier-Journal*, May 31, 1914; "Old Rosebud Put Out of Training," *Thoroughbred Record*, June 6, 1914.

37. "Old Rosebud Beaten for the Withers," *New York Times*, May 31, 1914; "Old Rosebud Quit in the Withers," *Nashville Banner*, June 1, 1914; John W. Fox, "Old Rosebud May Never Go to the Post Again," *Brooklyn Citizen*, June 1, 1914. The *Times* called the result "almost a tragedy" for Kentucky, "which loves its horses only one degree less than it loves its beautiful women and its incomparable whisky."

38. "Opening at Juarez," *Thoroughbred Record*, November 28, 1914; "Old Rosebud Is Wintering Well," *Louisville Courier-Journal*, December 6, 1914; *Daily Racing Form*, December 9, 1914.

39. Casualty figures from the revolution are imprecise, but estimates range from a million to a million and a half deaths. Peter Eisner, "Mexico," *Newsday*, November 13, 1988; "Mexico Land-Reform Plan Recalls Fears of U.S. Control," *Corpus Christi Caller-Times*, November 10, 1991; Francisco Cantú, "An American Story," *New York Review of Books*, March 23, 2023, 28.

40. "Francisco Villa, the Strong Man of Mexico," *San Francisco Examiner*, September 26, 1914; Margarita de Orellana, *Filming Pancho: How Hollywood Shaped the Mexican Revolution* (New York: Verso, 2009), 17, 39, 76; Nancy Brandt, "Pancho Villa: The Making of a Modern Legend," *The Americas* 21, no. 2 (October 1964): 146–62; John Reed, *Insurgent Mexico* (New York: Appleton, 1914); Kimberly O'Neill, "The Ethics of Intervention: US Writers and the Mexican Revolution," *Journal of American Studies* 50, no. 3 (2016): 613–38; "Villa, Bandit and Brute, May Be Mexican President," *New York Times*, December 14, 1913. Hearst had also been a consistent advocate for workers' rights until a well-publicized newsboy strike hurt sales.

41. "Strict Neutrality Behavior Urged by President Wilson," *Wall Street Journal*, August 19, 1914; "America Should Give an Example of Peace," *Boston Globe*, May 11, 1915.

42. "Notables at Juarez Track," *Daily Racing Form*, January 9, 1915.

43. "Meet Enters Final Week," *Louisville Courier-Journal*, May 31, 1915; "Louisville Favorite Training Well," *Louisville Courier-Journal*, June 3, 1915; "Little String and Little Nephew," *Daily Racing Form*, June 17, 1915.

44. *Louisville Courier-Journal*, July 5, 1915; *Daily Racing Form*, July 7, 1915; "Current Notes of the Turf," *Daily Racing Form*, July 15, 1915; *Montreal Gazette*, July 22, 1915.

45. *Cincinnati Enquirer*, November 28, 1915; Hy Schneider, "Old Rosebud Is Only Winner of Famous Kentucky Derby Which 'Came Back' Four Times," *Lexington Herald*, February 21, 1929.

46. Friedrich Katz, *The Life and Times of Pancho Villa* (Palo Alto, CA: Stanford University Press, 2009), 523, citing *El Paso Morning Herald*, October 8, 1915.

4. Miracle Horse

1. "How Old Rosebud Was Brought Back," *Daily Racing Form*, July 22, 1917. The stream was likely Foil Creek, but the Clear Branch of the Brazos River also crossed a portion of the McLemore Ranch.

2. *Chihuahua Vida Nueva*, November 21, 1915, cited in Friedrich Katz, "Pancho Villa and the Attack on Columbus, New Mexico," *American Historical Review* 83, no. 1 (February 1978): 111; "Massacre of Americans under Orders of Villa," *Leadville (Colo.) Herald Democrat*, January 13, 1916; "Mining Men Stripped Naked and Ruthlessly Shot Down by Band of Villa Savages," *El Paso Morning Times*, January 12, 1916; "Tragedy Declared Villa Reply to American Aid to Carranza Cause," *El Paso Morning Times*, January 12, 1916; Friedrich Katz, *The Life and Times of Pancho Villa* (Palo Alto, CA: Stanford University Press, 2009), 499.

3. William Randolph Hearst, "Citizens, You Must Now Protect Republic with Your Ballots," *San Francisco Examiner*, January 14, 1916.

4. "Villa, in Glee over Order," *Washington Post*, February 4, 1914; Katz, *The Life and Times of Pancho Villa*, 355; "Crowd Starts Riot on Broadway," *El Paso Herald*, January 14, 1916; "U.S. Army to Mexico," *Chicago Tribune*, March 10, 1916; "Seventeen Americans Killed by Murderous Villa Raiders in Savage Attacks on Columbus," *El Paso Times*, March 10, 1916; "From the Firing Line," *Kansas City (Kan.) Republic*, March 16, 1916; Clair Kenamore, "Military Men Satisfied with Columbus Record; Civilians Disappointed," *St. Louis Post-Dispatch*, March 11, 1916; Margarita de Orellana, *Filming Pancho: How Hollywood Shaped the Mexican Revolution* (New York: Verso, 2009), 184; Miguel A. Levario, "The Mexican Revolution and Tejano Communities," in *War along the Border* (College Station: Texas A&M University Press, 2011), 134–55.

5. Ralph Thomas Fulton, "Northern Mexico's Beef Cattle Industry 1910–1920: A Perspective" (master's thesis, University of Montana, 1974), 20. A house fire took the lives of Pershing's wife and three daughters in 1914. Only his six-year-old son survived. One of the many notes of sympathy that streamed in from around the world came from Pancho Villa. Andrew Carroll, *My Fellow Soldiers: General John Pershing and the Americans Who Helped Win the Great War* (New York: Penguin, 2018), 10; Eileen Welsome, *The General and the Jaguar: Pershing's Hunt for Pancho Villa* (Lincoln: University of Nebraska Press, 2006), 158.

6. "T. R. Rejects Invitation from Ford," *San Francisco Examiner*, May 20, 1916.

7. "Racing for Sport a Factor in Preparedness for War," *New York Sun*, May 3, 1916; "Thoroughbred Indispensable in War," *Daily Racing Form*, May 5, 1916.

8. "They Served and Suffered for Us," *London Daily Telegraph*, November 1, 2004; "The Horse in Transition: The Horse in World War 1, 1914–1918," International Museum of the Horse, archived from the original on September 26, 2010; "Proper Type of War Horse," *Daily Racing Form*, July 11, 1917; "Way to Secure Proper War Horse," *Daily Racing Form*, May 10, 1918. The *Daily Racing Form* put the number of American and Canadian horses exported for military service at two million by April

1914. *Daily Racing Form*; "Racing Should Not Be Curtailed," *Daily Racing Form*, April 13, 1917.

9. Jack Salee, "Turf News and Yarns," *Salt Lake Tribune*, February 11, 1917.

10. "Realizing Value of Thoroughbred," *Daily Racing Form*, June 28, 1917.

11. Paul Roberts and Isabelle Taylor, "Saratoga: The One Illiterate, Impoverished Irish Immigrant Who Got the Great Meet Started," *Thoroughbred Racing Commentary*, July 16, 2018.

12. Jim Bolus, *Kentucky Derby Stories* (Gretna, LA: Pelican, 1993), 73; "Churchill Downs Is Undergoing Repairs," *Lexington Herald*, January 17, 1915; "Derby Day," *Louisville Courier-Journal*, May 2, 1915.

13. Ulric J. Bell, "Great Crowd Makes Holiday," *Louisville Courier-Journal*, May 14, 1916; "Kentucky Derby Echoes," *Buffalo Morning Express*, May 17, 1916; "Derby," *Cincinnati Enquirer*, May 14, 1916.

14. Frank G. Menke, "You Can't Keep a Good Horse Down," *Pittsburgh Gazette-Times*, May 11, 1919. Menke would also help to write Matt Winn's autobiography, which would further enhance Winn's historical reputation as the person most responsible for the success of the Kentucky Derby.

15. "Current Notes of the Turf," *Daily Racing Form*, December 6, 1916; "Many Horses on the Oval," *Louisville Courier-Journal*, November 29, 1916; "Cold Wave Visits Juarez," *Daily Racing Form*, December 8, 1916; "Not Afraid of Villa's Men," *Daily Racing Form*, December 11, 1916; "Carranza Ends Bullfighting," *El Paso Herald*, October 10, 1916; Walter H. Pearce, "Carranza Reforms at Juarez Great Benefit to Racing," *Louisville Courier-Journal*, January 4, 1916.

16. "Public Invited to Witness Day's Sport," *Daily Racing Form*, December 16, 1916; Peter Clark, "Some Juarez Suggestions," *Daily Racing Form*, January 1, 1917; Jack Salee, "Turf News and Yarns," *Salt Lake Tribune*, February 11, 1917; "Only a Few Remaining at Juarez," *Daily Racing Form*, February 7, 1917; "Colonel Matt Winn in New York City," *El Paso Times*, February 17, 1917; "Juarez Season Not Big Success," *Akron Beacon*, February 5, 1917; "Racing in Juarez Proved a Failure," *Washington Herald*, February 11, 1917.

17. David Dorado Romo, *Ringside Seat to a Revolution: An Underground Cultural History of El Paso and Juárez, 1893–1923* (El Paso, TX: Cinco Puntos Press, 2017), 233.

18. "Auburn-Haired Amazon Leads Feminine Outbreak," *El Paso Morning Times*, January 29, 1917; "Bath Rioting Renewed at Santa Fe Bridge," *El Paso Morning Times*, January 30, 1917; "Statistics of the Juarez Meeting Abruptly Terminated Last Sunday," *Daily Racing Form*, January 31, 1917; Ian R. Tizard and Jeffrey M. B. Musser, *Great American Diseases: Their Effects on the Course of North American History* (Cambridge, MA: Academic Press, 2022), 170.

19. Will Englund, *March 1917: On the Brink of War and Revolution* (New York: Norton, 2017), 23, 74; "House Endorses T. R. Division," *Louisville Courier-Journal*, May 13, 1917.

20. "Fast Track Racing Near," *Daily Racing Form*, February 7, 1917; "Old Rosebud in Shape; May Meet Leochares," *Louisville Courier-Journal*, February 3, 1917; "Plan Race for Fast Trio," *Detroit Free Press*, March 11, 1917.

21. "Zim Defeats Old Rosebud," *El Paso Times*, February 19, 1917; Johnny McCabe, interview by Jim Bolus, tape recording, Elmont, New York, 1975, Kentucky Derby Museum (call number 1985.155.0031).

22. J. L. Dempsey, "Hot Springs Is Crowded," *Daily Racing Form*, March 4, 1917; "Senator Amis Dies Suddenly," *Arkansas Gazette*, January 1, 1908; "Want Amis Bill Repealed," *Batesville (Ark.) Daily Guard*, November 11, 1908.

23. "Rosebud Very Fast Breaker," *Ottowa Journal*, March 7, 1917; "Look Out! Old Rosebud Is In Again," *Cincinnati Enquirer*, March 9, 1917; "Old Rosebud in Comeback Role," *Hot Springs New Era*, March 9, 1917; "Old Favorite Wins Hot Springs Race," *Arkansas Gazette*, March 9, 1917.

24. "Old Favorite Wins Hot Springs Race," *Arkansas Gazette*, March 9, 1917 (quote); "Hot Springs Mayor Welcomes Return of Thoroughbreds to Arkansas Spa," *Munster Times*, March 12, 1917.

25. "Banner Day at Oaklawn," *Daily Racing Form*, March 25, 1917.

26. "Essex Park's Opening Day," *Daily Racing Form*, March 31, 1917; "After Lapse of Twelve Years Thoroughbreds at Essex Park," *Louisville Courier-Journal*, March 31, 1917. Gordon Russell would go on to service as a US Army Remount stallion and sire of Olympic show jumpers.

27. "Essex Opening Was Auspicious," *Hot Springs New Era*, March 31, 1917.

28. "Flames Sweep Essex Park," *Louisville Courier-Journal*, April 1, 1917; "Oaklawn Aids Essex to Meet a Misfortune," *Hot Springs New Era*, March 31, 1917; "Hot Springs Tracks Merge," *Lexington Leader*, December 29, 1917; "Horses Here Going Slow," *Louisville Courier-Journal*, December 1, 1917. Coincidentally, the Belmont Park grandstand was also damaged by fire days later. Blame was initially attached to the Germans, though it was later believed that unidentified domestic arsonists were responsible. Ed Cole, "Considerable Mystery to Belmont Fire," *Daily Racing Form*, April 11, 1917; "Preparations to Rebuild Belmont Stand," *Daily Racing Form*, April 11, 1917.

29. "Wilson Asks State of War Declared against Germany," *Boston Globe*, April 3, 1917; Alan Dawley, *Changing the World: American Progressives in War and Revolution* (Princeton, NJ: Princeton University Press, 2003), 133. The recently launched Russian Revolution that resulted in Czar Nicholas II's abdication allowed for a tidier framing of the war as a fight between democracy and totalitarianism. In recognition of his service in the Great War, Congress would re-create the title of General of the Armies of the United States, previously held only by George Washington, for Pershing.

30. George Creel, *How We Advertised America* (New York: Harper, 1920), 4; Alan Axelrod, *Selling the Great War: The Making of American Propaganda* (New York: Palgrave, 2009).

31. Axelrod, *Selling the Great War*, 22–23.

32. Axelrod, *Selling the Great War*, 40–47.

33. Charles Merz, *The Dry Decade* (Seattle: University of Washington Press, 1969), cited in Daniel Okrent, *Last Call: The Rise and Fall of Prohibition* (New York: Scribner, 2010), 101; Richard Hoffman, *Love and Fury: A Memoir* (Boston: Beacon Press, 2015), 93; "'Daylight Saving' Plan Is Approved," *Salt Lake Tribune*, February 1, 1917.

34. "End of Whisky Making," *Baltimore Sun*, September 8, 1917; "Facts to Face," *Wisconsin State Journal*, May 26, 1919; "Segregated Vice to Be Abolished from U.S. Military Zones," *Arkansas Democrat*, September 29, 1917; "Secretary of Navy Daniels Submits His Annual Report," *Chattanooga News*, December 10, 1917; Frederic J. Haskin, "Social Hygiene and the War," *Lexington Herald*, November 9, 1917.

35. "Racing Should Not Be Curtailed," *Daily Racing Form*, April 13, 1917; "War Horses in Greatest Demand, Says Gen. Wood," *Indianapolis Star*, April 14, 1917; Bob Silbernagel, "Demand for War Horses Created Army Remount Service in 1908," *Grand Junction Daily Sentinel*, April 22, 2018.

36. "Old Rosebud Is Insured for $10,000," *Daily Racing Form*, April 10, 1917.

37. "Additional Attraction for Derby Day," *Daily Racing Form*, April 19, 1917; "Hail Storm at Lexington," *Daily Racing Form*, May 10, 1917.

38. "By Great Stretch Running Omar Khayyam Wins Derby," *Nashville Tennessean*, May 13, 1917; "Long Shot Wins Rich Derby," *Cincinnati Enquirer*, May 13, 1917; "Derby Day Is Pervaded by Military Air," *Louisville Courier-Journal*, May 13, 1917.

39. "Derby Day Is Pervaded by Military Air," *Louisville Courier-Journal*, May 13, 1917; Helen F. Randolph, "Pretty Women and Gay Colors Form Setting for Running of Great Kentucky Derby," *Louisville Courier-Journal*, May 13, 1917.

5. King of the Turf

1. "Money Maker Wins Speculation Stakes," *Thoroughbred Record*, June 2, 1917; "Douglas Park's Opening," *Daily Racing Form*, May 27, 1917.

2. "Crack Racers Meet Today," *Louisville Courier-Journal*, June 2, 1917.

3. "Ready for Open at Milldale," *Louisville Courier-Journal*, June 11, 1917; H. W. Brands, *Woodrow Wilson* (New York: Times Books, 2003), 55; US Department of Commerce, *Statistical Abstract of the United States, 1917* (Washington, DC: US Government Printing Office, 1918), 353; Will Englund, *March 1917: On the Brink of War and Revolution* (New York: Norton, 2017), 5.

4. "Latonia Gossip," *Thoroughbred Record*, June 16, 1917; Bob Saxton, "Old Rosebud," *Cincinnati Enquirer*, June 12, 1917; "Latonia's Good Opening," *Daily Racing Form*, June 12, 1917; "Thousands Cheer as Little Maiden Unfurls Flag at Latonia Course," *Kentucky Post*, June 12, 1917.

5. Len Wooster, "Sport Topics," *Brooklyn Daily Times*, June 22, 1917; "Old Rosebud's Stable Hopeful of Beating Roamer Tomorrow," *Brooklyn Daily Times*, June 29, 1917; "Should Apply for License at Once," *Daily Racing Form*, January 26, 1917.

6. "Great Geldings in Present Racing," *Daily Racing Form*, July 13, 1917; Jim Bolus, *Kentucky Derby Stories* (Gretna, LA: Pelican, 1993), 85–86. Three Kentucky Derby winners would also appear in the same race the following year, when George Smith beat Omar Khayyam and Exterminator in the 1918 Bowie Handicap.

7. Len Wooster, "Brooklyn Handicap Proves That Race Riding Is Not a Lost Art," *Brooklyn Daily Times*, June 26, 1917.

8. Vincent Treanor, "World's Record Time Made," *New York Evening World*, June 26, 1917.

9. "Brooklyn Handicap Is Won by Borrow," *New York Sun*, June 26, 1917.

10. Len Wooster, "Brooklyn Handicap Proves That Race Riding Is Not a Lost Art," *Brooklyn Daily Times*, June 26, 1917.

11. "Old Rosebud Wins Carter Handicap," *Thoroughbred Record*, July 7, 1917; "Old Rosebud Is First in Carter," *New York Sun*, July 5, 1917; "Old Rosebud Won Carter Handicap," *Montreal Gazette*, July 5, 1917.

12. Frank O'Neil, "Old Rosebud Wins Tribute from Madden," *New York Tribune*, July 8, 1917.

13. "Old Rosebud to Race Again," *Brooklyn Daily Eagle*, December 15, 1918.

14. "Turf Potatoes Bring $1,730.75," *Louisville Courier-Journal*, December 8, 1917; "Churchill Downs Potato Crop Sold for Soldiers," *Honolulu Advertiser*, December 29, 1917; "Red Cross Will Gather Harvest from 1918 Racing: Yield for This Year Expected to Reach a Total of $750,000," *New York Tribune*, February 10, 1918; O'Neil Sevier, "Racing Will Contribute More than $750,000 to the Red Cross This Year," *Louisville Courier-Journal*, February 10, 1918; "Last Day at Churchill Downs," *Cincinnati Enquirer*, May 26, 1918. Novelist F. Scott Fitzgerald trained at Camp Taylor.

15. "Old Rosebud Takes Measure of the Field," *Buffalo Times*, July 15, 1917, says it was a crowd of seventeen thousand.

16. "Old Rosebud Greatest of Winners," *Daily Racing Form*, May 3, 1947.

17. "Old Rosebud Blooms Full," *New Orleans Times-Picayune*, July 15, 1917; Frank G. Menke, "The Miracle Horse," *Omaha Daily News*, July 15, 1917; *Buffalo Evening Times*, July 17, 1917; "Old Rosebud Picked as Best Racer of the Year," *Harrisburg Evening News*, July 23, 1917.

18. "Await Bugle Call at Saratoga," *Daily Racing Form*, July 31, 1917.

19. Vincent Treanor, "Roamer's Form Reversal and Spectacular Storm Shock Racegoers at Spa," *New York Evening World*, August 2, 1917; "Kempton Park Racing Contemplated," *Daily Racing Form*, August 7, 1917. Boots had been the early betting favorite in the race but would be scratched along with Stromboli.

20. J. L. Dempsey, "Old Rosebud Wins Again," *Daily Racing Form*, August 8, 1917; "Old Rosebud Clinches Claim to Handicap Championship," *Brooklyn Daily Times*, August 8, 1917.

21. "One of Old Rosebud's Peculiarities," *Daily Racing Form*, August 15, 1917; "Frank Weir Would Match Old Rosebud against Omar Khayyam," *Brooklyn Daily Times*, August 10, 1917.

22. J. R. Jeffrey, "Increase in Attendance," *Daily Racing Form*, August 14, 1917.

23. "Frank Weir Would Match Old Rosebud against Omar Khayyam," *Brooklyn Daily Times*, August 10, 1917.

24. "Old Rosebud Will Not Race for Some Time," *Brooklyn Citizen*, August 25, 1917; "Old Rosebud Falls Victim to Illness," *New York Times*, August 25, 1917; Mary Simon, "The Story of Old Rosebud," *Daily Racing Form*, April 18, 2014; J. L. Dempsey, "Rain Spoils at Saratoga," *Daily Racing Form*, August 25, 1917; Vincent Treanor, "Old Rosebud 'Faints' and May Not Race for Saratoga Cup," *New York Evening World*, August 25, 1917; Ed Cole, "Laurel Fall Stakes Filling Well," *Daily Racing Form*, August 25, 1917; "Superb Saratoga Racing," *Thoroughbred Record*, September 1, 1917.

25. Len Wooster, "Old Rosebud Being Reserved for the Aqueduct Meeting," *Brooklyn Daily Times*, September 6, 1917.

26. John W. Fox, "Old Rosebud Big Feature at Aqueduct Reopening," *Brooklyn Citizen*, September 18, 1917.

27. "Test for Old Rosebud," *New York Times*, September 19, 1917; "Big Races Are Off," *Washington Times*, September 20, 1917; "Special Race Plan Fails," *New York Times*, September 20, 1917; John W. Fox, "Matches for Race Meet at Aqueduct Called Off," *Brooklyn Citizen*, September 20, 1917; *Louisville Courier-Journal*, September 23, 1917; "Grainger Enthusiastic over Prospects for Fall Meeting," *Thoroughbred Record*, September 29, 1917; Len Wooster, "Old Rosebud Not to Start Against the Great Mare," *Brooklyn Daily Times*, September 28, 1917.

28. "Home of Old Rosebud," *Cincinnati Enquirer*, November 21, 1917.

29. *Thoroughbred Record*, October 20, 1917.

30. "Old Rosebud the King," *New York Sun*, December 30, 1917; "Rosebud Handicap King for 1917 Season," *Tulsa Daily World*, December 19, 1917; "Leaders in Nation's Sports in 1917," *New York Times*, December 30, 1917; "Old Rosebud Best Handicap Horse," *Lexington Leader*, December 23, 1917; "Leading Horses of Racing Year," *Houston Post*, December 30, 1917.

31. "Old Rosebud Being Pointed for Hourless and Omar," *El Paso Times*, April 6, 1918.

32. "Helped Save Racing in Maryland," *Daily Racing Form*, April 4, 1918; "For and Against Racing," *Baltimore Sun*, February 18, 1918.

33. O'Neil Sevier, "Halting of Racing Would Be a Big Blow to Breeders," *Washington Post*, June 23, 1918.

34. Matt J. Winn and Frank G. Menke, *Down the Stretch* (New York: Smith and Durrell, 1945), 159–60; *Louisville Courier-Journal*, May 12, 1918.

35. "War Coloring Given Derby," *Louisville Courier-Journal*, May 12, 1918; "Kilmer Wins the Derby," *Baltimore Sun*, May 12, 1918; C. A. Bergin, "Freecutter Is a Coming Horse," *Lexington Herald*, September 29, 1918.

36. "What the Owners Had to Say," *Louisville Courier-Journal*, May 12, 1918; Winn and Menke, *Down the Stretch*, 158–59.

37. *Daily Racing Form*, June 6, 1918; "Casualties among Handicap Horses," *Ottawa Citizen*, June 22, 1918.

38. "Mayor Strong in Stand against Racing Pastime," *Louisville Courier-Journal*, June 20, 1918.

39. Thomas B. Cromwell, "Oh, Boy!... Racing Under Fire," *Cincinnati Enquirer*, December 16, 1917.

40. Walter H. Pearce, "Geldings Are Barred in 1919 Kentucky Derby, Says Winn," *Louisville Courier-Journal*, August 5, 1918; O'Neil Sevier, "Geldings Will Be Barred from Kentucky Derby," *Washington Post*, August 4, 1918; "Geldings to Be Barred from the Lawrence Realization," *Collyer's Eye*, September 7, 1918; "Geldings to Be Barred Out," *Montreal Gazette*, October 19, 1918.

41. "Cassatt Would Bar the Geldings," *Thoroughbred Record*, February 24, 1917; "Geldings Should Be Barred," *Daily Racing Form*, February 22, 1917; "Discourage Gelding of Stallions by Making Them Ineligible to Stakes Races," *Daily Racing Form*, June 2, 1918; W. S. Vosburgh, "Bar Geldings from Our Standard Events," *Thoroughbred Record*, March 2, 1918.

42. "Important Jockey Club Action: Proposed Amendment Excluding Geldings from Certain Big Races Adopted," *Daily Racing Form*, February 14, 1919.

43. "Old Rosebud to Race Again," *Brooklyn Daily Eagle*, December 15, 1918; "Noble Old Rosebud a Wonderful Horse," *Anaconda Standard*, January 12, 1919.

6. Last Campaigns

1. "Greatest Comeback Horse of All Time If Old Rosebud Stands Up This Year," *Brooklyn Daily Times*, January 4, 1919; "Old Rosebud to Race Again," *Brooklyn Daily Eagle*, December 15, 1918.

2. "Many Withdrawals at Havana," *Daily Racing Form*, February 28, 1919; *Lexington Leader*, April 18, 1919; E. T. McCreight, "Only Four Weeks More until Races Begin Here," *Lexington Leader*, August 17, 1919; Andrew G. Leonard, "All Kentucky Race Tracks Will Be Merged under One Control," *Lexington Leader*, January 5, 1919; "Kentucky Tracks Are Sold: Biggest Deal of American Turf History Now Completed," *Daily Racing Form*, February 13, 1919; "Old Rosebud Arrives," *Louisville Courier-Journal*, June 4, 1919; *Collyer's Eye*, November 22, 1924.

3. See Jennifer Kelly, *Sir Barton and the Making of the Triple Crown* (Lexington: University Press of Kentucky, 2019).

4. Len Wooster, "Old Rosebud the Wonder Horse," *Brooklyn Daily Times*, April 26, 1919.

5. "Parr Colors Unbeatable," *Daily Racing Form*, May 11, 1919. The candy maker was George W. Loft, a former two-term congressman who filled the New York seat vacated on the death of Tammany Hall stalwart "Big Tim" Sullivan.

6. Frank G. Menke, "You Can't Keep a Good Horse Down," *Pittsburgh Gazette Times*, May 11, 1919.

7. "The Kentucky Derby," *Louisville Courier-Journal*, May 11, 1919.

8. Thomas B. Cromwell, "Sir Barton Wins," *Daily Racing Form*, May 11, 1919.

9. John O'Keefe, "The Phoenix Horse," *Pittsburgh Gazette Times*, May 11, 1919.

10. W. J. Macbeth, "Horse Lovers Throng Track at Jamaica," *New York Tribune*, May 16, 1919.

11. "Old Rosebud Has Gone Back," *Brooklyn Daily Times*, May 28, 1919.

12. "Latonia Form Chart," *Daily Racing Form*, July 2, 1919.

13. CJ Savage, "Fleet Filly Shows Speed," *Louisville Courier-Journal*, July 6, 1919; "Cincinnati Trophy Day," *Daily Racing Form*, July 6, 1919.

14. "Mexican Rebel Is Shot to Death on Ranch at Canutillo by Trillo," *Fort Worth Star-Telegram*, July 20, 1923; "Pancho Villa Slain," *Kansas City Star*, July 20, 1923; "Pancho Villa Killed by Own Bodyguard," *Santa Ana Register*, July 20, 1923.

15. See Eliza McGraw, *Here Comes Exterminator! The Long-Shot Horse, the Great War, and the Making of an American Hero* (New York: Thomas Dunne, 2016), 102, 111.

16. "Lucullite Clinches His Claim as the Turf's Champion Miler," *Brooklyn Daily Times*, July 18, 1919; Henry V. King, "Big Race Forces Public to Ponder," *New York Sun*, July 18, 1919. There were murmurs that Loftus had employed suspiciously unorthodox tactics on Sun Briar, though the stewards would take no disciplinary action.

17. "Old Rosebud to Race in the Fall," *Daily Racing Form*, August 26, 1919.

18. "Naturalist Wins Whirlwind Race," *New York Times*, September 5, 1919.

19. "Lord Brighton Lands," *Brooklyn Daily Times*, September 18, 1919.

20. "He's In Again," *Cincinnati Enquirer*, October 22, 1919.

21. *Washington Evening Star*, November 16, 1919. The Linstead Handicap winner, Tippity Witchet, would win 78 of 216 starts in a thirteen-year career, including wins at two and fourteen years of age.

22. The incident that resulted in McCabe's injury was near the spot where leading jockey Frankie Robinson had been fatally trampled at Bowie earlier that year.

23. "Blossom Stage Play Turned into Film," *Louisville Courier-Journal*, September 21, 1919; "'Checkers' in Film Form," *Louisville Courier-Journal*, October 5, 1919; "'Checkers' Film to Be Shown Here," *Louisville Courier-Journal*, October 2, 1919.

24. *Baltimore Sun*, April 28, 1920.

25. "Old Rosebud Wins from Fleet Field," *New York Times*, May 27, 1920; W. C. Vreeland, "Old Rosebud, at Nine Years, Still Retains His Speed," *Brooklyn Daily Eagle*, May 28, 1920.

26. "Man o' War's Smooth Way of Racing," *Daily Racing Form*, June 17, 1920.

27. David Nasaw, *The Chief: The Life of William Randolph Hearst* (Boston: Mariner, 2001), 270.

28. "Rail Bird Chatter," *Collyer's Eye*, June 21, 1919; "No Longer Allowed to Race at NYRA," *Thoroughbred Daily News*, January 26, 2022.

29. *Baltimore Evening Sun*, April 21, 1921; *Philadelphia Inquirer*, April 21, 1921. Farrell had sold the Yankees in 1915 and would miss out on the Babe Ruth–led dynasty that would win six American League pennants in the 1920s and become one of the most iconic sports properties in the booming American sports scene. Many of Farrell's horses would soon end up with Mack McLaughlin, Weir's former assistant.

30. Henry V. King, "Old Rosebud Returns to Races and Wins a Purse," *New York Herald*, September 7, 1921.

31. *Buffalo Courier*, May 9, 1922.

32. "Morvich Circles Track Unruffled," *Louisville Courier-Journal*, May 14, 1922.

33. "Greatest Derby Day Says Colonel Winn," *Louisville Courier-Journal*, May 14, 1922.

34. A chart in the *New York Herald* said he finished ninth.

35. David J. Walsh, "Rosebud's Career Ended as Morvich Races to Victory," *Washington Times*, June 6, 1922; "Weir Famed for Liking Horse," *Brooklyn Daily Times*, August 14, 1923; "Old Rosebud, Once King of the Turf, Destroyed," *New York Herald*, May 24, 1922; "Eyes Grow Misty at Jamaica When Old Rosebud, Derby Winner and One of Princes of Turf, Is Shot Down," *Lexington Herald*, May 23, 1922; Johnny McCabe, interview by Jim Bolus, tape recording, Elmont, New York, 1975, Kentucky Derby Museum (call number 1985.155.0031); telegram, May 26, 1922, Applegate family scrapbook. While many news reports assumed Old Rosebud had been stabled at Jamaica when he died, he was apparently still training at Aqueduct. "Old Rosebud Retired," *New York Tribune*, May 23, 1922; "Famous Old Rosebud Is Dead," *Daily Racing Form*, May 24, 1923; Ed Comerford, "Baldwin Man Led 1914 Derby Field," *Newsday*, April 27, 1976.

36. "Speedy Lady Madcap," *Daily Racing Form*, October 20, 1922; Zoe Beckley, "Man Can Learn from a Horse, Equine Not Much from a Man," date and publication unknown, cited in English Drews, "Old Rosebud: Prince of the Turf," unpublished (2019). Article preserved in an Applegate family scrapbook along with telegram communication between Weir and Ham Applegate.

Epilogue

1. *Daily Racing Form*, April 21, 1923; "Frank D. Weir Dies of Heart Attack in Chicago," *Louisville Courier-Journal*, August 12, 1923; "Frank Weir Dies of Heart Attack," *Thoroughbred Record*, August 18, 1923.

2. "Significance of Big Match," *Daily Racing Form*, October 20, 1923; "Big International Race of $100,000 Today," *Daily Racing Form*, October 20, 1923; James C. Nicholson, *Racing for America: The Horse Race of the Century and the Redemption of a Sport* (Lexington: University Press of Kentucky, 2021).

3. "Sister, Nephew Bequeathed Most of Applegate Estate," *Louisville Courier-Journal*, September 16, 1960; "John McCabe, 86, Was Derby Jockey," *Newsday*, June 26, 1980; Ed Comerfield, "Baldwin Man Led 1914 Derby Field," *Newsday*, April 27, 1976.

4. "Ben Jones Maintains Allegiance to Old Rosebud," *Daily Racing Form*, May 1, 1954; Warren Brown, publication unknown, May 12, 1938. Article in Applegate family scrapbook.

5. Discussing historical championships is a bit tricky. From 1935 to the advent of the Eclipse Awards in 1971, the publisher of the *Daily Racing Form* and *Morning Telegraph* produced an annual list of top Thoroughbred performers in the various age

divisions based on a poll of its staff. *Turf and Sport Digest* published its own list derived from voting by selected sportswriters. In 1950, racing secretaries from member tracks of the Thoroughbred Racing Association began producing a third semiofficial slate of champions. Kent Hollingsworth's 1970 book *The Great Ones* contained a list of historical champions beginning in 1870. Entries for the years 1870–1935 were retrospectively determined by Hollingsworth, editor of *Blood-Horse* magazine, through an examination of the historical record that included contemporaneous coverage of the sport in leading magazines and newspapers. That table became a foundation of the sport's de facto record of champions. (In the Eclipse Award era, championships for what had been called handicap males and handicap females were awarded to the top "older male" and "older female" until 2015, when the word *dirt* was added to emphasize that horses running primarily on grass should not be considered for the honors.) Designation of championships necessarily entails a certain level of subjectivity, even in the modern era of the single universally recognized Eclipse Awards. But the point is that Old Rosebud's accomplishments placed him in truly rarified company.

Bibliography

Axelrod, Alan. *Selling the Great War: The Making of American Propaganda*. New York: Palgrave, 2009.
Benbow, Mark E. "Birth of a Quotation: Woodrow Wilson and 'Like Writing History with Lightning.'" *Journal of the Gilded Age and Progressive Era* 9, no. 4 (October 2010): 509–33.
Bernstein, Matthew. *George Hearst: Silver King of the Gilded Age*. Norman: University of Oklahoma Press, 2021.
Bolus, Jim. *Kentucky Derby Stories*. Gretna, LA: Pelican, 1993.
Bowen, Edward L. *Legacies of the Turf: A Century of Great Thoroughbred Breeders*. Lexington, KY: Eclipse Press, 2003.
———. *Masters of the Turf: Ten Trainers Who Dominated Horse Racing's Golden Age*. Lexington, KY: Eclipse Press, 2007.
Braddy, Haldeen. "Pancho Villa, Folk Hero of the Mexican Border." *Western Folklore* 7, no. 4 (October 1948): 349–55.
Brands, H. W. *Woodrow Wilson*. New York: Times Books, 2003.
———. "Woodrow Wilson and the Irony of Fate." *Diplomatic History* 28, no. 4 (September 2004): 503–12.
Brandt, Nancy. "Pancho Villa: The Making of a Modern Legend." *The Americas* 21, no. 2 (October 1964): 146–62.
Brink-Johnsen, Kim. "Playing the Man: Masculinity, Performance, and United States Foreign Policy, 1901–1920." PhD diss., University of New Hampshire–Durham, 2004.
Burns, Eric. *1920: The Year That Made the Decade Roar*. New York: Pegasus, 2016.
Campbell, W. Joseph. *Getting It Wrong: Debunking the Greatest Myths in American Journalism*. Oakland: University of California Press, 2017.
Carroll, Andrew. *My Fellow Soldiers: General John Pershing and the Americans Who Helped Win the Great War*. New York: Penguin, 2018.

Carver, Nancy E. *Making Tracks: The Untold Story of Horse Racing in St. Louis, 1767–1905*. St. Louis, MO: Reedy Press, 2014.

Chambers, John Whiteclay. *The Tyranny of Change: America in the Progressive Era, 1890–1920*. New Brunswick, NJ: Rutgers University Press, 2006.

Cline, Howard F. *The United States and Mexico*. New York: Atheneum, 1971.

Cohen, Kenneth. *They Will Have Their Game: Sporting Culture and the Making of the Early American Republic*. Ithaca, NY: Cornell University Press, 2017.

Cooper, Jilly. *Animals in War*. London: Corgi Books, 2000.

Creel, George. *How We Advertised America*. New York: Harper, 1920.

Cunningham, Thomas N. "The Life and Career of Edward R. Bradley." Master's thesis, Florida Atlantic University, 1992.

Davis, Janet M. *The Gospel of Kindness: Animal Welfare and the Making of Modern America*. New York: Oxford University Press, 2016.

Dawley, Alan. *Changing the World: American Progressives in War and Revolution*. Princeton, NJ: Princeton University Press, 2003.

de Orellana, Margarita. *Filming Pancho: How Hollywood Shaped the Mexican Revolution*. New York: Verso, 2009.

Dos Passos, John. *U.S.A.* New York: Library of America, 1996.

Drews, English. "Old Rosebud and Colonel W. E. Applegate: A Collection of Lost Stories." Unpublished, 2019.

Edward, William. *Colonel Rockinghorse*. New York: Hastings and Baker, 1919.

Englund, Will. *March 1917: On the Brink of War and Revolution*. New York: Norton, 2017.

Fabian, Ann. *Card Sharps, Dream Books, and Bucket Shops: Gambling in 19th-Century America*. Ithaca, NY: Cornell University Press, 1990.

Freeberg, Ernest. *A Traitor to His Species: Henry Bergh and the Birth of the Animal Rights Movement*. New York: Basic Books, 2020.

Fulton, Ralph Thomas. "Northern Mexico's Beef Cattle Industry 1910–1920: A Perspective." Master's thesis, University of Montana, 1974.

Haley, P. Edward. *Revolution and Intervention: The Diplomacy of Taft and Wilson with Mexico, 1910–1917*. Cambridge, MA: MIT Press, 1970.

Hawley, Ellis W. *The Great War and the Search for a Modern Order: A History of the American People and Their Institutions, 1917–1933*. New York: St. Martin's Press, 1992.

Henderson, Peter V. N. "Woodrow Wilson, Victoriano Huerta, and the Recognition Issue in Mexico." *The Americas* 41, no. 2 (1984): 151–76.

Hodges, Gladys Arlene. "El Paso, Texas, and Ciudad Juárez, Chihuahua, 1880–1930: A Material Cultural Study of Borderlands Interdependency." Master's thesis, University of Texas–El Paso, 2010.

Hoffman, Richard. *Love and Fury: A Memoir*. Boston: Beacon Press, 2015.

Hollingsworth, Kent. *The Great Ones*. Lexington, KY: Blood-Horse, 1970.

———. *The Wizard of the Turf: John Madden of Hamburg Place*. Lexington, KY: Blood-Horse, 1965.

Hotaling, Edward. *The Great Black Jockeys: The Lives and Times of the Men Who Dominated America's First National Sport*. Rocklin, CA: Forum, 1999.

Ivers, Tom. *The Bowed Tendon Book: Prevention, Treatment, Rehabilitation*. Neenah, WI: Russell Meerdink, 1994.

Iversen, Eve. "Improving America's Horses: The Army Remount Program." *Army History* 38 (Summer 1996): 7–14.

Johnston, J. Stoddard. *Memorial History of Louisville from Its First Settlement to the Year 1896*. Chicago: American Biographical Pub. Co., 1896.

Katz, Friedrich. *The Life and Times of Pancho Villa*. Palo Alto, CA: Stanford University Press, 2009.

———. "Pancho Villa and the Attack on Columbus, New Mexico." *American Historical Review* 83, no. 1 (February 1978): 101–30.

Kelly, Jennifer. *Sir Barton and the Making of the Triple Crown*. Lexington: University Press of Kentucky, 2019.

Kennedy, David M. *Over Here: The First World War and American Society*. New York: Oxford University Press, 2004.

Lears, T. J. Jackson. *Something for Nothing: Luck in America*. New York: Viking, 2003.

Leuchtenburg, William E. *The Perils of Prosperity, 1914–32*. Chicago: University of Chicago Press, 1973.

Levario, Miguel A. "The Mexican Revolution and Tejano Communities." In *War along the Border*, 134–55. College Station: Texas A&M University Press, 2011.

Mankiewicz, Frank, with Joel Swerdlow. *So As I Was Saying: My Somewhat Eventful Life*. New York: Thomas Dunne, 2016.

Marcus, Emerson. "Reno at the Races: The Sporting Life versus Progressive Reform." Master's thesis, University of Nevada, Reno, 2015.

McGerr, Michael. *A Fierce Discontent: The Rise and Fall of the Progressive Movement in America, 1870–1920*. New York: Oxford University Press, 2005.

McGilligan, Patrick. *Young Orson: The Years of Luck and Genius on the Path to Citizen Kane*. New York: Harper, 2015.

McGirr, Lisa. *The War on Alcohol: Prohibition and the Rise of the American State*. New York: Norton, 2016.

McGraw, Eliza. *Astride: Horses, Women, and the Partnership That Changed America*. Lexington: University Press of Kentucky, 2025.

———. *Here Comes Exterminator! The Long-Shot Horse, the Great War, and the Making of an American Hero*. New York: Thomas Dunne, 2016.

Merz, Charles. *The Dry Decade*. Seattle: University of Washington Press, 1969.

Meyer, G. J. *The World Remade: America in World War I*. New York: Bantam Books, 2016.

Miller, Robert Ryal. *Mexico: A History*. Norman: University of Oklahoma Press, 1985.

Mooney, Katherine C. *Isaac Murphy: A Biography*. New Haven, CT: Yale University Press, 2023.

———. *Race Horse Men: How Slavery and Freedom Were Made at the Racetrack*. Cambridge, MA: Harvard University Press, 2014.

Nasaw, David. *The Chief: The Life of William Randolph Hearst*. Boston: Mariner, 2001.
Nicholson, James C. *The Kentucky Derby: How the Run for the Roses Became America's Premier Sporting Event*. Lexington: University Press of Kentucky, 2012.
———. *The Notorious John Morrissey: How a Bareknuckle Brawler Became a Congressman and Founded Saratoga Racecourse*. Lexington: University Press of Kentucky, 2016.
———. *Racing for America: The Horse Race of the Century and the Redemption of a Sport*. Lexington: University Press of Kentucky, 2021.
Okrent, Daniel. *Last Call: The Rise and Fall of Prohibition*. New York: Scribner, 2010.
O'Neill, Kimberly. "The Ethics of Intervention: US Writers and the Mexican Revolution." *Journal of American Studies* 50, no. 3 (2016): 613–38.
Ours, Dorothy. *Man o' War: A Legend Like Lightning*. New York: St. Martin's Press, 2007.
Parker, LeRoy. "The Trial of the Anarchist Murderer Czolgosz." *Yale Law Journal* 11, no. 2 (December 1901): 80–94.
Peck, Garrett. *The Great War in America: World War I and Its Aftermath*. New York: Pegasus, 2018.
Perreault, Matthew Saul. "Jockeying for Position: Horse Racing in New Orleans, 1865–1920." Master's thesis, University of Connecticut, 2016.
Ponce de Leon, Jose M. "Francisco Villa, Outlaw and Rebel Chief." *Current History* 19, no. 1 (October 1923): 124–27.
Proctor, Ben. *William Randolph Hearst: The Early Years, 1863–1910*. New York: Oxford University Press, 1998.
Reed, John. *Insurgent Mexico*. New York: Appleton, 1914.
Reiss, Stephen A. "The Cyclical History of Racing: The USA's Oldest and (Sometimes) Most Popular Spectator Sport." *International Journal of the History of Sport* 31, no. 1 (March 2014): 1–2, 29–54.
———. *Horse Racing the Chicago Way: Gambling, Politics, and Organized Crime, 1837–1911*. Syracuse, NY: Syracuse University Press, 2022.
———. *The Sport of Kings and the Kings of Crime: Horse Racing, Politics, and Organized Crime in New York, 1865–1913*. Syracuse, NY: Syracuse University Press, 2011.
Rieser, Marjorie. "Horse Racing in Central Kentucky and Jefferson County with Special Reference to Churchill Downs." Master's thesis, University of Louisville, 1944.
Robertson, William H. P. *The History of Thoroughbred Racing*. Hoboken, NJ: Prentice-Hall, 1964.
Robinson, Judith. *The Hearsts: An American Dynasty*. New York: Avon, 1991.
Romo, David Dorado. *Ringside Seat to a Revolution: An Underground Cultural History of El Paso and Juárez, 1893–1923*. El Paso, TX: Cinco Puntos Press, 2017.
Roosevelt, Theodore. *The Strenuous Life: Essays and Addresses*. New York: Century, 1902.

———. *The Works of Theodore Roosevelt.* Vol. 1. New York: P. F. Collier, 1897.

Royer, Jennifer Baugh. "A Dark Side of Dixie: Illegal Gambling in Northern Kentucky, 1790–2000." PhD diss., Texas Christian University, 2009.

Ruby, Earl. *The Golden Goose: Story of the Jockey Who Won the Most Stunning Kentucky Derby and How He Became a Millionaire.* Lexington, KY: Thoroughbred Record, 1974.

Sandels, Robert. "Silvestre Terrazas and the Old Regime in Chihuahua." *The Americas* 28, no. 2 (October 1971): 191–205.

Saunders, James Robert, and Monica Renae Saunders. *Black Winning Jockeys in the Kentucky Derby.* Jefferson, NC: McFarland, 2003.

Schmitt, Karl M. *Mexico and the United States, 1821–1973: Conflict and Coexistence.* New York: John Wiley and Sons, 1974.

Seely, Jack. *Warrior: The Amazing Story of a Real War Horse.* London: Racing Post, 2011.

Swanberg, W. A. *Citizen Hearst: A Biography of William Randolph Hearst.* New York: Galahad, 1996.

———. *Whitney Father, Whitney Heiress: Two Generations of One of America's Richest Families.* New York: Charles Scribner's Sons, 1980.

Tanner, Michael. *The Suffragette Derby.* London: Robson Press, 2013.

Thomas, Samuel W. *Churchill Downs: A Documentary History of America's Most Legendary Race Track.* Louisville: Kentucky Derby Museum, 1995.

Tinker, Edward Larocque. "Campaigning with Villa." *Southwest Review* 30, no. 2 (Winter 1945): 148–54.

Tizard, Ian R., and Jeffrey M. B. Musser. *Great American Diseases: Their Effects on the Course of North American History.* Cambridge, MA: Academic Press, 2022.

US Department of Commerce. *Statistical Abstract of the United States, 1917.* Washington, DC: US Government Printing Office, 1918.

Veach, Michael R. *Kentucky Bourbon Whiskey: An American Heritage.* Lexington: University Press of Kentucky, 2013.

Wahler, Brenda. *Montana Horse Racing: A History.* Charleston, SC: History Press, 2019.

Wall, Maryjean. *How Kentucky Became Southern: A Tale of Outlaws, Horse Thieves, Gamblers, and Breeders.* Lexington: University Press of Kentucky, 2010.

Wasserman, Mark. "Enrique Creel: Business and Politics in Mexico, 1880–1930." *Business History Review* 59, no. 4 (1985): 645–62.

———. "The Social Origins of the 1910 Revolution in Chihuahua." *Latin American Research Review* 15, no. 1 (1980): 15–38.

Welsome, Eileen. *The General and the Jaguar: Pershing's Hunt for Pancho Villa.* Lincoln: University of Nebraska Press, 2006.

Wilson, Edward O. *Biophilia: The Human Bond with Other Species.* Cambridge, MA: Harvard University Press, 1984.

Winn, Matt J., and Frank G. Menke. *Down the Stretch.* New York: Smith and Durrell, 1945.

Index

Page numbers in italics refer to illustrations.

Adirondack Handicap, 40, 155n30
Agua Prieta, 69
alcohol, 3, 17–18, 87, 112
Aldebaran (horse), 82–83
Amis, W. T., 82
antigambling movement, 1–2, 5, 9–18, 35–36, 50
Anti-Saloon League, 18, 87
Applegate, Bettie, 17
Applegate, Hamilton Clarke ("Ham"): early life, 20; estate, 145; and Kentucky Jockey Club, 122–23; at 1914 Kentucky Derby, 59, 61; Old Rosebud purchase, 17, 20–21; possible Old Rosebud sale, 31, 53–54; and New Louisville Jockey Club, 50, 153n6; sells distillery, 112; telegram to Weir, 142; and Withers Stakes, 64–65, 159n35
Applegate, William Edward ("Ed"): bookmaking operations, 18–20; early life and career, 17–18; enters racing business, 18–19; and Jack Hare Jr., 111, 113, 122; and Kentucky Jockey Club, 122; and New Louisville Jockey Club, 48–50; and Old Rosebud, 17, 36, 41, 53–54, 62, 81, 90, 92, 101, 103; separation from Weir, 122–23

Applegate, William Edward, Jr. ("Willie"), 19–20, 154n11
Aqueduct racetrack, 97–98, 101, 103, 105, 110–11, 132, 140–41, 168n35
Army Remount Service, 76, 162n26
Ashland Oaks, 55, 57–58
Aunt Mamie (horse), 152n22
automobiles, 35, 58, 63, 76, 96, 104, 129, 135, 144
Autumn Highweight Handicap, 132
Averne Handicap, 132
Avondale Stud, 21

Babylon Handicap, 136
Baldwin, Lucky, 16, 48
Bally (horse), 130–31
Barney Shannon (horse), 128
Bashford Manor Stakes, 26, 28
Bay View Park racetrack, 16
Beaverkill (horse), 128
Be Frank (horse), 130
Belle of New York, The (play), 19
Belmont, August, II: founding member of Jockey Club, 12, *13*, organizer of Race of the Century, 144; promoter of Thoroughbred racing as essential component of American military

preparedness, *89,* 114, 117; racehorse owner and breeder, 34, 36, 38, 98, 137, 156n29; volunteer for US military service, 87–88
Belmont Park, 14, 22, 62–64, 117, 132, 135, 139, 144, 154n11, 162n28
Belmont Stakes, 101, 117, 120, 137
Ben Ali (horse), 48
Billy Kelly (horse), 132, 135–36
Black Broom (horse), 37
Black horsemen, 22–23, 32, 55
Black Toney (horse), 28–29, 38, 56
Block, Benjamin, 141
Blue Grass Stakes, 55, 57–58
Boniface (horse), 123
bookmakers, 18–20, 34, 48, 50, 52, 63
Boots (horse), 95, 98, 104–5, 164n19
Borrow (horse), 98–100, *100,* 101, 103, 106, 110
Bradley, Edward R., 25, 28, 37, 56
Brave Cunarder (horse), 28
Breeders' Futurity, 29–30, 58, 106, 111, 153n8
Brighton Beach racetrack, 21
Bromo (horse), 101, 103–4
Bronzewing (horse), 55, 57–60
Brooklyn Handicap, 97–100, *100*
Brossman, Charles, 75
Brown, Elza, 22, 31, *32*
Burnett Woods Handicap, 128
Business Men's League, 82
Butler, James, *51,* 108, 110–11, 130–31
Butwell, Jimmy, 108
Buxton, Merritt "Happy," 30

Californian Handicap, 136
Camden, Johnson N., 29, 116
Campfire (horse), 106
Camp Zachary Taylor, 103, 164n14
Capra (horse), 108, 110–11
Carrancistas, 68, 129
Carranza, Venustiano, 65, 67–70, 72, 78–79, 129
Carr, John D., 40, 42, 65
Carter Handicap, 101–2
Cassatt, Edward B., 118, 155n25
Cassidy, Mars, 6, 8, 99, 132–33

Charlestonian (horse), 63–64
Checkers (film), 135
Chiclet (horse), 99, 101, 103–4
Chihuahua, Mexico, 41, 69, 71–72, 78, 86, 129
Chinn, Phil T., 54
Christophine (horse), 55–56
Churchill Downs: Ed Applegate involvement, 19, 47, 50, 122; cooperation with Douglas Park, 29; early history, 47–48; gelding ban, 117, 120; infield, 49–50, 58–59, 61, 103, 114; Kentucky Derby promotion, 53, 75–77, 90–92, 141; managerial shake-up, 49–50; Old Rosebud races, 26, 28, 57–61, 90, 92–93; Old Rosebud workouts, 21, 55, 57, 62; organization of New Louisville Jockey Club, 48–49; reimplementation of pari-mutuel wagering, 50–53; wartime patriotism, 74–75, 91–92, 103, 114
Cincinnati Trophy, 30–32
Citizen Kane (film), 61
Ciudad Juárez, 5, 7, 67, 69, 78–79, 129
Clark, Meriwether Lewis, 48
Clark Handicap, 61, 90, 92–93
Clinton Park racetrack, 82
Cole, Ed, 40
Colin (horse), 22–23, 38
Colonel Vennie (horse), 94
Committee on Public Information (Creel Committee), 3, 85–86, 121
Connelly, Danny, 91, 93–95, 97–99, 100–101
Consolation Handicap, 133
Corum, Bill, 141
Creason Handicap, 83
Creel, Enrique Clay, 86
Creel, George, 85–86, 121
Cromwell, Thomas B., 116
Cudgel (horse), 95–96, 108
Cum Sah (horse), 140

David Craig (horse), 83
Davison, Emily Wilding, 154n19
daylight saving time, 87
Delaware Handicap, 108, 130

Della Mack (horse) 152n22
Díaz, Porfirio, 6–7
Dolphin, USS, 46
Donerail (horse), 53, 55
Dos Passos, John, 3
Douglas Park, 29–31, 42, 53, 54, 94–96, 122
Dreyer, Joe, 123–25, 127
Dunboyne (horse), 124, 136

Ed Crump (horse), 95
Eden Park Handicap, 128
Edith W. (horse), 152n22
Elfin Queen (horse), 126
El Paso, Texas, 6, 67–68, 71–72, 78–79, 129
Emeryville racetrack, 16
Empire City racetrack, 129–30, 133
Equity Handicap, 124
Essex Park, 82, 84–85
Excelsior Handicap, 98, 107
Exterminator (horse), 116–17, 164n6

Fairbrother, Charles, 133
Fair Grounds racetrack, 81
Fair Play (horse), 37
Fairy Wand (horse), 132
Fall, Albert, 61, 71
Farrell, Frank, 12, 140, 167n29
Fator, Laverne, 130, 140
Finn, The (horse), 101–3
Flags (horse), 124, 126–27, 132–34
Flash Stakes, 35–37, 124
Flittergold (horse), 36
Follansbee, Jack, 6, 42
Food and Fuel Control Act, 87
Fordyce Handicap, 82
Fox, William, 135
Frontier Handicap, 104–5
Fruit Cake (horse), 104–5
Futurity Stakes, 40, 124, 136

gambling bans, 22, 24
Gainer (horse), 63–64
Gardner, E. S., 21
gelding ban, 117–18, 120
George Smith (horse), 76, 106

Georgetown College, 17
Gibson Hotel Handicap, 128
Glenn Springs raid, 72
Gloucester racetrack, 9
Goldblatt, Mose, 31, 56
Goldsborough, Jack, 63
Goose, Roscoe, 93
Gordon Russell (horse), 84, 162n26
Grainger, Charlie, 50
Grand Hotel Purse, 127–28
Grannan, Charles "Riley," 20, 153n20
Gravesend racetrack, 97, 112–13, 122, 124, 139–40
Grayson, Cary T., 114, 120–21
Griffith, D. W., 65
Grinstead, "Honest Jim," 50
Gruber, Michael B., 22, 28, 31

Haggin, James Ben Ali, 16, 48, 95
Harding, Warren G., 138
Hays, George Washington, 82
Hamburg Place farm, 21, 152nn22–23
Hampton Roads Purse, 134
Harford Handicap, 135
Harold Stakes, 31–32
Havre de Grace racetrack, 113, 123–24, 135, 139
Hart-Agnew law, 14, 16, 35
Headley, Hal Price, 157n8
Healey, Tom, 34, 155n25
Healy, Simon, 38, 155n25
Hearst, George, 16
Hearst, William Randolph: advocate for US military intervention in Mexico, 68, 159n39; coverage of Punitive Expedition, 72; gubernatorial campaign, 14, *16,* 151n13; support of Harding campaign, 138; and "yellow journalism," 10–11
Heflin, "Cotton Tom," 87
Hildreth, Sam, 22–23, 126, 129, 132, 153n26
Hirsch, Max, 124
Hitchcock, Frank, 118
Hodge (horse): Cherokee Handicap, 95; first start, 28; Frontier Handicap, 104–5; Inaugural Handicap, 96–97;

Kentucky Derby runner-up, 59–61;
    Kentucky Handicap, 95; pre-Derby
    attention, 55–58; possible sale, 57;
    Pendennis Club Special, 94
Hollister (horse), 108
Hot Springs, Arkansas, 81–84
Howe, Mabel, 19
Huerta, Victoriano, 41–42, 46
Hughes, Charles Evans, 14, *16*, 80

Ida Lavinia (horse), 152n22
Ida Pickwick (horse), 21, 152n23
Imperator (horse), 29–30
influenza, 120, 124
International Derby, 59, 83
Ivory Bells (horse), 21

Jack Hare Jr. (horse), 110, 113, 122
Jamaica racetrack, 126, 133, 136–37, 140,
    142, 168n35
Jim Crow laws, 22
Jockey Club, 11–13, 87, 97, 109, 118
John Gund (horse), 58–59
Johnson, Davy C., 12
Jones, Ben, 145–46
Juárez Jockey Club, 6, 42, 78,

Keene, James R., 6, 22, 155n27
Kenilworth Handicap, 105–6
Kentucky Association racetrack, 17, 21–22,
    25, 55–57, 65, 68, 122
Kentucky Derby: changes under New
    Louisville Jockey Club, 48–49;
    contributions of Matt Winn, 49–53;
    early years, 47–48; Exterminator wins,
    116; gelding ban, 117–18, 120; Morvich
    wins, 141; Old Rosebud prepares for,
    43, 47, 53–57; Old Rosebud wins,
    57–61; Omar Khayyam wins, 91–92;
    Regret wins, 76, *77;* reintroduction of
    pari-mutuel wagering promotes growth,
    50, 52–53; Sir Barton wins, 125–26;
    survives during World War I, 114–16;
    Woodrow Wilson supports, 114
Kentucky Handicap, 29, 62, 90, 94–96
Kentucky Jockey Club, 122
Kentucky Oaks, 55, 58, 110, 123, 128

Killingsworth (jockey), *32*
Kilmer, W. S., 116, 130
King Gorin (horse), 95–97
Kinney (horse), 106
Knapp, Willie, 99–100, 104
Knight Errant (horse), 26
Kohler, Charles, 23–24
Kuchen, Willie, 110
Kummer, Clarence, 136

Latonia racetrack, 19, 30–33, 68, 96–97,
    122, 127–28
Lawrence Realization Stakes, 98, 137
Lecompte Purse, 133
Leochares (horse), 101, 134
Life of General Villa, The (film), 65
Lillian Shaw (horse), 128
Linstead Handicap, 134, 167n21
Little Nephew (horse), 22, 24–26, 28–32,
    32, 38, 40
Livingston, Jefferson, 53–54, 56, 156n5
Loftus, Johnny, 28; and Boots, 95, 105; and
    Bromo, 104; and George Smith, 76; and
    Little Nephew, 25, 28–31; and Man o'
    War, 137; and Old Rosebud, 127, 131;
    and Sun Briar, 130, 167n16
Long, George, 33
Long Island Railroad, 98
Lord Brighton (horse), 132
Lorillard, Pierre, IV, 48
Louisville Jockey Club and Driving Park
    Association, 47
Lucullite (horse), 126, 129–30, 132
Luke Blackburn Handicap, 132
Lunsford, Harry, 130
Lusitania, RMS, 76

Macomber, Kingsley, 95
Madden, John E., 20–22, 24, 36, 55, 102,
    152nn22–24, 153n26
Madero, Francisco, 7, 41
Mankiewicz, Herman J., 61, 158n27
Man o' War (horse), 37, 137, *138,* 145
McAtee, Linus "Pony," 139
McCabe, Johnny: Cincinnati Trophy,
    32–33; defeated by Johnny Loftus, 28;
    early life, 26; falling out with Weir,

81; first race on Old Rosebud, 8–9; Flash Stakes, *37, 38*; at Hamburg Place for Old Rosebud's purchase, 152n22; Kentucky Derby, 59–60; Old Rosebud's Hall of Fame induction, 145; pre-Derby workouts, 53–54; recalls Old Rosebud's fatal injury, 142; return from military service, 131; United States Hotel Stakes, *39*, 57; Withers Stakes, 63–64, 159n35
McCreary, James B., 60
McCulley, R. W., 110, 142
McGuigan, "Umbrella Bill," 82
McKinley, William, 14, 44
McLaughlin, Harry "Mack," 42, 68, 167n29
McLemore, Wade, 70, 77–78, 160n1
McMeekin, Charles, 19
McTaggert, Tommy, 34, 37
Meadowbrook Handicap, 134
Menke, Frank G., 77, 105, 125, 161n14
Mexican Revolution, 5–7, 41–42, 65–69, 129, 159n38
Milldale Purse, 127
Milkmaid (horse), 123
Miller, Andrew, 38, 91–92, 107–8, 131, 108, 124, 131
Molesworth, George, 81, 88, 105–9
Morrissey, John, 34–35
Morrow, Edwin P., 141
Mt. Vernon Handicap, 129–30
Murray, Tommy, 127–28
Musgrave, Phil, 29

Nancy Hanks (horse), 152
National American Woman Suffrage Association, 35
Naturalist (horse), 132
Nellie Irene (horse), 152n22
New Louisville Jockey Club (NLJC), 48–50
New Moody Hotel Handicap, 83
New York Law and Order League, 35

Oaklawn Park, 81–83, 85, 88
Oakley racetrack, 19
Oakwood farm, 19
Obregón, Álvaro, 129

Old Ben (horse), 58–60
Old Koenig (horse), 126
Old Rosebud (horse): Applegates' purchase, 17, 20–21; in Arkansas, 81–84, 88; Bayview Handicap, 110–11; Brooklyn Handicap, 97–101; at Carr farm, 40, 42, 65; Carter Handicap, 101–2; and *Checkers,* 135; Cherokee Handicap, 95; Cincinnati Trophy, 32–33; Clark Handicap, 92–93; death, 142; Delaware Handicap, 108; Derby Day race against Roamer, 90–91; feinting incident, 110; first start, 7; Flash Stakes, 36–38; Frontier Handicap, 104–5; at Gravesend, 112–13, 122; Hall of Fame induction, 145; at Hamburg Place, 21; historical context, 146; Inaugural Handicap, 96–97; at Juárez, 5, 7–9, 78, 81; Kenilworth Handicap, 105–6; Kentucky Derby, 59–61; Kentucky Handicap, 95–96; last races, 139–142; Man o' War comparisons, 137–38; on McLemore ranch, 70, 78; pedigree, 21–24; Pendennis Club Special, 94–95; possible sale, 41, 53–54, 56; pre-Derby workouts, 42, 53, 55–57; pulls sulky, 68; Queens County Handicap, 101, *102;* questions about toughness of, 43–44; races in 1920, 135–137; Red Cross Handicap, 103–4; return in 1919, 123–135; rivalry with Little Nephew, 22, 24–25, 28–31; Saratoga Handicap, 106–8; sidelined in 1918, 113, 116, 120; United Hotel Stakes, 38, *39;* Weir assumes ownership, 122–23; Withers Stakes, 62–64
Old Rosebud Distillery, 112
Omar Khayyam (horse), 91–92, 98–99, 109, 164n6
Opportunity (horse), 95
Ormesdale (horse), 99, 101–2

Palo Alto Stud, 16
Pan Zareta (horse), 68, 83–84, 88
Papp (horse), 124–25
Papyrus (horse), 144
Payne, Oliver Hazard, 101

pari-mutuel system, 50, 52–53
Parmer, W. O., 61
Paumonok Handicap, 126, 129, 136
Peak, Charley, 7, 26, 56, 82–84, 97, 109–11
Pendennis Club Special, 94
Pennant (horse), 38, 40, 63, 155n27
Percy-Gray law, 11, 14
Pershing, Gen. John J., 72, *73*, 80, 85, 103, 160n5, 162n29
Peter Pan (horse), 38
Peter Piper (horse), 132, 136–37
Pif Jr. (horse), 94
Pimlico racetrack, 113, 124, 134
Preakness Stakes, 28, 34, 104, 113, 120, 125, 137
Progressivism, 1–3, 9–10, 44, 121, 138–39
Progressive Party, 44
Prohibition, 87, 118
Punitive Expedition, 72, *73*

Queens County Handicap, 101, *102*

Ramapo Stud, 23
Rancocas Farm, 120
Red Cross Handicap, 103–4
Regret (horse), 76–77, 90, 98–100, 103, 111
Remington, Frederic, 11
Richmond Handicap, 137
Riddle, Samuel, 137
RMS *Lusitania*, 76
Roamer (horse): blossomed in Old Rosebud's absence, 90, *92*, 124; Brooklyn Handicap, 98–99; Clark Handicap, 93; conception, 26; death, 131; Delaware Handicap, 108; Derby day win against Old Rosebud, 90–91; early races against Old Rosebud, 26, 30; Kentucky Handicap, 94–96; Queens County Handicap, 101; sale to Andrew Miller, 38; sent to New York, 30; Saratoga Handicap, 106–7; Saratoga Special, 38; Travers Stakes, 58; Withers Stakes, 63–64; Yonkers Handicap, 130–31

Robert Bradley (horse), 88
Robinson, Frankie, 99, 101, 167n22
Roosevelt, Theodore, 11, 14, 44, 71, 74, 79, *80*, 138
Root, Elihu, 14
Roseben (horse), 12, 14, *15*, 43, 151n12
Rose Tree II (horse), 26
Ross, Commander J. K. L., 123, 125, 132, 136
Rough Riders, 44, 88
Rowe, James, 38, 99
Runnymede Farm, 26

Salvator Handicap, 132–33
Sande, Earl, 123, 140, 142, 144
Sanders, Harland, 18
Sanford, John, 76
Sanford Memorial Stakes, 40, 124, 137
Santa Fe Bridge, 78–79
Santa Isabel attack, 71
Saratoga Association for the Improvement of the Breed of Horses, 75
Saratoga Cup, 98, 109–10
Saratoga Handicap, 36, 90, 105–8
Saratoga racetrack, 34–40, 106–10
Saratoga Special, 22, 38
Saratoga Springs, New York, 34, 145
Scheider, Hy, 152n22
Schuttinger, Andy, 91, 95, 101–2, 131
Scott, Gen. Hugh, *67*, 74
Sheepshead Bay racetrack, 26
Sinclair, Harry, 120, 140
Sir Barton (horse), 123, 125
Smith, George Weissinger, 116
Southern Maryland Handicap, 134–35
Spanish-American War, 11, 44, 74, 88, 118
Spence, Kay, 53, 56–57, 60, 122
Spring Trial Stakes, 30–31
Spur (horse), 106–7, 130
Stanford, Leland, 16
Stanley, Augustus Owsley, 76, 91, 125
Star Shoot (horse), 22, 26
Stirling, Dave, 134–35

Stromboli (horse), 34, 36–38, 40, 98, 164n19
Suburban Handicap, 98, 117
Sunbonnet (horse), 110–11
Sun Briar (horse), 116, 129–30, 167n16
Superintendent (horse), 63
Surprising (horse), 56, 58–60
Sweep On (horse), 124

Taft, William Howard, 44, 80
Taylor, Walter, 59, 158n21
Teapot Dome scandal, 120
Tennessee-bred horses, 21, 28, 53, 56
Terrazas, Alberto, 6, 42
Terrazas Park racetrack, 5–7
Thanksgiving Handicap, 134
Thompson, Lewis, 101
Ticket (horse), 92, 106–7
Tippity Witchet (horse), 167n21
Toboggan Handicap, 136–37
Torres, Carmelita, 79
Toto (horse), 133
Travers Stakes, 58, 98, 106, 130

Uncle (horse), 21–23, *23*, 24, 157n8
Uncle's Lassie (horse), 139
United States Hotel Stakes, 38–39, 124
USS *Dolphin*, 46

Vanderbilt, Alfred Gwynne, 76
Vandergrift (horse), 29
Veracruz, 46, 67
Viau, Wilfrid, 98
Villa, Pancho: attacks Juárez, 7, 41; attends horse races, 42–43, *67;* Columbus, New Mexico, raid, 3, 71–73; death, 129; note to Pershing, 160n5; struggles against Carrancistas, 68–69; subject of American filmmakers, 65, *66*
Villistas, 71–72, 129
Viva America (horse), 116, 128
Vosburgh, Walter, 103, 105, 113, 130
Vreeland, W. C., 136

Walker, William, 23, 55
Walker-Otis antigambling bill, 17

War Pennant (horse), 136
Watermelon (horse), 55, 58–59
Weir, Frank: assumes Old Rosebud ownership, 123; conceals Old Rosebud's 1913 injury, 40–41; conflict with photographer, 62; death, 144; decision to put down Old Rosebud, 141–42; declining fortunes, 122–23, 139–40, 167n29; early training career, 9, *10,* 12, 14–17; purchases Old Rosebud, 20, 151–52n22; relationship with Old Rosebud, 29, 142–43; visits Old Rosebud in Texas, 77–78
Weir, Ida, 139
Welles, Orson, 61
Westchester Racing Association, 63, 117
whiskey, 17, 20, 112
Whitney, Harry Payne, 37–38 63, 76, 98–99, 101, 103, 137
Widener, Joseph E., 103, 132
Willard, Jess, 86
Wilson, Henry Lane, 155n34
Wilson, Richard T., 34, 102
Wilson, Woodrow: advocacy of American neutrality, 67; authorization of military incursion into Mexico, 72; creation of Committee on Public Information (Creel Committee), 3, 85–86; declining health, 121; election to presidency, 44–46; in Europe, 120–21; Food and Fuel Control Act signing, 87; military intervention in Veracruz, 46, 67; and "moral diplomacy," 46; recognition of Carranza regime, 69–70; reelection to presidency, 80; request for declaration of war, 85; support of Kentucky Derby, 114; wartime implementation of regulations, 86–87
Windsor Jockey Club, 104–5
Winn, Martin J. ("Matt"): advocacy for Thoroughbred racing, 74–75, 103, 113–15, *115;* announces race for Old Rosebud and Roamer, 90; death, 141; and Exterminator, 116; gelding ban, 117–18; joins Churchill

Downs management, 50–51; and free infield policy, 58; and Juárez Jockey Club, 6, 42–43, 78, 112; Kentucky colonelship, 18; and Kentucky Jockey Club, 122; and pari-mutuel system, 50, 52–53
Withers Stakes, 23, 62–64, 106, 117, 137, 140
Woman's Christian Temperance Union, 18
Wood, Gen. Leonard, 88

World War I, 3, 66–67, 69, 74, 87, 96, 117, 119–20, 162n29

Yanke, W. G., 58
Yonkers Handicap, 130
Yucatan Stakes, 7–8

Zev (horse), 140, 144, *145*
Zim (horse), 81
Zimmerman telegram, 85

Horses in History

Series Editor: James C. Nicholson

For thousands of years, humans have utilized horses for transportation, recreation, war, agriculture, and sport. Arguably, no animal has had a greater influence on human history. Horses in History explores this special human-equine relationship, encompassing a broad range of topics, from ancient Chinese polo to modern Thoroughbred racing. From biographies of influential equestrians to studies of horses in literature, television, and film, this series profiles racehorses, warhorses, sport horses, and plow horses in novel and compelling ways.